FROM THE AUTHOR OF THE FULL ENGLISH

# FAT IN PARIS

CAMELS     SUCK

2017         2021

Creative Writer PRO
Chicago

First Printing
November 2023

Produced in the United States of America.

Library of Congress Cataloging-in-Publication Data
Garlington, Bull.
Fat in Paris
ISBN 979-8-9882669-0-7

www. creativewriter.pro
www.bullgarlington.com

## DEDICATION

This book is dedicated to my ride and die, my best friend in the whole world, and
the woman who told me to marry her,
[My Attorney]
Colleen "Scooby" Garlington.

## DISCLAIMER

This happened. Most names have been changed by request, as a matter of privacy, because I don't want to get sued, because God told me to, and/or, in the case of the mother of my children, because she has a real career and is a damn professional and doesn't want anyone to know she married a fat, howling, crazy person (which is why she is referred to in every publication and book of mine, exclusively, since my first column in 2010, as [My Attorney]).

Also, please bear in mind that though I am a working writer and a published author and can spell and stuff, I have a hard-wired inability to stay in tense both in the paragraphs and the structure of a story and even, sometimes, within a single sentence. However, this artifact of my personal crazy seems to work with my style, though you may experience moments of temporal dislocation. Whoops.

## Epigraph

They say that travel broadens the mind
till you can't get your head
through the door.

Elvis Costello, "God's Comic," Spike, 1989

## CONTENTS

### Prebuttal
#### by Lt. David "Biscuit" Haynes

This is not a foreword. It is a prebuttal.

This prebuttal is the result of a settlement in the civil lawsuit titled Haynes v. Garlington. I will get into the specifics of the case and provide some context in a short while. In the meantime, I will stipulate some things.

I will stipulate that I have a long acquaintance with Mr. Garlington.

I will stipulate that I have read Mr. Garlington's work, and even participated in Mr. Garlington's work. I co-wrote "The Beat Cop's Guide to Chicago Eats" with Mr. Garlington.

I will stipulate that, generally, I enjoy the assorted writings of Mr. Garlington. My problem with this manuscript do not extend to the larger canon of Mr. Garlington's work. I will also stipulate that most of this manuscript is enjoyable and funny. I will not go so far as to say that you made a mistake in spending your money on this book. Obviously, I have no reason to lie about that. I do not benefit financially from the sale of this book, and Mr. Garlington has already taken your money, and with an evil laugh he has placed it in a mason jar and buried it somewhere on his vast estate.

My problem is with the chapter entitled "Fish Camp."

When I attempted to discuss my feelings with the way I was represented in this chapter with Mr. Garlington, we was less that sympathetic. I believe his exact words were: "I don't care about your feelings, I have mason jars that need filling." Or words to that effect. At this point, I filed a lawsuit in Cook County circuit court.

During the first hearing, the judge ripped into the lawsuit as frivolous and irresponsible. Obviously he was a fan of Mr. Garlington's work. He was able to quote long passages of "Death by Children" by heart. He should have recused himself. I realized that Mr. Garlington had the courts held tightly in his web. I then took my case to the People's Court.

This was a mistake. Actually the mistake on my part was underestimating the reach of Mr. Garlington's influence. Judge Wapner hurled abuse at me and Doug Llewellyn quoted chapter and verse from "The Platinum-Level Transluminal Vacation Package of Your Dreams!" That book hadn't even been released at that time. Mr. Garlington had actually given them early access to his manuscript to influence the case.

Finally I took my case to the only forum left. A kind of "neighborhood court." An off-the-books court that is scrupulously fair. Hearings and settlements are negotiated at Jones BBQ and Foot Massage on the South Side of Chicago. It was there that I finally got a settlement I could live with. Namely, the chance to write this prebuttal, to tell my story, to clear my name. So, here goes.

I can fish. I can fish well. *I catch lots of fish.* The only time I don't catch fish is when I fish with Mr. Garlington. Therefore, and quite obviously, the problem lies with him. He is the repeller of fish.

Thank you for allowing me to set the record straight. I hope you enjoy the rest of the book, and you can just skip over the chapter of lies called "Fish Camp."

# Introduction

Our driver races through the outskirts of Giza. He lurches and skids through a convoluted path of switchbacks, narrow alleys, and dirt roads. Shops rush past the narrow windows of our van in a blur, their open storefronts spilling car parts, groceries, electronics, and ten million other everyday things onto the sidewalks where bored Egyptians sit in rickety plastic chairs, on upturned boxes, and on the bare ground. The long face of a donkey looms suddenly as it passes, drawing a flat two-wheeled cart piled high with cauliflower. On the sidewalk a very sick, very old man in a wheelchair breathing from an avocado-green oxygen tank is served coffee by a child. A family takes lunch in the median surrounded by camels.

We shudder to a stop. I look out the window at a kid selling small glass pyramids balanced on a black velvet covered board. He races toward us but before he gets close he's hit by a car. Thrown ten feet. His baubles shatter in a crystalline spray across the dirty black asphalt. The kid jumps up. Runs away.

I watch a girl wade into a shallow trash pit next to the sidewalk. She pulls KFC boxes out of the rubble then flattens them against her jeans. An old man lurches out from the traffic to glare at her from the edge of the pit. He yells angrily, but she flatly ignores him. He bends down and shoves his hand into the riot of spent cellophane, old food, dusty bottles, Styrofoam clamshells full of chicken bones, and tin cans. He snatches a wadded newspaper page and as I stare, he carefully unwads it, smooths it against his gebellah, then walks away reading. The girl looks up and catches my eye. I brace for some kind of rebuke—just another judgmental old man. But I'm not an Egyptian. I'm obviously a tourist. Obviously a rich tourist since I'm in a private van and not a bus full of three-hundred people. She can see my plump shoulders and my waggling jowls, so I am also a man made entirely out of food. Holding my gaze, this poor girl in her dirty shirt, with her hair flying all over the place and a streak of soot on her face, a face which hasn't held hope for, probably, ever, this poor girl pretends to eat. She holds one hand under her chin like a shallow, empty bowl and with the other raises an imaginary spoon to her mouth and my heart, my fat, overfed, struggling white American heart breaks. I mouth the words "ok, ok, wait a minute," and start stuffing our unfinished lunches into a bag. But our driver punches the gas, swerves around a disabled Tuk Tuk, then zooms off down the road. I don't know what I expected from Egypt, but it wasn't this.

I'm traveling with [My Attorney] and our mutual best friend, Adelaide. We're on our way to meet a local purveyor of camel excursions who will guide us into the broad Sahara.  Our trip is scheduled for two full hours. Instead of the parking lot of The Great Pyramid of Giza, we're mounting our animals at a locals-only spot two miles away in Nazlet al Samaan, a historic neighborhood of noble camel drivers and legendary equestrians. Our selfies will be stunning.

We get out at the end of Avenue Gamal Abd El-Nasir next to a motorcycle mechanic shop and a garage-sized nightclub hand-painted in bright yellows and greens. The street is heaped with garbage. Strewn with spent coffee cups, candy wrappers, and empty water bottles. Wild dogs sleep in the middle of the road in lazy, flagrant disregard for the cars hurtling by a hair's breadth from their bony marimba rib cages. Horses burst out of nameless alleys, whipped savagely by barking Egyptians riding bareback in dress slacks and expensive shoes.

Four enormous camels are parked against the curb and before we get any instruction other than "lean back," we're mounted on our gargantuan animals, captains of our own personal ships of the desert. I glance over at the girls with the town behind them and the people and the brick-a-brack of an Egyptian postcard and a tiny little smile peeks out from my grizzled visage. However, in this crucial, almost symbolic moment things go, as they always do, fucking sideways and I am hurled into the open air.

Camels get up ass first which is why riders are instructed to lean back. Waaaay back. And I am leaning back. Waaaay back. For a second. But I can't get my feet into the stirrups. I hunch forward to get a look down at my feet which are hanging six inches above the metal footrests because I have legs like a Corgi. I tilt even further forward to figure out how I'm going to get stirruped but the second my posterior lifts off the camel's back, the camel wrangler whistles 'giddyup' through his teeth and my camel pops his ass into the sky, allowing me to take full advantage of the inescapable power of gravity.

Suddenly I'm hurtling face first toward oyster-colored sand ornamented with dog shit and cigarette butts, florid with camel piss, and savagely fanged by serrated chunks of spent concrete like upturned scimitars.

Camels are surprisingly low to the ground when they're kneeling, patiently waiting for you to throw a leg over. So I am barely four feet off the ground when I begin to fall. My pudgy fingers are curled around the pommel in a death grip. I think maybe I can brace for this, it's not that different from falling out of bed. It's sand, after all, right? Then the camel stood all the way up. The front of its body blasted skyward, and because I'm holding onto the pommel, it drags my falling carcass with it. Now I'm falling up. The momentum flips me out over the camel's long neck, ripping fingers off the pommel, as I'm flung into the air. Now I'm falling. I'm sixty feet off the ground (this is a rough estimate), arms flailing, feet kicking, howling my favorite word, eye to eye with a man-eating dromedary.

And so, this is where we are now, gentle reader, here at the beginning of this book. Time has stopped. The world is an alarming, frozen tableau of [My Attorney], Adelaide, our camel driver, Achmed, our personal Egyptologist, Ahmed, and our driver, frozen in mid-shout, hands outstretched toward me, eyes wide with dread, while I hang suspended midway between a camel's hump and the pee-stained dirt of Nezlet al Samaan and it is here, in this instant, as I am about to enjoy permanent disfigurement and probable quadriplegia that I think to myself: I am not, as I once believed, a man of adventure.

I am not cut from the same cloth as Hemingway. I'm not even Paul Bowles. Instead, I'm Otis Campbell, the town drunk from The Andy Griffith Show, mopping my brow in a jail cell with my fat floral tie, petulanting: "I declare, it is a might warm, isn't it now Sherriff?"

I want to be an adventurer. I do. I want to Anthony Bourdain my ass across Spain. I want to drink whiskey and smoke cigarettes in a cheap Parisian bar. I want to walk across India, pilot a narrow boat through the floating cities of Thailand, paddle bravely toward the headwaters of the Amazon.

Or so I thought.

Evidence tells a different story. I had two years to prepare for this trip. A trip I knew involved a ridiculous measure of walking in an unforgiving African heat. I spent a few minutes at the gym, but my family was concerned about Covid exposure, so I quit going. I have plenty of excuses for why I didn't get into shape for this trip; but the truth is, as much as I'm not a man of adventure, I'm also not a man of gymnasiums.

I hit the ground pretty hard. I get up, dust myself off, insist that I'm fine before I yell "Fuck camels!" perhaps too loudly in a       historic   camel wrangling neighborhood.

I should have seen a chiropractor because when my three-hundred and twenty pounds landed on my dainty feet, damage occurred. As Achmed hauls me in a hastily procured buckboard carriage up the hills to a Bedouin camp overlooking the pyramids, I realize with growing alarm that I've fallen off a camel on the first day of a two-week trip featuring daily hikes of three to five miles into the goddam Egyptian desert and yeah, it's November, but it's still pretty hot for a guy from Chicago where we wear sweaters in June.

As the backside of Cheops rises over the dunes, and the jarring cart lurches and bounces across every single boulder the horse can find and as my spine and hips and all the muscles in my legs send damage reports filled with exclamation points, my shoulders sag and I rub my forehead, sigh heavily, and whisper to the indifferent Sahara: not again.

Not again will I experience a hideous, truncated, idiotic, poorly timed, stupid-ass vacation.

Not again.

For thirty years, [My Attorney] and I have made every effort to book the perfect holiday. We've tried hard to take a grand tour, to hit the global highlights, to lounge on a pristine beach, to travel like pros on a flawless junket from our humble home in Chicago to a magical place where magical things magically occur magically. We thought we'd return refreshed and inspired, forty pounds lighter, tanned to within an inch of our lives, our minds so broadened we'd have to carry them in a wheelbarrow.

But no. Every single trip has been at the wrong time of year. Every single journey has borne a hidden agenda of catastrophe. Never, ever have we looked into each other's eyes and said, "This is it; this is the one: this vacation is perfect."

Look: the mayhem that follows in this book is dumb. I know that. You're probably suspecting it by now. If you're standing in a bookstore thumbing through these pages, you've already made some kind of resignation about your own capacity for handling a massive glurge of stupid since you have turned to the intro with the hope of discovering the author is, perhaps, just putting on. That it's all tongue in cheek. That maybe he's just piling up bullshit, grinning all the way to the bank.

I'm not. Everything in this book is absolutely true and though I hold fast the rights of an author to exaggerate for effect, I have not exaggerated into the realm of prevarication in these pages.

Much.

I try, very hard, when telling these stories, to be dignified. Honestly, the man you meet on these trips is not the man I aim to be. I want to wear a cardigan and smoke a pipe and read the paper and laugh about golf with my dignified friends. But that is not my life. I wear dirty T-shirts three days in a row and doom scroll through the dark gutters of Reddit and sure, I laugh with my friends, but we're laughing at public freakout videos because we are shallow, bilious, post-punk thrash freaks riding it out at the end of the world and we haven't been in a bookstore in three years. Dignity does not always obtain.

As much as I try to live the cardinal virtues and have a positive outlook and always use my dinner forks starting with the one furthest away from the plate, I still find myself erupting into righteous, furious indignation at the ridiculous, stupid, completely unfair, caterwauling vicissitudes of an observer of the twenty-first century. Also, and I'm serious here, God loves me.

I don't mean God loves me like God loves Her favored creatures; I mean God loves to watch me like [My Attorney] loves to watch Intervention: with a glass of Chateau Neuf de Pape as she cackles with glee at the wild misfortunes uncoiling before her. I think, and again, I'm dead serious, that the divine (or whatever she calls itself) is sagely indifferent to our daily struggles. However, sometimes it remembers we're here. In those moments it finds an individual to play as if their life is a highly glitched Mario Kart side quest.

Someone like me.

For example: I recently went to Alabama to visit my family and hang out with my sister to explore Lay Lake on a borrowed pontoon boat. Returning to the marina, a storm gathered itself up into vast dark purple anvils. As we approached the dock, the storm unloaded. Rain like it can only rain in Alabama: in buckets. In torrents. And lightning. Close.

There are too many boats tied up. They cram against each other. They take up too much dock space. It makes our berth almost exactly wide enough to fit, which is not enough during a storm, or really anytime as barges are big, stupid, and unwieldy. Yet there we are trying desperately to wield it into the dock so we can get off the water and wield ourselves into the truck and maybe, you know, live. My stoic brother-in-law pokes the nose of the boat in and out of the slot, but he can't get it right because the wind is blowing us back out into the lake and, as I mentioned, it does not wield well.

Meanwhile, my niece yells "Hey is there supposed to be smoke?!" We all freeze. Thin greasy vapor is boiling out from under the driver's console.

Also, we're not docked yet. Also, rain. Also lightning.

"Where is the fire extinguisher?!" I scream.

"It's in there!," my sister explains, pointing at the space under the steering wheel. It glows like a forge.

Acrid smoke billows out. Flames lick the fiberglass hull. For a moment there is a perfect dreadful silence except for the song playing over the sound system from my phone (which has, as we discover later, started the fire) the incomparable 70s funk anthem "Le Freak," by Chic, the lyrics of which are as follows:

Freak out! Freak out!

It's just too much. Too on the nose. I shed my normal composure of calm, professorial dignity. I leap onto the dock in the rain and howl into the sky.

"Really? REALLY? CAN I JUST HAVE ONE FUCKING DAY? CAN I JUST GO ON VACATION FOR ONE WEEK AND NOT HAVE ALL THESE CRAZY WEIRD THINGS HAPPEN? I HAVE ENOUGH STORIES! YOU CAN STOP! JESUS!"

And it's not like this is an isolated incident. When Covid-19 delayed the Egyptian excursion, we rescheduled. I should have at least glanced at my passport. Because a few short months before our departure, my second wife, Adelaide, noticed it had expired. Because of Covid, the time it took to issue passports had been expanded by eight to twelve weeks. Getting a new one would involve crippling stress, talking to the Post Office, and having a coronary.

I can only assume God reached out to her bestie.

God: [calls Satan] Yo, Goat, whassup?

Satan: G dog! Just chillin'. Torching some souls.

God: TORCH!

Satan: TORCH!

God: Remember that Job thing?

Satan: (sighs) Good times, God. Good times.

God: Wanna do it again?

Satan: Oh shit, serious? I am all in.

God: I think this Garlington character would be perfect.

Satan: I mean, I'm already working on his space down here . . .

God: Wanna do it?

Satan: Come on, God. Dude's always in the middle of a grand and luridly ornamented fuck up. I think you're already Jobbing the shit out of this guy.

### FRANCE, FINALLY.

And so, we begin in Paris. Well, not exactly Paris—our French journey starts at Charles de Gaulle International Airport where we fight our way to baggage claim then fight our way to the taxi stand where Sally welcomes us into her cab to hurl us into Paris proper, texting all the way down the A1, lurching around the Arc de Triomphe, then barreling down Avenue des Champs Élysée's across the Seine into the seventh arrondissement to our hotel.

Kind of. Sally drives like she just stole the Mona Lisa and the French foreign legion's hot on her tail. She accomplishes this in a sleeveless brick-red Public Image, Ltd. t-shirt with her arm thrown over the back of her cracked Naugahyde seat so she can sell my wife and son on her little Airbnb rental, as if we came to Paris without a place to stay.

"Eet ees the steel," Sally says. By now we were in the Avenue Franklin Delano Roosevelt roundabout locked in traffic, creeping forward. You could lounge your way to the hotel and beat us there. Sally, adept at the face-to-face sales pitch, throws the car into park. In the roundabout. She whirls around to hand talk at [My Attorney]. "Eemageen eet: a beautiful leetle ateel lee ay weeth a view."

"Should we be parked here?" I stare at the driver next to us. I can't read lips and he was parlaying some serious Francais, but I felt like I got the gist of his communiqué:

"Mon Dieu, c'est Sally!? Parle-t-elle de son appartement?! C'est un placard à balais. Vous allez tous mourir."[1]

Sally throws her hands up at the traffic swerving around us. "Zey are eediots. You want me to move?" She resumes her position as the pilot of our obstructioning. "I move."

She throws the car into gear, and we lurch toward the Eiffel Tower.

We get out at Hotel le Derby Alma. Sally and the hotel staff unload our

---

1 "Oh my god is that Sally? Is she talking about her apartment? It's a broom closet! You're all going to die!"

luggage. She shoves a hastily written note into [My Attorney]'s hand with the address of her apartment and her phone number then screeches back into traffic, cursing out the window at a guy in a sky-blue Citroen.

And here we are. Paris. I'm almost fifty-three years old. I've dreamed of being a world traveler my whole life. Sure, I'd been to England, but does England really count? Except for the Scottish lorry drivers, I understood almost everyone there. But in France, we're foreigners! I take in this emblematic moment with the Eiffel glaring down at us, the hotel bellhop rolling our luggage into the lobby, and a guy just standing there on the corner next to a kiosk smoking a cigarette and reading a magazine.

"Holy shit, can I smoke?" My nineteen-year-old son lopes joyfully to the cancer stand and buys cigarettes decorated with diseased lungs. He lights up then blows smoke into the air in fluent French.

I am overcome by a wave of emotion. My eyes are suddenly slick with tears and there's a lump in my throat. I choke up.

Fuck. Paris!

I have endured so much disappointment in my life, so much glurge and grumbling2. The long ribbon of my lifeline unfurls in my mind. It's mostly blank, mostly stained with ink and bruises and the faint scrimshaw illustrations of my frigates of hope broken into kindling against the indifferent and jagged rocks of hope. Mostly.

You don't realize you're on a journey. You just don't know. Your life picks you up like a cork in the water and sweeps you along and you think you're making good decisions. You believe you're pulling your weight; you focus on being a good person, being a good father, being a good husband, and being a good son. And Jeebus Homerian-epic Crass, after a few years that focus narrows down to a pinpoint until you're just trying to shoulder your way through a single fucking day. Just one day more. Then it's a year later; five years later; ten years. You have a Tom Joad moment standing there in the dust cloud of the road of your life. You're just trying to change a tire but the sweat's in your eyes and the kids are crying and you look back down that highway fading away into the desert and wonder what in the living hell you've been doing? The road should look like it's supposed to end up where you are, but you're dissolving in the glare of the unwavering sun, and it doesn't feel like a meaningful trajectory. It feels like you're lost. It feels like you're in the middle of nowhere.

So you put your head back down and you shoulder on and then one day you and your wife and your newly adult son fly to Paris and now you're

2 Over crap that I had caused.

there and all those memories and regrets that have kept you up at night staring into the dark, rolling your mental finger down the endless taxonomy of failure, all those brilliant literary projects that came to nothing, all those journals filled not with brilliance or even half-way decent prose but, instead, stuopid to-do lists and phone numbers; all those sunup-to-midnight days, all the spurious lurches into dead-end jobs, the dead pets and dead parents and car after car after car; all of it snaps into focus: suddenly it all seems like its part of a plan. A narrative stands up and shakes the dust off its waistcoat and doffs its hat and shakes your hand and you realize it's all led you here, to stand with your family a stone's throw from the Avenue des Champs Èlysée's with the Eiffel tower practically leaning its knobby head down over the top of the Hotel to say Bienvenue! Bienvenue à Paris! and it's just, it's too much.

A wave of emotions that have been trailing in your wake—in my wake, this is me, I'm talking about me—a wave of emotions I've been trying to avoid, a wake of little joys eclipsed by all the mundane horror and splenetic madness of parenting, of evoking a new career out of thin air in my late fortiess, of holding a marriage together through constant explosive trauma, law school, and all of it like the dark towering walls of a great chasm choking out the light—but now you've skidded to a full stop and those sparkling little joys well up and you—I mean I—have to lean over and put my hands on my knees to choke back tears.

I am here. We are here.

We made it.

"Hey, you can nap later. Let's unload," [My Attorney] says. I sniff my emotional tidal wave away and wipe my nose on the edge of my sleeve. We unload into our room and we shower and we dress for dinner at the Eiffel Tower and I am grinning ear to ear because I have no idea how much it's going to suck.

## Fuck the Eiffel Tower

We're only in Paris for three days so our first job is finding ham.

That isn't the purpose of our trip, but [My Attorney] and I want to take a romantic stroll around the arrondissement which we do, not preparing at all or even asking questions like hey, where's a good place to take a romantic stroll around the arrondissement? But no, we're from Chicago and we don't need no help over by der. We snatch our coats, wish Dr. Cigarettes best of luck, and head out. We stroll along the Seine in the shadow of a drab apartment building, and it quickly becomes apparent that March in Paris is not significantly different from January in Chicago which isn't significantly different from winter on Pluto.

We make it around a corner and halfway down a block of buildings that must've looked cool in 1973 before we admit that we're not feeling a twinge of romance because were cold and hungry.

Me: (shivering) Romantique, no?

[My Attorney]: (shivering) I'm cold and hungry.

Me: Oui, I am zee handsome one.

[My Attorney]: Look, ham!

We duck into Bellota-Bellota whose business card says "Comptoir de vente & degustation" which sounds really cool, but it means "sales and tasting counter" which could be a 7-11 or your mom's house. What their business card should say is "Bellota-Bellota is a regional chain of luxury meats and specialty foods like caviar and smoked salmon" and not a one-of-a-kind ham cavern. We don't know that. It feels like a ham cavern, and they have a hell of a wine list, but it's still a chain which means we're in a French Chili's.

Afterward, we grab the kid for dinner at the Eiffel Tower. You may be surprised to know the Eiffel Tower only has three floors, accessible by an elevator that holds an entire tour bus of impatient Brazilian tourists. On the first floor is 58 Tour Eiffel which is where I booked us a table.

We stroll leisurely along Avenue Rapp. We don't need directions because at night the Eiffel Tower is lit up like the sun. When we arrive, there is a steady trickle of tourists but no crowd. I relax, knowing we won't have to fight for a spot or stand in a long line. The elevators, which are a mere half a football field away from the ticket booth, stand empty and inviting, their doors wide open. [My Attorney] nudges me with a sharp kick.

"Hurry up, we have to get there before anyone else!"

I look around at the vast emptiness of the site. "Babe, it's March, nobody's here. We're fine."

"Just get the tickets and hurry up!" She glares at the empty elevator. I feel panic rising as she growls, suddenly and viciously protective of what is rightfully hers. I finally get the tickets. I mosey toward the open, empty elevators.

"Faster!" [My Attorney] yells, trying to drag me along, but it's no use. I gaze up through the ornate guts of the tower and lose myself in wonder. I feel pressed upon by ten thousand tons of steel and glass. It weighs on me and I slow down.

This is the great danger of travel, of wandering and wondering. You get sucked into the endlessly fascinating detail of a place and your thoughts race away and time gets quiet and slips off and leaves you there agape and maybe drooling a little at all the magnificence and beauty. God help anyone if I take out a notebook because I will take me some notes.

I slip my notebook out of my pocket but before I click my pen, [My Attorney] exasperates.

"What are you doing?! Run!" She charges toward the elevator, still yawning its invitation. Suddenly she's hammering me in my ribs because a parade of Brazilian teens comes out of nowhere.

"You see!? I told you!" [My Attorney] grips my jacket in her tiny fists and tries to jerk me forward out of my reverie. The Brazilians barrel toward the elevator. She lets go of my sleeve, skittering across the wide-open space, looking over her shoulder at me and our son with a panicked grimace. The kid is trying to find a place to have yet another cigarette right out in the open like it doesn't even matter. I'm struggling with the overwhelming architectural beauty over my head and furiously refraining from taking notes. But we are trying, we are shuffling in the right direction, and we're picking up steam because the Brazilians are roiling toward the lift like an army of post-apocalyptic zombie soccer players.

"They're young! They have training!" yells [My Attorney].

"Babe, relax, none of these kids have their tickets yet. They got in line without paying. We don't need to run. They have to follow the rules."

[My Attorney] looks to see if I'm right and I am. The kids are slowing down, talking nervously when a voice behind me cries out in a thick accent, "Eu tenho os bilhetes!" I turn to see a man with dual fanny packs and a flag on a stick waddling out of the ticket booth waving a bouquet of tickets.

Now I'm panicking. I don't really care if we make the elevator, I mean we have a good half an hour before our reservations. But [My Attorney] can hold a grudge and she turns cruel when her victory is threatened. Me and fanny packs are neck and neck, but he's young and he pulls ahead. Still racing toward the open doors, [My Attorney] whirls mid-stride like a teacup ninja. She points at him and snarls "Sweep the leg!"

But it's too late. The Brazilians see their tickets and they see the elevator doors and they break into excited scurrying. We still have the lead, and we have something like a home court advantage because, again, we were there first. But it's no use, not only am I slow, but I'm also Southern which means I'm half Canadian which means I'm polite.

As the tour guide gains the lead, brushing past me in his pink and teal windbreaker, he employs a tool which, let's face it, in games like this where the stakes are high and divorce is on the table, should be banned.

"Excuse, Señor, but those are my kids," he says, with genuine concern and love in his heart, that son-of-a-bitch. I actually stop, sweep my arm out in front of me like I'm showing him to his seat, and mumble "of course, of course;" or maybe I say "remember me to your grandchildren," because I let him go first WHICH IS A SIN, according to [My Attorney] who makes the elevator just as the Brazilian line of defense washes up against the doors like a tidal wave, driving her further and further away as if she's a buoy in a storm, her eyes twin beacons of alarm flashing the international signal for you fucking idiot, we could've beaten them.

We get in line forty-seven miles behind the Brazilians. We have a good thirty-five minutes of queue in front of us which means we'll have to wait until after dinner to tour the tower but worse, and unforgivably, we've squandered the serendipitous real estate of being first in line which has [My Attorney] glowering in silent fury, trying to trepan the Brazilians with the power of her withering glare.

Dinner is fine. It's not particularly special and as I live in Chicago which sports a bejeweled crown of Michelin starred restaurants and five hundred more trying to score their own little constellation, I have dined fine. But whatever, 58 Tour Eiffel knows their customers: the people who want to eat at the Eiffel tower but can't afford the expensive one[1]. We settle in,

---

1 This has changed in the few short years since we were there. 58 Tour Eiffel was replaced by Madame Bras-

pretending we understand a single word on the menu and wishing they'd take a cue from Denny's and use pictures.

We have a great seat, looking out over a broad steel girder at the City of Lights sparkling in the dark. The waiter brings champagne. We order. He brings our appetizer and I think, well, this isn't so bad. I mean, it's not The French Laundry or anything, but we won't starve to death. I look at my lovely family and a tiny ember of warmth flutters to life, a gleaming spark of joy from my emotional moment earlier and I think, well shit, maybe this will all work out. I lift my champagne and clear my throat. A deeply heartfelt toast is poised behind my teeth as I smile at [My Attorney]and my boy and open my mouth.

The restaurant erupts in thunderous applause. I admit, I am pretty good at toasts, but they're early. We look around and see a Frenchman kneeling in front of a teary-eyed woman with her dainty hand laid delicately against her chest, her head bobbing yes, yes, a thousand times, yes. We join the applause, because it really is adorable and let's face it, pretty classy. I mean, if you're going to propose, this is the place for it: on your knees in the very heart, the actual icon of Paris, the City of Love.

[My Attorney]and I share a moment, staring into each other's eyes with the burnished, polished love of a long marriage, remembering when we got engaged at in a Chi Chis over a bowl of guacamole at eleven in the morning on a Tuesday. Look at me in 1991:

"Hey," I say, my hair pulled back in a mullet, wiping my hands on my stone-washed parachute pants, spraying tortilla crumbs all over her enchiladas. "We should probably get married or something."

Fucking romantic.

Back in France in the 21st century, I raise my glass again and so does my family. I open my mouth to—

Thunderous applause.

Another one. He kisses his new fiancé. A nearby table buys them a bottle of champagne. More applause.

I raise my glass again, clear my throat to—

Thunderous applause.

Son of a bitch! Across the restaurant, a future groom stands triumphantly, planting a big sloppy kiss on his betrothed then throws his arms wide and cries out, "Thank you Paris!" Which earns even thunderouser applause and

---

serie, run by a Michelin starred chef. The Jules Verne is the new expensive restaurant, offering an unparelled truly French gastronomic experience that will surely leave you gasping for more and short a couple hundred bucks per person.

a little patriotic table banging. Someone orders the happy couple a bottle of champagne. [My Attorney] buries her attention in the wine list.

Hmm.

I turn back to my table with a grin. My son stops his food halfway to his mouth. I look at our bottle of expensive champagne then cut my eyes around toward the room as my mischievous grin turns into a brilliant idea.

"Dad—no." My son knows this look and he's scared.

I scoot to the edge of the booth and loom my corpus forward, clearly preparing to take a knee. People turn toward us, their hands poised over the escargot, ready to applaud thunderously.

"Dad, I swear," My son growls.

"Shut up, kid. Champagne's expensive." I glance at [My Attorney]. "Darling will you—"

"I will gut you like a fish," she says quietly, not even looking up from the menu.

I stand up and saunter off toward the restrooms. A guy at the table who was ready to applaud makes eye contact and shrugs a private what the hell, dude? I jab my thumb over my shoulder at [My Attorney], mouth the word 'sister,' and keep walking.

## Sᴛ. Gᴇʀᴍᴀɪɴ ɪɴ Sᴛ. Gᴇʀᴍᴀɪɴ Wɪᴛʜ Sᴛ. Gᴇʀᴍᴀɪɴ ᴀᴛ Cᴀғᴇ Sᴛ. Gᴇʀᴍᴀɪɴ

The next day, we split up and [My Attorney] and my son go shopping while I walk to Rue St. Germain. It's only a forty-five-minute walk, according to Google, but it takes me an hour and a half because of my short little legs and because I have to stop and get some Dr. Scholl's.

I have beautiful feet. They are wonderfully shaped with high, graceful arches. But I weigh three-hundred pounds so every time I take a step I'm throwing one-hundred-fifty pounds—or the weight of a normal person—onto each of my beautiful, delicate feet.

Since arriving we've walked forty-five miles around the Eiffel Tower to find ham, then sixty miles this morning trying to find the Louvre, which I'm convinced is a myth. Normally, I walk at least six or seven arduous yards every day as part of my exercise regimen but walking over seventeen-thousand steps was killing my feet as they were really carrying two people so it's more like I walked twelve miles or thirty-seven-thousand steps which is about how far it is to the moon.

I duck into a Parisian version of a Walgreens (les Walverdant) and buy some Dr. Scholl's which leads to another problem—where to put them on.

I'm not easily embarrassed but I'm in a fairly upscale part of the city with no public restrooms and nowhere to sit down that isn't already taken by exhausted French philosophers.

But I'm hurting pretty bad. My feet are finit. I walk around looking for a bench or a flat rock or a small car so I can sit down and upgrade my shoes. Finally, I find a grassy spot and plop down in front of God and everybody and take off my shoes, exposing my naked socks while filling my sneakers with the healing power of foam inserts.

I decide to find a cafe and have a seat and do some people watching. I take a table at Café St. Germain directly across the street from a souvenir shop, order a drink and open a music app with a flourish. I am about to fulfill a stupid dream.

A long time ago, I managed a music shop in a major bookstore chain that rhymes with Harmes & Goebel and if you're standing in a Harmes & Goebel reading this, just think about how cool that is and, also, hug the nearest bookseller because their job is hard.

I had a staff of eight and I did my job, so the manager never came back to my department, and I pretty much ran the joint like a tiny little kingdom. One year we got a promo CD by a French DJ named St. Germain. I looked him up and discovered he was named after a neighborhood called St. Germain. It's good music, very chill, groovy, brainy tunes and we sold a metric ton of it.

One day we were listening to this music when I revealed my great dream.

"Wouldn't it be cool to go there?" I said, back in 2001 to a couple of bored booksellers.

"I can't come in tomorrow," one of them informed.

"Me neither," the other one said.

"I mean," I continue, not listening to them. "Imagine it: sitting in a cafe in this neighborhood where this guy is from."

"Seriously, no one in coming in tomorrow," someone said. I continued to ignore them because I was a good manager.

"You know there's a liqueur called St. Germain?"

"I need January off."

"Hey," I snap my fingers like it's 1943. "I bet there's a coffee shop called St. Germain."

"Cafe"

"What?"

"It would be called a cafe. Also, I need the rest of my life off for band practice."

"Imagine it," I said, forgetting they even existed, lost in the dream. "There I am at a little table at Cafe St. Germain, in St. Germain, drinking a St. Germain while I'm listening to St. Germain!"

"That's the stupidiest thing I've ever heard."

"Yeah, there's no song called St Germain on the album," said the little one. It breaks the chain."

"Your fired," I explained, logically.

But now, sixteen years on, here I am. I'm sitting at a small table at Cafe St. Germain, halfway through my ice cold St Germain cocktail. I plug in my headphones and call up "Montego Bay Spleen," the best song on the CD, and sit there grinning ear to ear, bobbing my head with maybe more expressive lilt than is necessary, waiting for someone to notice how cool I am.

It's just after eleven in the morning, so there's just a smattering of customers, since people in France sleep in until the next day. I look around, bobbing my head like an idiot. I catch the eye of a slim Frenchman a few tables over. I point at my headphones and make the 'damn, this music is good' face but he just looks away, terrified.

It occurs to me that no one can hear the song and even if they could, they might not recognize it, and sice they probably live here, they'd never make the connection between the DJ, the neighborhood, the drink, and the cafe.

Well, sometimes you have to make your own fate. The waiter comes over.

"Pardon moi monsieur, weel zer be zumzing ails?"

I hold up my phone, kind of wave it around.

"St. Germain."

"Ah."

"I'm listening to St. Germain," I show him the album cover.

"Ah heff nevier 'eard off eem."

"But..." I look around, waving my hand to indicate all that one can see of the neighborhood of St. Germain, "This is—he's from here!"

"Ah leesen to cown tree muzeek. Zee Gyerth Broogs and zee Weelco."

"ST. GERMAIN!"

"I weel breeng anozer," he says, rolling his eyes, as excited as a cold lizard.

I pay my bill and leave. If a French waiter can't see the delicious irony of what I had accomplished, then my art means nothing.

I walk seven hundred more miles to find myself utterly and completely lost. I could have opened up Waze but [My Attorney] had only asked me to call our cellular provider and tell them we were going to Europe like three hundred times, so I forgot, and we had no credits. Just looking at Facebook would have cost me thirteen bucks. Using Waze would have meant remortgaging the house.

I power forward into the unknown, your intrepid raconteur, your laconic flaneur strolling the back streets of the City of Lights looking for intellectual conversation and prepared to...ready to...

Man was I ever lost.

I sat down on a bench, a beaten man. A limp flaneur. I called [My Attorney]. They were still shopping. Well, I can shop too, I thought.

Except there's not much I want that I can afford. I would have been very happy to have broken down in front of a cologne shop as I am a big fan of

Creed's Irish Tweed and would have bought a half an ounce of that precious potion just for the hell of it. I would have loved to find a stationery shop, a pencil boutique, a pen chalet, or...A hat shop! There it was, literally across the rue. An outdoor vendor's hovel bewigged with colorful scarves and bedazzled with berets. I had to have a beret. Hell, I was in France. Along with beating up a mime, the whole St. Germain thing, and declining to eat snails, a beret was one of my top five things to do in Paris.

I saunter across the rue, pay way too much money for a beret and a scarf. I am filled with the joie des vivre of sartorial splendor. Surely I look like Gerard Depardieu on a good day. Surely I'm elegant. I take a selfie (see inserts). I'm so handsome.

[My Attorney] calls.

"Did you buy a beret?"

"Did I wha—no. I'm sitting on a bench—"

"We can see you."

"I—"

"Oh my God, you bought a beret!"

"Well, I'm in France!"

"You have a head like a pumpkin. That doesn't look like a beret, it looks like you're wearing a bed skirt."

I toss my scarf rackishly and ignore her. Whatever. I look French which is important since tomorrow we're going to the Louvre and I'll need to blend in.

## THE MONA LISA HATES YOU

The next day, we take a boat to the Louvre, which is lovely, though I'd like to remind you that it's March so it's twenty-eight degrees with a light drizzle. Paris is gray, bitter, huddled in its doorways in a trench coat with a cigarette. Only insane people and Americans are outside so as we are both, we walk an endless path along the Seine to find our boat, climb clumsily aboard, then float along the slate gray waters staring out the plexiglass windows at architectural ennui.

I'm sure the Palais Royal gleams golden in the sunlight. I'm certain bougainvillea and lilacs spill over the balustrades along the water as if it were a luridly floral Maxfield Parrish hallucination. I'm convinced wan, beautiful couples entwine along the bridges, occasionally looking down into our boat with the exhausted, laconic disdain of oversexed youth. Of course, they do. But those scenes are from the Paris of summer.

Ours is the Paris of winter. Ours is the Paris of overcoats. Ours is the Paris of empty riverwalks. Where are the famous bookstalls? I find one with its clapboard walls and shadowy interior, a couple of political tracts pinned to the wall. The purveyor's face, glimmering dully deep in darkness like a worn coin on the bottom of a lake, daring me to walk all the way over through the rain. Why would I? All his books are in French.

Our boat disgorges us fifty-seven miles away from the Louvre, so we walk along gravel paths and beside normally picturesque streets until we find the museum which we identified by the incredibly long line of grim people wrapped around the glass pyramid and across the yard. There were easily nine-thousand Franks in line. No place to sit. My thighs are on fire and my head is swimming from having walked the distance to the goddam moon because [My Attorney] won't cab. I find a place against the low wall where the anti-pigeon spikes are just far enough apart that I can sit down.

My face is rigid with dissatisfaction. My eyes stare holes into the gravel walk. I'm curled into a tight ball against the cold and though I am not smoking a cigarette, it looks like I'm smoking a cigarette with absolute disregard for all this bourgeois bullshit and the sheer force of my bitterness makes the next guy in line think I'm French, so he says "c'est une abomination capitaliste, cette ligne pour l'art," ruefully, pffhting at the end and shooting his pockets with frustrated resignation. I just glance at him then look away as if he doesn't exist, which is proper French etiquette. It warms his heart.

But [My Attorney] didn't suffer eight hours in third class to stand in line. She uses the power of l'internet to find us fast passes. She sprints away, leaving me and the kid wondering if she's finally just given up, but she returns to rescue us from the queue. I glance at my compatriot who is glaring at me for my class betrayal and for impersonating a Frenchman. I turn my weary visage to him with feigned Frank resignation:

"La vie n'a pas de sens. La mort est inévitable. Tout est souffrance. J'aime les pain pardue."[1]

For the next eighteen days, we roam the endless hallways of the Louvre. It could use a few more strategically placed benches. There are nine miles (sorry, 14.5 kilometers) of art-splattered hallways in the Louvre. If you don't stop at all, it'll take five hours. If you were to grace each work of art with a mere ten seconds, skipped all meals, and didn't sleep, it would take you three days, and you'd die.

Our single goal, of course, was to see La Giaconda. We didn't really know what other art the Louvre contained[2]. We're familiar with the various wings of the Chicago Museum of Art. We're not savages. I can direct you to the renaissance wing, the Druer rooms, Van Gogh's Bedroom, and the dollhouse in the basement. I could lead you blindfolded to the impressionists, to the Monets, to the lone John Singer Sargent, and to the cafe for a sandwich.

But at the Louvre we were clueless so our path to La Giaconda was full of false starts, brief misadventures in rooms filled with hilarious statues like the life-sized marble atrocity of a young man strangling a goose which, if it's not a French analogue for the American idiom 'choking the chicken,' should be.

Finally, we arrived at the infamous Italian painting. What a disappointment. What a shitshow. What a scam.

La Giaconda, or "The Mona Lisa," is fucking awful.

I know you probably heard about the guy who stole the Mona Lisa, and you probably imagined him sneaking out through secret janitor tubes and dark stairwells with a gilded painting wrapped in canvas that barely fits under his armpit, but your imagination is crap, and your grasp of art history

---

1 Life is meaningless. Death is inevitable. All is suffering. I like pancakes.

2 Fucking all of it.

is even crapper. As was mine. It's small. It's only 2'6" by 1'9" with the frame. If you sliced it out, as a good art thief would, you could easily fold it up and slip the Mona Lisa into a notebook and walk out through a phalanx of glaring gendarme and they'd never know.

Which begs one to ask why would anyone steal it? Why, in fact, does anyone give this sad lifeless image a passing glance? You're in the fucking Louvre! You can, if you so desire, sit down in a room whose walls are hung with The Raft of Medua or The Intervention of the Sabine Women. You could spend hours staring at The Winged Victory of Samonthrace or Vermeer's Lacemaker. You could get lost in Psyche Revived by Cupid's Kiss. Just getting an adorable pastry and a cup of cafe noir for fifteen minutes is a better use of your time than backhanding your way through a mob of vicious art snobs to get a glimpse—and I mean just a glimpse—of a portrait of a woman who hates you.

Lisa Gherardini's visage has had a weird effect on people over the five-hundred years since her placid disdain was captured by Leonardo da Vinci. It is the only painting in the Louvre which receives its own mail. People have written sonnets about this painting. Claimed to be in love with Ms. Giaconda. Fought duels over her while she stares out from her painting with the world's first recorded snapshot of "I can't even".

Why would you give this painting a single second of your time? The Mona Lisa hates you. Look at her face. So much has been written about the look on her face but may I present my theory here, based on having raised a daughter, having strong female friends my entire life, and being married to a woman-type person: Lisa Gherardini's face was captured in the middle of having just about enough of Leonardo's shit.

I can only imagine the situation here. Leonardo is an old man, 51, broke as hell, wild hair all over the place, probably drunk, eyeing the male servants in Señor Giacondo's mansion with a lurid grin and smelling like the 16th century.

And here is Señor Giancondo's young wife, so beautiful and distant he commissions a painting by the genius da Vinci, who took his goddam time over the next ten years—TEN years—and never even finished the fucking thing. Here she is, married at fifteen to a man twice her age who makes some of his living selling women into slavery and has such a kowtowing relationship[3] with the Medici that when Lisa rejects their overtures, her

---

3 It was awful. The guy was a fastidious bootlicker and abuser and inglorious merchant pimp who threw his wife under the carriage without hesitation, and I wish he were alive today so I could punch him in his 16th century dick. Not because I'm particularly fond of Madame Lisa (finish the chapter)

husband actually apologizes—to them. She has to sit with Leonardo and breathe his stank and fend off his lewd groping—which you know he did. Worse, as she looks down from wherever she is now, the rest of the world goes completely ape shit over her terrible portrait which she had to sit in with Da Vinci choosing out of fashion items from her jewelry box and her closet, so she looks like she was dressed by a racoon and to top it off they call her Mona Lisa.

We don't even know if that's the name of the painting or if the painting even has a name. The name comes from Giogio Visari's biography of Da Vinci, written thirty years after he died wherein the writer barely mentions the painting. He writes "Leonardo undertook to paint, for Francesco del Giocondo, the portrait of Mona Lisa, his wife". But Visari was Italian so what he actually wrote was 'Monna Lisa,' which is like saying 'Madam' or "m'Lady". Worse, Mona was a vulgar idiom for vagina so for five hundred years people have been staring open mouthed and maybe breathing a little too heavily at Lisa Gherardini, who had six kids over the next decade of her marriage, who was married to the Renaissance version of Epstein,[4] and saying, "Vagina Lisa." For five hundred years! So yeah, she hates you. She hates you hard.

But when you walk into the room dedicated to the Mona Lisa, you will be lucky if you get anything more than a glimpse of a topmost corner around the tousled hair of a Japanese tourist. When we arrived—again, in March—the room was packed. We couldn't get close, so we gave up. We finished our trek taking pictures of 15th and 16th century art that clearly showed people using cellphones and taking selfies. We ejected ourselves up the spiral staircase and made a beeline for Les Deux Palais for a midday cocktail and espresso before heading over to Notre Dame. I was overdue for a religious experience.

At Notre Dame I have another moment where I choke up a little because I'm participating in broad history, Notre Dame being a personal pilgrimage site, and also I'm standing there with my gate hanging open looking at alchemical medallions sculptured into the wall and rearing back to gaze up at the gargoyles, looking for the Old Puffer which I will not find because he's three hundred stairs up, inside the north tower which (a) was closed and (b) are you kidding me?

Notre Dame is more than a cathedral. It's an encyclopedia. In my days

---

but because men like that—even dead men from the dusty depths of history—deserve to suffer.
4 Who cares if he did or didn't as long as he's dead.

as a bookstore haunt I picked up a copy of the mysterious and brilliant Les Mysteries des Cathedrales, by Fulcanelli, a guy with only one name so you know you can trust him. Fulcanelli was an alchemist. He was, apparently, the last true alchemist[5]. The book is stacked to its eaves with ornate verbiage and luridly esoteric phrases relating to the practice and history of alchemy in the early days of Notre Dame, which was a popular meeting spot for alchemists because, according to Fulcanelli, alchemists designed and built the cathedral.

You may be looking for a way to get out of this now thinking to yourself, oh crap, he's talking about alchemy. Just when I thought he was cool. I wonder what's on Hulu? But stay with me. Look, maybe the old alchemists were batshit crazy and maybe they were chasing a pipe dream trying to turn lead into gold and maybe they were devoted scholars and not just batshit crazy pederasts. Maybe. But they certainly believed they were onto something and so did a lot of well-heeled merchants who paid them to build Notre Dame. And the merchants were completely all-in on the alchemy angle. In the 16th century, alchemy was the rage. And good business.

Alchemists did a lot more than look for the philosophers' stone. They made ink, dyes, tinctures, mirrors, and more. They were a combination of industrial chemists and pharmacists, and they made bank. All that orthological blather in the woodcuts they left behind was esoteric only in the sense that it was good business to keep their industrial secrets behind a paywall, which in 1635 meant language like this:

*"In our water is required first fire, second the liquor of the vegetable Saturnia, third the bond of mercury. The fire is the mineral Sulfur, and yet it is not properly mineral, nor metallic, but a medium between the mineral and metallic... It is a Chaos or Spirit, because our fiery Dragon, which conquers all things[6] ..."*

It goes on and on like that. Insane writing that has fascinated occultists for centuries but it's not as demonic as most people think. It's a recipe for a chemical mix that creates a material that merchants would have paid for. Is it really any less weird than this passage?

*"Aluminum and iodine react energetically to produce aluminum iodide. The heat of the reaction vaporizes some of the solid iodine as a purple vapor. How many moles of I2 are required to react with 0.429 mol of Al?"*

Moles? Purple vapor? Sounds like alchemy to me, but it's just part of the

---

5 Which sounds like the kind of thing a working alchemist would put on his business card to get more work.
6 Eirenaeus Philalethes, 17th century.

recipe for a pretty chemical reaction from a contemporary online textbook.[7]

What fascinated me about Fulcanelli and the work at Notre Dame were the stories embedded in the architecture. There are stories in the stained-glass windows. Chronicles in the cloisters. On the very face of the cathedral at eye-level you will discover seven round Alchemical medallions affixed to the wall sometime around 1170.

The thing is the stories behind many of the alchemical emblems and series of images are not Catholic. They are pagan as all hell and in Les Mysteries, Fulcanelli acknowledges that the alchemists in charge got an enormous kick out of using seemingly Catholic imagery to build a sculptural white paper on how alchemy works.

*"Other ceremonies, very attractive with the common people, were held there during the beautiful medieval period. It was the Feast of Fools—or the Wise—a processional hermetic fair, which set out from the church with its pope, dignitaries, enthusiasts, and its people—the people of the Middle Ages, loud, mischievous, facetious, overflowing with vitality, enthusiasm, and ardor—spreading throughout the city...A hilarious satire of an ignorant clergy, subject to the authority of Science in disguise, crushed under the weight of an indisputable superiority. Ah! The Feast of Fools, with its triumphal chariot of Bacchus, dragged by a male and female centaur, naked as god himself, accompanied by the great Pan; obscene carnival taking possession of the ogival naves! Nymphs and naiads coming out of the bath; Olympian divinities, without clouds and without tutu: Juno, Diana, Venus, Latone meeting at the cathedral to hear the mass! And what a mass! Composed by the initiate Pierre de Corbeil, Archbishop of Sens, according to pagan ritual, and where the flocks of the year 1220 made the cry of joy of the bacchanalians: Evoe! Evoe!—and the delirious answer:*
*Hæc est clara dies clararum clara dierum!*
*Hæc est festa dies festarum festa dierum!*
*[This day is famous among the famous days!*
*This day is a holiday among the holidays!]"[8]*

These are my kind of people, the kind of back of the bus rock and roll scholars that in the eighties would have read Augustine but played in a punk band called Sebum Thrash! These are the kinds of brothers and fellows who

7 Chemical Recipes. (2019, June 5). https://chem.libretexts.org/@go/page/98549
8 Les Mysteries Des Cathedrales, pg 18, translated by Daniel Bernardo from the 1926 edition: Sojourner Books, 2019

would use blatantly esoteric vocabulary as if they were on the level and square, as if their text had two entirely separate meanings. And look, my copy of L.M.D.C. is dog-eared and fringed with color-coded flags. I have at least thirty index cards in my notes devoted to this thing. I can quote parts of it from memory. Prominent in the book are photographic plates of the medallions, poorly reprinted from pictures taken in 1922. Yet there I was, standing three feet from these legendary emblems.

Here is where we get into a weird subplot for a humorous travel memoir: beneath all the dad jokes and the puerility and the poop splattered excursions is an enduring search for the divine. And look, if you're an atheist and you're preparing at this moment to throw this book across the room, don't. Or do, you paid for it so do as thou wilt. But you're not going to find an ounce of preaching or proselytizing here. I support your atheism. I'm 98% atheist myself. But I'm also 2% chimp9 and like with atheism, that 2% makes a big difference. Traveling or not, I spend a chunk of every day thinking about faith—which is to say I spend a good long couple minutes thinking about cosmology and theology. My suspicion is that such pondering may eventually lead to some kind of all-encompassing definition which will bring me comfort in this vale of tears. But the pragmatist in me knows that's not how spiritual growth works and more than likely these musings will bring me ever deeper into the bracken of theological confusion or the poorly organized library of hermetic books with cool pictures about alchemy and honestly, I can't tell the difference between them.

Inside the cathedral, a hush came over me, and I shuffled along with my face turned up into the rafters that soared so far overhead. I wandered well behind the choir pews, dwelling on the stained glass and the sculptures, and then found myself in a side room where there was a thing that looked like a coatrack for a saint. Its brass tag said it was a something something10 something representing Matthew, Mark, Luke, and John but the only figures on it were carved into the wood at the very top, each the size of a basketball: an eagle, a lion, a man, and a bull.

A few years later, I would stand in my living room and wipe away tears as all of Paris stood around Notre Dame watching her burn because of a beehive.

Back outside, I tried to get close to the medallions one last time but

---

9 If you've ever seen me at the pool, you'll understandably amend this to read three maybe four percent depending how the light hits my back hair.

10 It is a representation of the tetramorph in the form of a totem or herald which would have been carried at the front of a procession and if you're catholic and have laid your eyes on such an object with veneration and ardor know that you have venerated a pre-Christian pagan artifact, you haggard blasphemous heretic.

could only get a bead on the lobster, near the exit about ten feet up. It's there. I swear it is.

## BARTHELONA

Our next stop was Barthelona. We got up early, Ubered to the airport, and looked around warily to see if Sally was there.

We have, as a traveling family, faced what I believe is an overabundance of machine guns. France did not disappoint, as someone had gone déránge dans, fired off some ordnance in public, then ran off. Europe was on a hair trigger.

I had no complaints. Crazy people must be with crazy dealt. We stood around the airport pretending to be French until our jet to Barthelona was released for take-off and here is where my non chalanted.

Barthelona isn't that far from Paris. It's like flying from Chicago to Milford, Iowa.[1] Why in the hell anyone would fly to Milford is a mystery, but Milford is exactly as far from Chicago as Barthelona is from Paris, or exactly as far as any single member of the Proclaimers[2] would walk (presumably from their base in Edinburgh all the way to Valognes which is the closest place they can find decent French food) to fall down at your door.[3]

As we arrived at our seats I was faced with the unsavory necessity of cramming my august presence into a seat carved out of a thimble. It was designed for a plague-thin Barthelonian contortionist. Finding my seatbelt required excessive thrashing from side to side like a grouper trying fit into a bait box. The ends of my seatbelt came up to just below my pockets, so I craned my neck out into the aisle and waggled my eyebrows at the terror-stricken stewardess and made the universal sign for MORE SEATBELT, CHRIST ALMIGHTY, which sent the stewardess into paroxysms searching her tiny compartment for a cinturión de vergonzoso.4

---

1 If you've never partied in Milford, then you haven't partied. Midwest much? Have you seen their grain elevator? Do you even gravel?

2 They did that song in the 80s that goes "I would walk five hundred miles . . ."

3 Of course, if they walked 500 more miles they'd be in Barthelona which would make this whole passage passe.

4 belt of embarrassment

Yet none could be found. The stewardess oscillated between cultural indifference and legal obligation. She conferred with another stewardess who took it upon herself to reach down and try to buckle the belt, as if, perhaps, I hadn't used enough machismo. She used plenty of machismo. She drove her tiny little fists down past my corpulent hips and wrenched the ends of the seatbelt up, then planted both her tiny feet on the edge of my seat between my knees and reared back with all her might.

Nada. They conferred. Then the first stewardess looked down at me, placed her finger against her lips for silence, and walked away leaving me unbelted. Not that I was concerned. We'd have to crash into a mountain to get me out of that seat.

In Barthelona, we decamped into a hotel directly across the street from the Sacreda Familia, the most luridly decorated and insanely architectured cathedral in all history, still under construction, festooned with ceramic doves, biblical scenes sculpted in exquisite detail, and lacey adornment. It is a beautiful acid trip of a church. I took the elevator to the roof of our hotel and stared at it. Right there. Right across the street. I could almost touch it.

I never did. Not even close. We are, in fact, not on speaking terms and it's all my fault. Mine and Ernest Hemingway's, Salvador Dali's, Pablo Neruda's and all the absinthe one can drink on a Tuesday evening at Bar Mariella's where each of these famous people got historically inebriated.

Bar Mariella's is my kind of bar. It hasn't been painted in a hundred years. None of the chairs match. There's graffiti all over the outside, frightened saints on the inside, and a bar carved by the dipsomaniacal minds of artists and poets. It was staffed by distant cousins of the owner, all too young to be in a bar. Of course, we ordered the absinthe service as I had really enjoyed the petit service at Doctor Lupin's in Paris, which was ornate and fancy and had all the rigor and pomp of a neon-lit Japanese tea ceremony, but Bar Mariella's was different.

They served us yellowish absinthe in shitty bar service cups with a plastic fork laid across the top to balance a dollar-store sugar cube over which we squirted tepid water from used mini water bottles with a hole drilled through their lid. You know, fucking fancy.

Didn't matter because absinthe does not give a shit what kind of glass it's served in. It just wants to party and so we had a few snorts then the green fairy turned into a wildly inebriated baby hulk, and we got, as they say in the districts, turnt.

We waddled out of Bar Mariella's because we were hungry. We somehow made it to a nameless bar populated by locals which offered shitty local beer and giant plastic jugs of olives in various brines. Somehow, we made it from the nameless local olive bar to the main drag, La Rambla, and my son, loopy with booze, wooted with joy as we found ourselves standing in a pool of warm golden light puddling on the cobblestones in front of an authentic Irish pub, the Temple Bar, where we drank more until we found ourselves becoming increasingly, lugubriously, joyous.

However, we needed food. We left the bar of our forefathers to stumble into the restaurant of our arch enemies, the sober wait staff at Restaurante Don Fernando. We fell into chairs, and I ordered page one of the menu, knocked over my waterglass, knocked over my wine glass, knocked over [My Attorney]'s wine glass, and laughed a lot.

The wait staff cashed us out immediately and brought all but one dish in to-go containers. There were two giant bags with eight clamshell containers and a plastic-wrapped tub of soup handed to me with the receipt and the hairy eyeball of rebuke. I'm not saying we were kicked out,[5] but our exit was brilliantly curated by the staff, and we found ourselves swaying on the sidewalk in the late moonlit evening of Barthelona with our hands full of food.

[My Attorney] expressed her desire to maybe go lie down and with the vast wisdom of drunken dumbasses, I called her an Uber and we shoved her into the backseat and sent her away. In Spain. At two in the morning. Not even worried about it. Not a care in the world. Just, here, have my wife, in slurred American.

The kid and I stumbled all up and down Carrer de Ferran and its side streets and back alleys, but it was almost three a.m., and everything was closing. Until we found Bar Americain.[6]

Bar Americain was an American bar. I didn't know American bars were a thing. Irish bars litter the international landscape like discarded Guinness cans and Outbacks introduced us all to Kangaroo steaks so why not an American bar? I assumed it would offer a surfeit of Pabst Blue Ribbon and lukewarm hot dogs under a soundtrack of Nickleback and the Star-Spangled Banner. But it was just a bar owned by some Americans and staffed by some Americans and they served us decent bourbon against all known wisdom and local laws.

I was staggeringly inebriated in a bar in Barthelona at three in the morning. My son was beside me, less besotted than I was. Much less. We

---

5 We were definitely kicked out.
6 Not its actual name. I can't remember what it was called or where it was. I was drunk. I was absinthed. It was three in the morning.

didn't talk and we didn't move and eventually we finished our bourbon and they closed and we Ubered back to our swank hotel.

What a perfect moment; a standard but great father and son interlude, the two of us joyously silent after a late, late-night prowling around a Spanish city, turning down poorly executed scams, avoiding three-card-monte tables, somehow safe from pickpockets and free from worry and just existing together in the warm Barthelonian evening by the sea. The cobbles of the Rambla bounced the moonlight back into the dark sky. All was quiet, save a few drunks singing to themselves. And my son and I, arm in arm, swaying along, going nowhere, perfectly happy.

## SAGRADA FAMILIA AND WHY I DIDN'T GO THERE

After returning, still hammered, the kid went to his room, but I was on fire. I ordered a snifter of brandy, which at 3:30 in the morning in Barthelona, is not that big a deal, and went to the roof to stare at the Sagrada Familia.

The elevator doors opened. I staggered over to the wall with my hand full of brandy. A Japanese couple watched me with concern.

I wasn't going to see the cathedral. I was this close, yet we were headed out in the morning, so I had no time. Here I was spitting distance from the world's most ecclesiastic architecture, yet I would never step inside.

Going inside was important not merely for the experience of the Gaudi interior, not merely to see the soaring arches and the way the light flows in and almost comes alive, not only for that. But because it is unfinished and because it won't be finished before I reach the creaking impossibility of being the ancient age of—oh, they pushed it back? It'll be done in 2026? Oh, well, no sweat. I didn't really miss anything.

But in the early morning rooftop darkness, I was angry at myself for not scheduling things properly. I'd blown it. I should have gone to church instead of getting drunk on absinthe like a nineteenth century libertine. I can get absinthe anywhere. But standing inside Gaudi's church would have been something singular and I'd missed it.

I had wanted to feel the presence of the divine in that building because I was certain it is thicker there than it is in the streets; like a dense fog of deity. Because of course it is. Of course God is lurking in the cathedral of Gaudi because God likes crazy people, and this building is maximum crazy set in stone. I'm sure God gets a kick out of watching the builders interpret the blueprints and figure out how to spackle three layers of ornamentation on every square inch and I wanted to get in there and get next to God and just be cool, right, just no big deal. Cross my arms and nod and wait for an opening and just kind of lean over and say, "Mad genius, am I right?" and deity would reach over blindly for a low-key fist bump, and it would be amazing, but no.

Instead, I was swaying on a rooftop like it was the deck of a ship, observed closely by the Japanese who knew something was up. I needed to connect with the spirit of that church. I needed to do something worthy of note: I had to make a grand gesture.

I snatched my notebook out of my pocket and scribbled something down. I don't remember what it was.[1] I'm 100% certain it was illegible. I tore the page out, took a swig of brandy, then dropped the illegible note into the glass and, like a great and noble scrivener, dramatically hurled it at the side of the church.

What a stupid fucking thing to do.

What a stoooooopid fucking thing to do.

First of all, I was a good fifty yards from the Sagrada Familia, and I have the throwing arm of a teacup schnauzer. The snifter whirled out ten feet, then dropped like a stone onto a parked car below and set off its alarm. I continued glaring at the Sagrada for a moment, you know, for effect, then I about-faced and staggered into the elevator.

---

1 Here's the thing. Sometimes writers, when unobserved, when no one can record us on their phones, when our wives are off in the produce aisle, and we're left alone, sometimes we do things that can only be interpreted as "writerly." We don't do it because these things are authentic. They aren't. Writing is mostly sitting and staring. Also, 99% percent of it is internal and unobservable. Any gesture or proclivity that declares "writer" is by definition arrogant and stupid and a lame, ridiculous, pathetic, attention-whoring, pose. But sometimes you want to connect to the popular zeitgeist. you want people, the world, God, and everyone to recognize and so you submit to this passion and sit in a cafe typing very loudly and occasionally muttering GODDAM VERBS! then kind of looking around to see if anyone gets it. I probably wrote WERDS MONKEY POOP.

### Pʟᴇᴀsᴇ Sᴀᴠᴇ Mᴇ I'ᴍ ᴛʀᴀᴘᴘᴇᴅ ɪɴ ᴀ Sᴘᴀɴɪsʜ Rᴏᴜɴᴅᴀʙᴏᴜᴛ

Driving in Spain is perfectly normal except that it's terrifying. Outside of England and Japan, most countries drive on the right side of the road. I had no problem with it. It was easy. Perfectly logical, clear, and weirdly familiar. Except for the roundabouts which are like little traffic whirlpools you can get lost in and maybe never get out of until you grow a beard or die.

However, as much as the roundabout is useful and ubiquitous there are, apparently, degrees of the level of lane change and swerve and combat one encounters based on two factors:

A) HOW BIG IT IS. The more lanes go round about the roundabout, the more likely you are to be flattened by a swarm of mopeds.

B) HOW MANY BUSES. Even one bus turns a lazy roundabout into a death trap. But as more and it becomes a desthtrap as giant whalish coaches lunge across three spinning lanes scattering smart cars and motorbikes into your path. Then one looms over you and you drive into its leeward side and and your simple right turn becomes full-on Indiana Jones-level stunt driving as you ram your ridiculously small car into the sharp, snapping pincers of a busy bus lane.

C) WHERE IT IS. If it's downtown then forget it. Just tear on through and hope for the best because everyone will be trying to kill you and they might succeed if you don't get the hell out of the way.

The roundabout at Placa de les Drassanes is a final boss roundabout composed of a large, five-lane outer circle, and a three-lane inner circle that swallows you whole as you drive underground into, I assume, another goddam roundabout.

Worse, the main roundabout is abutted by two malformed loops in case you go the wrong way. You just shove your car into one of these loops and try again. It adds up to nine circles and was the source material for Dante's Inferno.

The Barthelonian traffic arteries pump hundreds of thousands of cars into this monstrous coil every day along with countless tour buses and rental cars and scooters and mopeds. It is near the Royal Shipyards and a couple other major tourist destinations and is also, if you're an idiot and a glutton for punishment, the best route out of Barthelona on one's way toward, let's say, Madrid.

We'd been stuck in it for eleven years because I couldn't get out of the inside lane. I needed to be in the outer circle so we could exit before we starved to death. We'd already established a pee corner in the back and my son had eaten his shoes. If I didn't exit soon we were going to die. But I just couldn't figure it out.

"Be aggressive!" [My Attorney] yelled.

"I am being aggressive!" I said, continuing to circle in the inside lane as the gas needle fell closer and closer to E.

"Just, do it! Just swerve!"

"We'll wreck and die!"

"Death is inevitable!"

"Dad," my son croaked through parched lips. "I wanna go to college."

"Think about his future," [My Attorney] yelled. She rolled down her window and leaned out, gesticulating at a bus to let us in. He slowed down, but a flock of scooter models swooped in.

I managed to work my way over one lane. I could hear my son's stomach growling over the sounds of the horns commenting on my efforts. I was aimed for the exit, but a fleet of delivery vans cut me off and hid the exits.

"I can't see anything!"

"Have faith!"

"I threw whiskey at God!"

I cut in between the vans and saw another exit coming up one lane further over. I took a breath and zoomed out, narrowly missing a tricked-out scooter piloted by a cellist. I took the exit on two wheels.

"This is the wrong one!"

"How do you know!?"

"It says Barcelona!"

"Shit!"

I caromed across the connecting strip and raced back into the gyre. We eventually found the right exit before I grew a beard and headed off toward Madrid, never to see Barthelona again.[1]

---

1 Right!

## A Brief Guide to Truck Stop Cuisine, Gas Station Wine, and Rude Chinese Women between Barthelona and Madrid

After escaping the vicious vortex of the Barthelonian roundabout, we headed west toward Madrid by way of going south to Baleenthia.

The coast between Barthelona and Baleenthia is a beautiful, scenic drive. I'm reminded of thouthern California but altho of Oregon but altho of Miththigan but altho of jutht outthide Denver Colorado but altho downtown Beththemer, Alabama. I'm reminded of how expectations color one's experience. My expectations for Spain came from old Westerns, bad versions of Don Quixote (which I never finished), and my own imagination. I'd built up a clumsy mental model of Spain and Spain was having none of it. Sure, there are castles, there are bullfighting arenas, sure. But there are also gas stations, Ikeas, convenience stores, and truck stops.

My preconceived ideas of any country I've ever visited have always been off by a country mile. It's an American jingoism infection that no level of intellectualism can scrub out. Americans are necessarily of America and even the cool America that is still here, the America of the 30s and 40s who came back from the war and gave us Film Noir and chess clubs and American intellectualism,[1] is often blind to the realities of the rest of the world.

Soldiers know. Traveling business professionals know. Expats and students and even some missionaries know. They all know that the rest of the world is too busy being the rest of the world and just trying to get by every day to live up to their subconscious insistence that, for instance, Spain is just wall-to-wall bullfighters or some kind of mishmash Daliesque desert dreamscape. I never imagined Spain to be nearly identical to Ohio, but from the window of a stick-shift diesel speeding along the E-901, it is.

We could be anywhere. We could be in Wisconsin. West Georgia. North Texas. The scene from the highway is cross-country-generic—until we hit the tollbooths.

---

1 Not the America of the 50s who gave us McCarthyism.

There are two things about Spanish tolls that were very different from American tolls. One, I didn't know how they worked. There was no attendant. I didn't have an E-Z-Pass. I didn't have cash. But it turns out a tollbooth in the Spanish desert is very much like an ATM in reverse.

The second thing were the machine guns. There had been a terrorist action in France so Spain was keeping a close eye on travelers. As soon as I paid, a man with a machine gun leaned into the driver's window to yell at me and search my nethers for bombs.

"¡Tengo una ametralladora! ¡Dónde está el baño! ¡Qué hay debajo de tus bolas!" He points the tip of his machine gun toward my family jewels.

I took high school Spanish just like the rest of you which means I hid a Spiderman comic behind my book then copied off of Efrain between classes, so I had no goddam idea what this terror monger was saying. I just know he was yelling at my face.

"¿Donde está la biblioteca?!!!"

I wanted to respond but I was hypnotized by his AR-15. He tried again.

"¿Te gusta el futbol?!!!"

I racked my brain. I really should have paid better attention in school. The soldier closed his eyes and reared back like I had insulted his mother. He took a breath, then, his face screwed into a mask of fury, tried again. A torrent of incomprehensible Spanish filled our tiny car.

"Agua por favor! Buenos días! Buenas tardes! Buenas noches! Hola, me llamo Juan! Me llamo… Me llamo… Me llamo… sombra delgada! ¿Cómo te llamas? Mucho gusto! ¿Cómo estás?!"

"DO I BRIBE YOU NOW?"

"Oh, you are Americans?"

"SI"

"Oh, well, we're not looking for Americans. Move along."

"WE COME BARTH ELONA! WE GO MADRID!"

"Madrid is that way, Señor." He pointed the nozzle of his steel death hose in a direction we were not going.

"MADRID THERE?" I pointed.

"I speak English, you know. I went to Oxford."

"WE GO NOW?"

"Get the hell out of here."

I kept driving the wrong way into the desert, passing machine gun-toting soldiers and getting stuck in roundabouts. This was all exacerbated by my realization somewhere around Tarragona that I'd left my $600 phone lying on the toilet paper holder in the lobby bathroom at our hotel in

Berthelona[2]. Mierda!

We turned around, managed somehow to pass by the soldiers without pissing our pants, and headed east. West? Toward the city we had recently vacated.

My family was already suspicious of me driving us across Andalusia because I drive like an old man, and they worried we'd never get there. But I was the only one who could drive stick so, yay. When we picked up the car at the airport rental it took me fifteen minutes to get off the level where the car was parked because I didn't understand the signs for the invisible exit ramp and cursing ensued. So they don't want to go back. Also, we'd have to do the big roundabout twice and by the time we got there, it would surely be starving.

But we did all that. They had my phone at the front desk, the roundabout was napping. By this time we were hungry. I had read that Spanish truck stops had great food, so we headed west on E-90, and I found a truck stop and we pulled in and O.K., this was when things got all foreign.

First of all, overland trucks in Europe are adorable. They'll fit in the palm of your hand. Secondly, the truck stop served leg of lamb roasted over a fire pit with a glass of red wine that only cost a dollar.

"Eet ees the dolaro per reefeel?" asked [my attorney], Spanishing.

"No ma'am. Just one dollar. We fill it up as much as you want."

"Eeet eess free reefeels?"

"Yes. I mean ci. Yes. All you want."

"It's a truck stop!"

"Yes, but it's also Europe. Enjoy your endless glass of cheap ass day wine."

We had the lamb with roasted spring vegetables and even though sweaty truck drivers were passing us to hit the showers, we had a marvelous lunch. We hit the road in the afternoon then, somewhere in the Andalusian mountains, I attempted familiacide.

It was not premeditated. While most European road signs are clear and easy to understand, some of them are dangerously enigmatic. For example, most Spanish highways are divided, you know, like they are in the rest of the developed world, with cars on one side all going in the same direction. But sometimes they are not and when they are not, I mean, when they allow two-way traffic, those brief stretches of one-way traffic highway change into

---

2 If you think for one minute I'm going to eventually spell this right because, ha ha, everyone gets the joke about how pedantic dickheads always correct you when you say *Barss eh loana* by qietly saying, *Barth eh loana,* as they bob their pathetic man-bun and drink their Whiteclaw, you are fucking wrong.

screaming death traps without telling you.

I mean, they try. There are tiny blue signs the size of a doll's open hand with an arrow pointing up, meaning "You're fine; You're going the right direction. It's all good," or pointing down, meaning "THIS IS WHERE YOU MEET YOUR MAKER, GRINGO!" But they are useless. We passed one of these postage-stamps and I remarked,

"Isn't that an adorable, delightfully enigmatic— AAAAAAAAAAAAAAA!"

Suddenly we were hurtling head-on into a wave of angry Spanish drivers coming at us like they're powered by dynamite trying to ram themselves through our grill and shove our diesel engine block through our knees. Somehow, and memory fails me entirely, probably an artifact of trauma, I got us off the one-way highway and back onto the my-way highway and we made it out into the desert just as the sun went down so the bulk of our gorgeous road trip across Spain happened in the dark, liberally seasoned by post-traumatic stress syndrome.

We stopped for gas and so I could do the thing you know I'm about to do. We walked into a Repsol Station which was similar to any basic American gas station. It offered candy, snacks, essentials, parts—and a wall of beer. Not just cans. Not just bottles. There were small kegs of beer. Chilled. This was in the middle of the empty desert, not in a town. The only people buying those kegs were the truckers hunched over the lunch counter staring at me in lurid Spanish. I went into the men's room and that's when things got weird.

I like to use the bathroom alone. It's a habit I picked up ever since I was alive. But about halfway through my occupation of the solitary stall the men's room door burst open and three hundred Chinese women hove in to pound on my door.

"Occupado!"

[Shrill urgent Chinese—pounding]

"I'm in here!'

[Shrill urgent Chinese—pounding]

"This is the Men's room!

[Shrill urgent Chinese—yelling, stomping, pounding]

Normally, I'd wield the power of occupation mercilessly in the face of such blatant disregard for gender tagging and a classless invasion of privacy, but normally it would be some drunk dude who deserved it, not three hundred elderly Chinese women who probably hadn't peed since Zaragoza. So, I gathered myself and unlocked the door to walk out but it slammed open on me as all three hundred women piled in, and one of them took off her pants.

While I admit I have fantasized in my distant youth about being assaulted by a hoard of Chinese women taking off their pants, this was not playing out with the same kind of flair, so I pushed through them out onto the tarmac where my wife was huddled angrily in the car as an entire busload of Chinese businessmen smoked cigarettes right next to her.

The rest of the trip into Madrid happened in the dark so it could have been anywhere. Strange, illuminated visions of industry and commerce floated by on distant hills like constellations in space. Spanish drivers swooped up to my bumper, fell asleep on their horn, then finally passed me as I Americanned my placid way toward the capital.

The only drama came from my son and I because his idea of giving directions was to tell me WHEN I WAS AT A TURN to TURN, TURN NOW! I tried to explain how one should inform the driver of upcoming turns well before hand so they can apply the brakes and perhaps keep him in the will, but he was having none of it and I am overly cautious, so we got stuck in a couple more roundabouts before we finally found our hotel and I wedged our rental between two cars that I swear had those scratches when I got there.

### Rᴀᴛ Sᴏᴜᴘ ᴀᴛ Bᴀʀ Aɴᴅᴀʟú

We settled into the lovely apartment I'd rented, then the next morning my family ditched me to go buy stuff they could get in any well-appointed Walmart leaving me to wander alone, tired, and freezing to death in Madrid.

They do this all the time. I'm a slow walker when I'm feeling good. When I'm tired, I mosey. I shamble. Worse, I was cold which is saying a lot since I live in Chicago where it's colder than the north pole from December to May. I'd adopted the Parisian fashion of strangling myself with a scarf, but it didn't matter. It was March in Spain, and it was cold as hell, and I needed soup.

I walked halfway around the Playa Mayor, my tourist senses jacked up from over exposure to trinkets. I grew up in Orlando so I'm sensitive to tourist trap crap and the Playa Mayor is packed to the eaves with knick knackage of the worst order. I passed every one of them with a sneer until I came to the bright green door of La Torre del Oro's Bar Andalú, through which I glimpsed a giant bull's head adorning their wall and knew I was home.

I ordered a beer and was given a cup of warm sopa jamon, which I drained in a single gulp. I barely tasted it. Might have come out of a can. I have no idea. It was broth and it was hot. I ordered some shrimp, which I ate with a toothpick because tapas. I dined erect at the bar under the watchful gaze of dead steers. I took ironic selfies. The barkeeps wore bright green vests, which lent me comfort as I am a sweater vester from way back and it was good to be with my people. The guy behind the counter made a joke and his friend laughed and I laughed, and the soup and the beer warmed my wintery bones. Then they served me rat soup.

One of the smiling barkeeps reached over the counter with a meaningful look, like I get you, this is amazing and set down a shallow bowl full of stewed meat. It looked like oxtail soup in miniature which should have made me ask, hey, what kind of tiny little ox is this? But I was starving to death, so I dug in, sucking the savory meat off the tiny brittle vertebrae.

There was one bony piece in the center of the bow, about the size of a large strawberry. When I pulled on a nugget of flesh, it flipped over and stared back at me from an empty eyehole it's bowed yellowed incisors grinning up from out of a paper-thin skull.

Some kind of wordless ape knowledge welled up inside me, some kind of hindbrain measurement from the creature's eye socket to the end of its jaw. This was the same kind of bone-deep reaction I'd have if I accidently picked up a spider, or stepped in an anthill. I willed myself to refuse my body's panicked urge to flee and I looked more closely, trying to be reasonable, trying to take in the details to prove to myself it was just normal food but my gaze lingered on the teeth. Oh god the teeth. Those were rat teeth. I was eating a rat!

"What the hell is this?" I pointed to the plate full of pest.

"Pobre de popa."

My Spanish is almost as bad as my Esperanto, so I had to roll these words over in my head for a long time while I was staring at the curved, stained dentures on my plate. Poor pope? Is that slang for rat? It sounded like it could be slang for rat. If I were going to make up street jargon for a rat, I'd call it a poor pope.

It gets worse. The skull had been split. Before I'd turned it over, I'd sluiced some jiggle meat right out of it. I'd slurped a spoonful of rat brains.

I turned to my nearest companions at the bar to ask for help.

"Hey– "

"Oh, my Gawd, are yallermerican?"

Jesus Houston Astros Christ.

I signaled the bartender and waved at my rat then ordered two for Texas and smiled nervously and they started complaining about how nobody here speaks the language. I nodded and paid my bill and said no habla Engles and burst out into the frigid atmosphere of España.

We'd booked this trip at the last minute, my wife leaving the arrangements to me, a rarity in our marriage, as she was in the middle of transitioning from one life altering law firm to another and was working four-hundred-thirty-seven hours a day. If she didn't use her vacay time she'd lose it. I had to act fast.

Anything with a beach in a sunny climate where they serve Margaritas out of a bucket was already wall-to-wall Spring breakers and even if I did get a room in Cozumel or Playa del Carmen I wouldn't be able to sleep from the sound of college freshmen plunging to their deaths from every balcony at the hotel.

I'd looked long and hard at Tenerife, but the flight was insane, and it wasn't that warm anyway. Ultimately, we decided to fly into Paris and take the Eurail to Spain.

In March.

But hey, we're from Chicago. Fuck winter. I've walked from my car to the grocery store in a sleeveless t-shirt in January and didn't care because I hate bulky jackets and I'd parked close. I could hack it.

But winter cold is warmer than vacation cold. You expect to be chilly in February. You fight back. You tough it out. You don't expect to be cold on vacation so the slightest dip in the mercury turns even the hardiest Chicago native into a desperate trembling moron.

I caught up with my brood. We had lunch at the oldest restaurant in the world, Sobrina d'Botin, a meal I had pined for nearly my entire life. A meal I had hoped to have with my pop. I toasted the ghost of my dead father and enjoyed my roast suckling pig with a bottle of red, but my heart wasn't in it. Every forkful was ruined by the faintest aftertaste of roasted rodent. Goddam bar andalú–you ruined the meal of a lifetime.

We shivered down Calle de Cuchilleros to get a cab. My jacket was buttoned all the way to my chin; my scarf was tight around my neck; my mouth tasted like a small mammal. I was miserable and disappointed and sober.

Then it started snowing.[1]

In Madrid.

We napped off the pork in our hotel, cabbed back to the Mercado San Miguel which is delightful and loud and crowded and warm. I found a cart selling oysters caught that very morning next to a shop selling flutes of Spanish cava. My wife appeared out of thin air with a glass then my son sauntered up at the same time bearing beer and a plate of cheeses. We spent some time enjoying the multilingual chatter and the convivial vibe and the booze. I planted myself between them, two-fisting bubbly and bivalves until a smile crept warily onto my face.

It had been a good trip.

I'd drank absinthe with my boy in Café Mirabella's in the quarter in Barcelona, the same shitty joint where Dali, Neruda, and Hemmingway got hammered. The paint was peeling off the walls. The tables were wobbly. They didn't have cool absinthe fountains like we'd enjoyed at Dr. Lupins in Paris. They poured pine needle colored liquor over a sugar cube on a fork laid over the rim of a glass with an 8oz bottle of lukewarm water with a hole

1 More on this later.

in the cap. We drank ourselves into a hallucination then went to a classy restaurant where we ordered everything on the menu, spilled our drinks, and I'm not saying we were kicked out, but our exit was expediently curated.

We'd had dinner at the Eiffel Tower, every course interrupted by thunderous applause as some idiot took a knee and set his girlfriend's Facebook feed on fire by proposing. We'd dined at La Petit Canard where, true to its name, each dish was duck. We'd learned expensive escargot is worth the money. We'd dodged professional beggars at Notre Dame.

Our tapas tour had been glorious. We'd made friends with Belgian tourists who dragged us into a Belgian bar where we drank the world's rarest beer. We'd eaten strange and wonderful foods thousands of miles from our home. We'd photographed the landmarks and snaked our way through narrow alleys to impossible stores filled to overflowing with outlandish wares.

So I ate a rat[2]. I mean, when you balance that against everything else it was small and insignificant. And you know what? Stewed rat brain is tasty. Until I realized I'd dined on a varmint, I was fine with it. Rat[3] was good. And it's not like it was an accident. It didn't fall into the soup. It was the main ingredient. Who am I to question the delicacies of another culture? I'm from Alabama, my people eat boiled peanuts and chitlins.

---

2 Please note: limited research and a few phone calls to Madrid, while not definitive, have broadened the zoology of my meal at Bar Andalú to include all species in the families of leporidae, sciuridae, and hamsters. However, I have been reassured that the habit of Peruvians in turning to the easily farmed Cavia porcellus for inexpensive meat may have migrated to Spain and more than likely I did not eat a rat but instead a common guinea pig which is still a rodent and more than often a charming household pet so I'm no happier, only slightly more informed.

3 I think it was a squirrel. The skull was split open to expose the brain, which I apparently consumed. I know my grandfather used to hunt squirrel in Alabama and had squirrel brain with scrambled eggs for breakfast sometimes. They're rodents and they have big eyes and well maybe it was a squirrel. This isn't better than guinea pig, and guinea pig, frankly, only marginally exceeds rat. None of this is good. I'm becoming a vegetarian.

### Freezing to Death in Madrid

There was a moment in Madrid so sublime, I still think about it. In a sense, it was mundane. It was food. It was drink. It was people. It was a small, brief, golden moment and we'll get there in a second. First things first: the saga.

I've been able to read since I was alive. I swear I came out of the womb with a book in one hand and a library card in the other. I ran wild through the orange groves and gator infested swampland of my youth with all the other kids, but I was just as happy completely alone on the living room floor with my nose in an encyclopedia.

My dad, a master plumber and union rep, loved books. Our house had the National Geographic collection of picturesque hardbacks, the Tree of Knowledge encyclopedia, and A Treasury of Great Recipes by Vincent and Mary Price.

Yeah, that Vincent Price.

The Treasury is oversized. It's four inches thick, has a silk cover with a ribbon, crimson edged parchment-colored pages with brilliant illustrations, and full-bleed color shots of insanely beautiful dinners, of restaurant tables sagging beneath mountains of beef and lobster and the influence of one of the 20th century's most refined cinematic luminaries.

The Treasury isn't exactly a cookbook. It is, in that there are recipes, but the recipes are written with the same maddening neglect as a recipe written by a New Orleans mansion cook before the Civil War (I've checked). No steps, no order, no thought about the person using the recipe. Just ingredients and madness.

Of course, I didn't know this as a kid. I skimmed through this thing with my eyes wide, my heart pounding against the avocado-green shag carpet beneath my chest, like it was forbidden, like it was porn.

My people are biscuit forward—and biscuit backward, come to think of it. Our cuisine begins with fatback and doesn't go a whole lot further. It's soul food. You probably think of soul food as a Black thing, and it definitely is,[1] but it's also a Southern thing, a dirt-poor blue-collar Alabama thing, and that's what we ate growing up.

Here is a Garlington/Whitfield menu from any typical day in the early 70s:

Breakfast:[2]

Buttermilk biscuits with sorghum syrup

Fried eggs

Fried sausage

Fried bacon

Sausage or red-eye gravy

Fresh tomato right from the garden

Coffee with sugar and evaporated milk (depression-era coffee)

Lunch:

Sink sammiches: fresh thick tomato slices on white bread with Duke's mayonnaise, salt, and pepper

Leftover biscuits

Fresh biscuits

Sweet, iced tea

Dinner:

Fried chicken, or Chicken Fried Steak, or Salmon croquets

Church-style mac and cheese

Collard greens

Butterbeans

Fried okra

Mashed potatoes and gravy

Boiled yellow corn with butter

Crowder peas or black-eyeded peas or cow peas

Fresh, raw cow horn peppers

Leftover biscuits

Sweet, iced tea

Blackberry and peach cobbler with ice cream

---

1 Like all great things in America, soul food is an artifact of slavery. Africans brought the seeds and know-how and grew the food they loved. They planted okra, collard greens, watermelon, black-eyed peas, peppers, yams, and more. They were given scraps from plantation production—chicken necks, hog jowls, the gritty residue leftover from making corn meal, and pretty much whatever the cooks didn't use to feed the slavers. They incorporated African cooking techniques and recipes and gave birth to hybrid dishes that were so good the slavers started eating them and pretty soon this is what people ate from Savannah to Salt St. Marie.  Soul food is damned delicious, it's cheap, and it sticks to your ribs. It is the defacto cuisine of the south. if you like it—if you enjoy anything of worth in America—thank a slave.

2 It should be noted here that I wrote an entire book about breakfast, *The Full English*, and there is a chance the Southern morning repast is a trans-Atlantic declination of that classic meal. A full English is the U.K. breakfast consisting of fried eggs, blood sausage, fried mushrooms, a fried tomato, toast, and beans. If you change everything except the eggs, the two dishes are virtually identical.

Lemon merengue pie

This may seem like a luxurious and unusual meal to those of you who grew up rich and think soul food is an quixotic ethnic excursion. However, when fried chicken is your baseline you begin to wonder if there's something else. Don't get me wrong here, it's delicious and I still crave it now. But when you eat that way every day, it becomes a routine. And it becomes more than a foundation, it becomes a kind of shelter from other foods. We thought spaghetti was exotic. I didn't have a taco until I was twelve-years-old.

Dining out meant drive-through at Maryland Fried Chicken, a blatant rip-off of KFC that was ten thousand times better, or Fat Boy's Barbeque. In the summer, I'd go out on jobs with my dad, and we'd meet up with the other blue collar business elite of Ocoee at the lunch counter in the back of Eckerd's Pharmacy where we'd have the same breakfast together: watery grits, rubbery bacon, undercooked eggs, limp toast, and weak coffee. I remember those days so clearly. My pop and the other guys talking about their future in Central Florida, about politics, and about things I didn't understand. On Fridays, we went to Red Lobster.

This was the extent of my culinary life—until I discovered The Treasury in a cabinet over the stove with the other cookbooks and cracked it open and suddenly the gastronomic world opened up.

I'd never thought about other countries. I assume that as a somewhat bookish kid I knew there were other countries. We had a globe. I went to school. But I never thought about people actually living there and I sure as hell never thought about what they ate but here it was in living color: poached trout with shaved truffles and salmon mousse from France, garlic soup from Spain; even the food from the American cities was alien. From Gage & Tollner's in New York, there was a recipe for Cornish hen cooked in clay. Oysters Rockefeller. Gumbo from Antoine's. There were pictures of men in tuxedoes pouring wine for other men in tuxedoes and their hyper elegant, beautiful wives. The names of the recipes were in French, Spanish, German, and Slav—Sauté de Scupions à la Niçoise, Paella al la Valencia, Gurkhas Norge. And somehow, in all this, I found Sobrino de Botin, the oldest restaurant in the world.

Some of you just choked because you are under the impression the <u>oldest restaurant</u> in the world is [insert your mistake here].[3] You're wrong.

3 For the sake of completion, here are some of the oldest restaurants still operating and the year they opened. Botin is considered the oldest that has been in the same spot from day one.

Gostilna Gastuž—1467

Sobrino de Botin is accepted among brothers and fellows as the oldest continuously operating restaurant upon this globular thing we live on, and it is amazing.

Price gets Sobrino de Botin right. He gets how Dumas was a waiter there, how Hemingway loved it, how it opened in 1725 and part of the original oven is still down there in the kitchen. Their specialty is roasted suckling pig and ok, you vegetarians need to turn to another page because I'm about to drool all over this story about the consumption of a sentient being, but whatever. You can have my crispy suckling piglet when you pry it from my cold dead fingers.

I knew about this place. My dad and I talked about it. Talked about going there. I had kept this idea alive my whole life and finally, 14 years after his untimely death thanks to mesothelioma, my wife and my son and I walked through the door.

Pictures of me from that day show a man trying to hide the fact that he's a little sad because this was supposed to be my pop and me sitting at this table. I mean, my wife and kids too, but he'd be there. We walked in and I wiped away a tear and we crept down into the basement, my six-foot son crouching to fit through the tiny opening and there in the dining room, there among the ghosts of almost three hundred years of diners, I ordered crispy piglets for all of us and [My Attorney] ordered an expensive wine and men in tuxedoes served us until we couldn't take it anymore.

Our dinner was legendary, and I loved it but we had to go and so we climbed up out of the basement then trudged out through the lobby, handshaking everyone as we went, to kick open the front door like Hollywood bosses into a Madrid that had lost its goddam mind.

It was snowing. I mean, it was blizzarding—a lot. People were running out into the street staring up into the bright silver sky as fat snowflakes drifted down into their hair, onto their tongues, coating everything in a sheen of frost. Howling Spaniards threw their arms around each other in wild celebration. The whole city stopped what it was doing to

---

Honke Owariya — 1465
Hotel Gasthof Löwen — 1380
The Sheep Head Inn — 1360
La Couronne in France —1345
Brazen Head — 1198
Ma Yu Ching's Bucket Chicken House — 1153
The Old House in Wales — 1147
Wurstkuchl — 1146
St. Peter Stiftskulinarium — 803, a restaurant in Austria which served both Mozart and Clint Eastwood (according to NetCredit who apparently looks into these things).

go play in the snow while we walked slowly down the sidewalk shaking our heads and muttering Jesus Mary and Joseph, we're on vacation over here.

But this isn't the sublime moment.

Even though we just ate tiny baby pigs, we were starving so we hit the tapas trail. Look, I'm not a guidebook writer. There are eighty-five-thousand YouTube videos about tapas and at least that many books. Do your homework. But here's where we went: Bodegas Ricla and I didn't want to leave. Most people think Vermouth is just part of a Manhattan, but in Europe they drink it straight from tiny little glasses like gentlemen. At Riclas, we had tiny glass after tiny glass of Vermouth, and it was wonderful. I'm almost positive there were tapas because of course there were but I don't remember what they were. Or if they were. I had vermouth brain.

We met two Belgians and got to talking and turns out the guy loved the same weird fucking ambient records I do and/or knows how to bilk an American out of decent beer. They drug us up the street to Cafeeke, the best Belgian bar in Madrid where I spied a beer crate labeled Westvleteren in Old German capitals and I lost my composure. Surely they didn't have crates of the world's best beer?[4] Yes. Yes they did. I bought one for each of us. I'm sorry, [My Attorney] bought one for each of us and we proceeded to get Belgian drunk on a beer made by God.[5]

There were more. There were tapas bars up one side and down the other. Finally, we ended up at the 100-year-old Saint Michael market, a stand-alone joint with steampunk ironwork decor and stall after stall after stall of good stuff to stick in your mouth which I did. A lot.

We split up as we always do. [My Attorney] went off looking for cheese. My son stepped out to openly smoke a cigarette. I wandered.

Wandering is my strong suit. I aspire to be a dapper elderly flaneur, wandering ancient late-night markets smoking a pipe and wielding a fearsome cane at unyielding youth, shouting non sequiturs in my screechy old man voice. I have yielded easily over the last thirty years as [My Attorney] has molded me from the rough ashlar stone of a man I used to be—savage, wild, lost in the weird places in Florida, Alabama, and New Orleans, hunting down hard to elusive bookstores, beering with fishermen and truck drivers, grabbing a canoe and a notebook and a pack of cigarettes and paddling off into the swamps—to a portly placid pedestrian powerwalking a fanny pack

---

4 Depends on who you ask, of course. There are capricious, poorly educated morons who think it's down around #51 but they work for BeerAdvocate and they put Pliny The Younger at 13 and I'm not an expert or anything but fuck no.

5 $300 for a six-pack—if you can find them. And those are the little guys. I bought each of us a tallboy, so they had to be OW! they were probably about OW!—I'm sorry, [My Attorney] won't let me type that number.

around the pool at an all-inclusive resort. I have given in to itineraries and traveling with a three-ring binder that's color-coded and alphabetized. I bought a—we bought a—I got [My Attorney] drunk and she bought—a time share. We don't wander.

But I did. I flaneured the shit out of San Miguel's and after passing on the baby eels (yuck) I scooched around a crowd and found myself bathed in a golden light. On my left, a man selling freshly shucked Ostras de Cambados, from Galicia. On my right, a man selling frigid flutes of cava.

Oysters and champagne.

On my third bivalve, I spot my son towering over the Spanish housewives and tourists. He catches my eye then pretends he didn't then he's standing next to me and just as he takes the ice-cold oyster I hand to him, [My Attorney] is there with a little plate of crackers and Manchego. We eat in silence. I hand them more champagne.

I don't know how, how on earth, how in the wide complex madness of the universe anyone can stand in a quiet spot at San Miguel's eating fresh flat-shelled Galician oysters, then wash them down with Spanish bubbly, in the presence of one's cherished humans, the people who matter[6], the people who you hope will tearfully crowd your bedside as you slip away. I don't know how anyone in a moment like this can possibly doubt the existence of God.

As I slurped another oyster and chased it with cava I caught my wife's eye and we glanced at our son then back at each other then around us and silently wondered if perhaps we'd managed, despite the bitter cold, despite the snow, despite how everyone was smoking, and despite two Belgians hitting us up for world-class Trappist tripel, despite my gout sending me back to the apartment we'd rented, despite nearly freezing to death in a desert city, and despite the Scottish bartender at the Irish bar in the Spanish Capital we dipped into who, when he realized we were Americans who'd just voted in Lil' Bitchler to the executive high chair, slammed his hands on the counter and yelled, "What the hell is wrong with you people?!" despite all that, we were having a good time.

---

6  I wish to hell my daughter had been able to come with us, but we forgot all about her because she'd moved out and lived in an apartment in Des Plaines. We were at the airport when I turned to [My Attorney] and asked what Sarah thought about us going to Spain and [My Attorney] said: I thought you talked to her. We sent her a card. *We're good people.*

### My Balls are Broken in a Jet Ski Disaster

We come now to another entry in the growing list of ways [My Attorney] busts my balls. In this entry, however, I did it myself.

Let me state here and now: we have a close, loving relationship punctuated by insane levels of pointless competition. Also, let me state here, that in 2005 when we were racing go-karts in Alabama, I let her win. I am a champion go-kartist and there's no way she'd win on her own. That's insane. I was being generous WHICH SHE WOULD KNOW FOR HERSELF IF SHE WOULD CONSENT TO A REMATCH. THE TROPHY ISN'T YOURS IF YOU CAN'T DEFEND IT, LADY!

When I met her, [My Attorney] was a timid Notre Dame graduate, a good Catholic, and suspicious of pretty much everything. I am not talking out of school when I tell you she was afraid of avocadoes, drank Bartles & James, thought red wine was dangerous, and had never been inside a Subway. That's not to say she was some kind of sheltered half-punk half-prep who'd recently escaped the doldrums of the Midwest to relocate in sunny Florida, but yes, she was.

I was not a slim Catholic School girl but was instead a lunatic Floridian skate-punk-head-neck with a penchant for libraries and Cuban food living in a condemned shotgun apartment across the street from Lake Eola in Orlando where I lived mostly by candlelight because I didn't have the money to turn on the electricity.

I'm telling you this because she's come a long way. Today she collects Mourvèdre, drinks filthy martinis, and is about as timid as a tiger shark. However, our dynamic sometimes reverts to shy-Catholic-School-girl-married-to-a-worldly-lunatic-swamp-beast when I introduce her to something about which she is cautious. Then she gets it and immediately outstrips my talent and capabilities by several orders of magnitude.

Like Jet Skis.

We were in the Bahamas at an all-inclusive adult resort I don't want to get sued by whose name may rhyme with Flandals. It was April because of course it was April, so the Atlantic was a warm sixty-six degrees, the sky was a whorl of steel blue clouds, and the wind was blowing the deck chairs into the pool. You know, JetSki weather.

"How much for an hour of jet skiing?" I asked the uniformed equipment clerk at the rental hutch overlooking the ocean. Yellow warning flags snapped violently from every corner. The clerk stared at me for a minute, recognizing a lunatic.

"I'm sorry, sir. No one is allowed on the water today," he said, pointing to the yellow flags. "The weather is dangerous. The waves are more than three feet high in the bay. I am sorry. Perhaps tomorrow."

"Yeah but the pool is open," I said, presenting him with the unflinching logic of an idiot.

"Sir," he paused, his eyes closing briefly to allow him to gather the necessary energy to explain to a grown man why he can't rent him a high-powered water rocket when the waves are four feet high. "The pool is unaffected by the wind. You are welcome to swim there all day."

I glanced down the slope at another beach hut that had six beautiful Jet Skis parked in the sand.

"What about those, can I rent those?"

The clerk leaned forward over his counter to see what the hell I was talking about. Then he uttered words which should have given a sane man pause:

"Sure—if you want."

I waved [My Attorney] over. We trotted down the sandy hill to the line of waterbikes and we looked them over like professionals.

The rental hutch for Vandals Resort where I'd just been judged a lunatic was a well-crafted building made from two-by-fours and slat wood and painted a happy lemon yellow. It had signs and a register and flags. The rental hut for these slightly battered waterbikes was a fluttering tarp sretched over a folding card table manned by a couple of Bahamian guys and a large woman in a colorful blouse who was crafting knickknacks out of palm fronds. There were no signs. No special messages to the guests of Handles.

"Must be their auxiliary hut," I said. I smiled at a young Bahamian in bright gym shorts and nothing else. "Hey, we're in room 804."

"Fascinating; you want a JetSki?"

"Yeah! How much!"

"$200 for an hour."

"Two hundred—is that for all of them?"

"Ha ha. No, sir. Each."

"Hon, let's just do it. You've been wanting to go jet skiing since we got here," [My Attorney] said, giving in before I even put up a fight. We picked out two nice looking Jet Skis and the young man gave us our instructions.

"This one makes them go," he said patiently, his hand lightly gripping the throttle. Then, he stood up and looked at us very sternly, and said in all caps: "DO NOT GO INTO THE OCEAN! STAY IN THE BAY!"

And we were off. I had ridden a Jet Ski once in Alabama, so I was a damned expert. I opened her up and shot out into the jade green waters of Scandals Bay. [My Attorney] was more cautious. She rode her Jet Ski slowly into the open water as she calculated all the ways we could die, sorting them from "instant" to "lingering." I swung around and rode in circles around her, giving her the kind of support she needed, like a good husband.

"Oh my god, crank it!"

"I'm fine."

"OPEN IT UP!"

"I'm fine!"

"We're not paying four hundred bucks for you to go this slow!"

"I'M FINE!!"

This would not do. I wasn't put on this earth to slow roll a damn Jet Ski.

"I'm literally driving circles around y–"

And she broke. Cautiously, she cranked it up. In a matter of seconds, she'd mastered Jet Skiing and was hauling her pert little ass across the choppy waters of the Caribbean. Suddenly I was falling behind. Way behind. [My Attorney] was skipping over the waves, timing her approach just right so she ramped into the air off of every one of them like a goddam stunt skier. It was completely unfair. There's no way I was going to let my legal counsel out jet ski me. I cranked my throttle all the way open, stood up to give it some relief, then blasted directly into a five foot wave that slammed the seat up into my precious family heirlooms with the force of a runaway train.

I almost fainted. I slowed waaay down to administer first aid, comprised entirely of me breathing heavy while I reached down to take inventory as it seemed like the Caribbean may have stolen one of my coconuts or maybe knocked it back up around my spleen. As I breathed steady and slow, trying to blunt the force of the pain, I saw [My Attorney] shoot off a wave into the sky, her wake sparkling behind her, grinning a mile wide, howling with joy, in slow motion. At the apogee of her Instagrammable leap, she waved.

I am not a competitive man, dear reader. I am gentle and kind and can't stomach the cutthroat disposition of the sporting life, but this was too much. Even for a professional bystander like myself, it was clear a line had been crossed. A gauntlet flung. Testicular agony be damned, this was about decorum!

I cranked it. I aimed for [My Attorney] with a grim determination. No way was she a better jet skier than me. Jumping? On her first run? No. Look at me. Look at me! I'm the captain now.[1]

I got closer. The waves got bigger. Just as we synched up and just as she waved at me again, filled with joy and love, laughing and having a brilliant time, I saw my chance to ruin her.

A seven foot wave crested off my port bow. If I hit it exactly right, I'd fly into the air at least eight feet higher than her. I craned my neck and squinted up at the leading edge of the wave as it loomed fourteen feet over the surface of the bay. I was going approximately seventeen-thousand miles an hour when I hit it—exactly right, like a wet Evel Knievel. I swept up its face. I knifed through its foamy crest. I soared four-thousand feet into the air.

Grinning with joy, drunk with the power of victory, I glanced down into the slough behind the wave and there, directly beneath me, lurking under the aquamarine surface, was a shark-like shadow. There were fins. A tail whipped through the water. And against all logic, against all known wisdom, against just plain every day horse-sense, I thre my hands up to my head in the classic oh shit gesture.

An icy fear shot through me as the Jet Ski fell away and I plunged into the shark-infested waters to be eaten alive.

I hit hard. The waves buried me quick. I flailed under water, trying to fight a shark while fighting for air. I broke the surface, gasped for air, and whipped around looking for the shark. Then I realized why three-foot waves were a big deal.

Because I have a six-inch head.

I paddled like a terrified chihuahua to keep it above the surface while I scanned the suddenly opaque water for the shark, and all thirty-five feet of those vicious waves loomed over me.

My Jet Ski did what Jet Skis are supposed to do, which is to circle as they power down. But I couldn't exactly whistle here boy to get it to come back. And also, I was drifting away. And also, sharks.

Suddenly a shaft of golden light cut through the clouds, the wind died down, the waves fell away, and heroic music played. There was [My Attorney], the woman I loved, racing toward me as fast as she could go.[2] I

---

1 I am perfectly aware at just how lame that joke is but if you think for one second I'm going to edit it out simply because it is over used and dad-jokish and sad, you are wrong. It's funny. You laughed before you read this footnote.
2 This is essentially the story of my life. We met when I was a young man and she's been saving my

grabbed onto the stern. She looked down into my panic-stricken visage.

"Why are you freaking out?"

I tried to yell shark, but the ocean punched me in the face.

"SHAMP!"

"What?"

"Shark! I saw a shark!"

"There aren't any sharks in the bay. It's walled off."

"I saw a shark! There's a shark!"

She's right. There aren't any sharks in Bandals Bay. They made a big deal about it. It's all protected and safe. You could swim around with a side of beef around your neck and only the seagulls and vegans would attack you.

"Get on your Jet Ski, babe."

I'm floating in the surging waves, knocked around like a cork, and the Jet Ski is right there, waiting for me. But now the Naugahyde saddle is bobbing high over my head. Getting on would be like climbing onto the roof of my house. I can barely pull myself up onto a couch. How the hell am I going to haul my slippery ass out of the ocean onto a floating Jet Ski?

"You want me to tow you back into shallow water so you can–"

"NO!"

"Maybe there's a rock–"

"I got this!"

A half an hour later, I've managed to heave my torso onto the back of the machine after it's slid away from me fifty times. People on the beach are watching me and I'm pissed. I'm not here for their entertainment, goddammit! THERE WERE SHARKS! I knuckle down and make a massive and considerable effort, dragging my carcass all the way onto the seat leaving only a melon-sized bruise on my upper thigh.

I aim myself back toward Glandals.

"We still have another fifteen minutes!" [My Attorney] yells.

"We're done."

She drops in beside me as I pilot my machine gingerly toward the beach, wincing as I plow through every wave and every wave plows the saddled up into my taint. She's riding circles around me.

"We can go slower if–"

"I'm fine."

"Are you ok?"

---

ass pretty much daily ever since. It is rare that I am the Jet Ski savior in our relationship. She has saved me from financial ruin, from torching my reputation, from getting my ass handed to me by enormous bouncers at a piano bar, and from an accidental porn subscription I couldn't get out of, all with grace and dignity and endless calm.

"I'm FINE."

"Maybe you should stand up?"

"I'M FINE!"

Only for a minute, however. Our host helps us drag our water bikes onto the shore then makes sure we we're well satisfied. I shake his hand and tell him "we're in room 804" to which he replies, "We're not with the resort."

"Pardon me?"

"We are an independent, cash-only business. Your rental fees come to $400 dollars."

"But I told you our room number when we checked them out!"

"That was very entertaining, yes. However, we require a cash payment."

"I thought it was $200 an hour?"

"Each," he explained at length. Ok, so I should have figured that out up front. I should have noticed his lack of a uniform. Or shoes.

I drag my wallet out of my waterproof bag and stare down into its dark shadowy emptiness.

"I don't seem to...Um..."

"It is ok, I can take you to an ATM," he offers in the same tone of voice in which Vincent Corleone makes you an offer you can't refuse. "Your wife will stay here." I assume to be sold into slavery if I can't raise the money.

We get into his rusty pick-up truck. Trash and debris crowd in the deep well of the windshield. He wheels us out across the street abutting a parking lot next to our resort, then into a Publix grocery store with adjoining shops that would have been at home in any suburb in the United States.[3] I flounce into the Publix and shove my card into an ATM and receive no money at all. I have money, I can see my money. But I left the United States without informing my bank I'd be traveling to a place where bank fraud is a normal career, so my bank isn't issuing me a thin Roosevelt dime. I climb back into his rusty truck.

"I can't get any money."

"Mebbe dat Ay Tee Em is broken, man. Let me take you to another."

We drive through the real Bahamas. He takes me a mile to a Bank of America. My bank. I walk into the little lobby. I shove my card into the ATM. It laughs. I punch all the buttons. It puches back. I get into the truck empty handed.

---

3  And once again I flaunt my ignorance of the world as I reveal how I believed everyday life in the Bahamas was somehow exotic or foreign. They're only fifty miles off the coast of Florida (this is of course a specious comparison as I am talking about the outer islands of the Bahamas, not the main islands which are 313 miles away, but this is my book, not yours, and I can do what I want). Assuming you don't get sucked into the Bermuda triangle.

"Ok, mon, I been patient. If you can't get the money then we're going to have a problem.

I envisioned [My Attorney], slaving away in the hot Bahamian sun for the next twelve years to work off our debt. Then I remembered we had cash in a drawer back in our room. We pull up to Scandals.

"Just come with me and I'll get your money."

"I can't go in dere, mon." I look at him and he explains slowly, as if I'm an idiot, because I am an idiot. "It's a members only resort, mon." Then he smiles a broad and genuine smile. His face lights up like he's in a tourism ad and he says, "It's ok, mon. I trust you. I'm sure your lady won't mind waiting." Suddenly his smile, still warm and welcoming, is sharp as a knife. They're going to kill her. How will I tell the kids? How will I pay my bill?

In our room, I rip open the drawer under the bar where we put the money. It's not there. I rifle through the drawers, flinging carefully folded clothes all over the place like a meth-addled burglar. I look under the bed, throw open our suitcases. I can't find it.

There's a knock. I freeze. How'd he get in? I cautiously open the door. It's our evening butler, James.

"Hey, James; uh, I didn't call."

"I know mon, but my cousin Gerald sent me to check on you. He is worried," James frowns over my shoulder at the mayhem displayed behind me. "Are you ok?"

"Gerald?"

"He rents Jet Skis down on the beach."

"You know him?!"

"Do I know my cousin Gerald?"

Fuck! They're family! They're like a warm, friendly mafia. My blood turns to ice. I lean toward him, "I can't find our money," I whisper.

"Did you look in the safe?"

"The—" I shut the door in his face. I punch in the numbers and the door pops open. There it is. A thin envelope of twenties. I run back through the resort. Gerald's sitting in his truck, idling in the exit road with his hazards going as the Candles guards give him side eye. He's wearing sunglasses and looking grim. I get in. He snatches the envelope out of my hand, licks his fingertips, then counts it methodically. It's stuffed with four-hundred and forty dollars i(he deserved a tip for not cutting my throat).

"Nice doin' bidness wit you."

He drives me back. I hug [My Attorney] like she just got out of prison. She laughs and shows me the little knickknack she made with shells like she hadn't just been held hostage by the Bahamian Mob.

"Can we go home now?" I ask.

"What? No, we have three more days. Tonight's the piano bar."

"I'll have to drink a little to sing out loud in front of people."

"Well, it's all inclusive so you can drink all you want."

And then some, as it turns out.

## HOW TO THROW UP AT AN ALL-INCLUSIVE RESORT

*[Trigger warning: the following passage is luridly disgusting and definitely should not be in print, but alas, it is, and you can, without damaging your enjoyment of this book, skip to the next chapter. However, should you continue, gross things happen.]*

I pretend I don't like all-inclusive vacations. But [My Attorney] adores them as her only goals are to save money and do laundry. Although most all-inclusive vacations don't come with a washer-dryer combo, they do come with free booze and this is, perhaps, not a good thing.

At Handles Resort, we had our first real taste of all-you-can-drink all-inclusiveness when we waded into their pool wide-eyed and trembling with excitement at the vision taking up the shallow end: an entire bar, with stools and everything, in the pool. In. The. Pool. That excitement turned to giddiness when I ordered drinks.

"Uh, I'll have two of those," I said, pointing to a red-white-and-blue frozen slushie.

"Of course! Here ya go: two bebbe mekkers." The Bahamian bartender handed me the drinks.

"Room 804," I said, trying to pay for my drinks. He laughed.

"Mon, you don pay. E're ting is free. All inclusive, mon."

Holy. Shit. I froze to the bottom of the pool as my world shrunk like one of those this-guy-is-having-a-moment Steven Spielberg zoom shots. I cut my eyes slowly back to the bar, its well was loaded with booze, massive towers of pastel-colored frozen cocktails chilled, ready to be squirted into plastic cups on demand. I did a slow-motion turn, taking in the enormity of the pool now recognizing that the joie de vivre of an all-inclusive resort like Prandals which I'd previously besmirched and derided as false and shallow was, in fact, genuine and fueled by vodka, tequila, and rum.

I'd found my safe place.

I'd found my unsafe place.

Our room came with a staff of butlers available 24-7 via cell who would pretty much do anything we wanted. I'd already had my most racist moment earlier that day when our butler offered to press my trousers while he was unpacking our suitcases into the dresser.

"I mean, sure. Shit. What else do you do?"

"Shine shoes?"

I waited a moment while my inner liberal took a series of deep calming breaths as my inner Alabaman racist shot his cuffs and whispered, finally.

"Are you fucking with me?"

"What? No, mon. You are in the Bahamas, mon. Everybody 'ere is Black. This is my full-time job; I'm paid a salary and you Americans guilt-tip me like I'm royalty. Shining your shoes is a service provided by the resort. I don't have a shine box."

My inner liberal exploded because it couldn't tell if it was guilty of insensitive white colonialism, being racist, or just working with a professional.

"We're going to tip big at the end of the week," I squeaked.

"Oh, I know. I know you will." He started to leave with my pants and shoes, then turned back. "Should I prepare a romantic bath this evening while you are at dinner?"

"What?"

"Come on, mon. Flowers, candles, champagne? For you and your lady." He said, not even twerking an eyebrow in ironic bon homme regard.

My mind lost the thread for a second because I realized I didn't have to pay for this luxury, that this was an all-inclusive resort, that a romantic bath with candles and champagne after getting drunk at a piano bar–for free– was exactly the kind of thing that made [My Attorney] feel pretty damn all-inclusive. I snapped out of it, my class concerns fading in the sudden glare of potential sexy time. I rose to my full dwarfish height and proclaimed:

"Prepare the bath!"

Later, we walked into the piano bar, a dignified married couple. We'd dressed island formal, meaning I looked like the old guy from Jurassic Park while [My Attorney] looked like a hot supermodel. She'd bought knitted pants for the trip so she's wearing a sheer top and white doilys and her skin is tan and I couldn't stop staring at her and thinking about that romantic bath and mmmm hrrrmm phmmm, it was gonna be a good night.

Despite the lighting. The lighting at the piano bar in the main resort building at Blandals just after sunset has the luminal subtlety of the back corner drink section of an off-brand rural convenience store at two in the morning. It is harsh, unforgiving, and reaches deep into even the farthest corners, leaving no shadows and no aesthetic grace. It is unwelcoming. It's gross. And I think it contributed to the birth of a tragic evening.

I have told this story before, in The Full English, a book wherein I savagely pursue an old woman around a bus for ten days to steal her seat. It's told in the footnotes, and I worry that I didn't give it enough room. It's not a pleasant story. It's not at all endearing. It will paint me as an overwrought, aggressively boorish, outrageous psychopath. A fair portrait. I'm not making any excuses for my behavior, except to say this. It had been a rough year. We'd lost family. We'd moved. My newest book came out the same day as a major comedian's, so it got spined while his got faced out on the shelves because he's a big baby and booksellers feel sorry for him.

This was our first vacation as a couple in years. I'd never been to an all-inclusive resort and my nascent greed and gluttony were in full regard. I was gorging on free food. I spent the day in the pool with four margaritas on my float at all times. By the time we hit the piano bar, I had been drinking all day and I mean all-inclusive drinking. I've never had that much alcohol in my life. I'd slowed down for dinner then leveled off a little bit. I walked up to the piano mostly sober, somewhat dignified in a white tropical shirt and khakis. I looked normal.

We were greeted by the nice British couple we'd met earlier at the pool who I was convinced were swingers. They were to our left. On our right, more Brits. Two lovely older women with big character-actor smiles, light pastel sweaters, and sensible shoes. More people drifted in to surround the grand piano. I procured perfectly executed, utterly frigid, double dirty martinis. The piano player sat down. We applauded lightly. He launched into "Sweet Caroline." We smiled at each other as we sang.

We worked our drinks through a truncated version of "Hey Jude," a rousing rendition of "Great Balls of Fire," and perfect recitations of "Don't Stop Believing," "Friends in Low Places," and "Baby Got Back." I got more drinks while [My Attorney] sang "Joy to the World," and "No Diggity" with the British Empire. I slid in next to her as the piano player was discussing song selection with someone at the far end of the bar. [My Attorney] took a sip of her drink.

"Oh, babe. It's gin."

"What?" I sip her martini. "No, it's vodka."

"Well, it's horrible." She slumps on her stool, slightly deflated by the low quality of her drink. I leap to my feet, gallant and tipsy. I head back to the bartending bar and the bartender sets down two dirty martinis like I'd ordered them with my mind. They're so dirty they're almost green. Slivers of ice slide down the outside of the glasses. Perfect. I hand one to the woman of my dreams, she takes a sip, and her eyes roll back in her head.

"Oh My God, that's so good."

"American Pie," "The Real Slim Shady," "Jesse's Girl," and "Billie Jean" later, she waggles her glass suggestively, singing silently to me the siren song of her people. I pull up to the other bar. The ancient, quiet, almost reptilian bartender is already pouring two jade green filthy martinis. I come back as the whole crowd launches into the Pina Colada song. I put the martinis down and now there are three. Oh yeah, the one she didn't like. I sip it. It's fine. Shame for it to go to waste.

For those of you who didn't go to bartending school, that's five for me. A single martini is 2oz vodka to half an ounce of vermouth. Multiply that by five and you have this fucking horror show:

"I can't finish this," she says. I smile and hug her.

"Itsh okay, beb. I can furnish id."

"Are you drunk?"

"Are I drunk?" No, I'm charming. "No, I'm sharming." The British guy next to her chuckles. Finally, an audience.

The two British ladies ask for "Short Skirt, Long Jacket," which is [My Attorney]'s fight song but the piano player doesn't know that one. I turn to them, full of sharm.

"ISTHATANACCENT?"

One of them looks at me suspiciously, which I interpret as her recognizing my wit.

"ARE YOU FROM ALABAMA?!"

Ok. I just . . . if we can pause for a minute in this narration to allow me to prepologize for that and for what follows. Look, I am well aware that it isn't funny. I know that what happens here is quintessential "Ugly American" behavior. I know it's boorish and I know it's just fucking awful. I know that what the people around the bar saw was a dipshit in full regalia. They saw a flagrantly inebriated asshat showing off his lack of class. They saw a poor woman pretending not to notice. I carried on with this ridiculous 'it's funny because it's not funny' joke about the British people having an accent and me thinking it was southern for way too long and somewhere on one of my air-gapped hard drives is a video I took in that moment, a crazy selfie of my massive jowly countenance framed by two women looking like concerned librarians as I howl "SAY YOUR FROM ALABAMA! SAY IT!"

Sigh.

Clearly against their better judgement, they laugh politely.

Quickly, I prepare for the rest of my set by securing two more martinis. [My Attorney] looks at them like they're live grenades.

"I don't think we should drink those."

"Babe," I reassure her. "Babe," I make sure she is assured. "Babe, ish all ink loose shiv."

"I love Rock and Roll," "Brick House," and "Like a Virgin Later," I'm singing in loud falsetto. The piano player keeps glancing up at me. He plays "Bye Bye Bye," which bores me to tears tears tears, so I flip through the songbook until I find "Sweet Home Alabama," a song I hate with all my heart.

"HEY PLAYSWEE THOMEALA BAMA"

The guy is already playing Backstreet Boys. But no one is really singing so he glares at me for a second then plays the opening riff and everyone joins in, going duh duh duhhna, but I throw the songbook open on the bar, slide it over in front the British ladies, point to the lyrics for "Take Me Home Country Roads," and say, "BUT WITH THE WRONG LYRICS!"

Because I'm hilarious.

I sing John Denver all the way through Lynyrd Skynyrd until the piano player slams the keyboard shut in the middle of the song, stands up, looks right at me and growls, "I went to Juilliard!"

I was summarily sent to my room by the quaint British swingers protecting my wife.

Upon arrival, I realized I was experiencing the sad and typical effects of drinking eleven dirty martinis as my stomach had decided to leave me for another man. Through my mouth. I managed to get into my room and barely made it into the doorway of the bathroom before those eleven martinis and red wine from dinner exploded like the Tonga Volcano and I stood there, a slave to my body, as it erupted all over the bathroom, all over the walls, the sink, and the toilet.

I took a shuddering breath. I looked around.

I'm going to deploy some euphemisms here because I value your time. I want you to read the rest of this book. I want you to think of me as a man of letters, an auteur, a contemplative. I know that's who you are. You're a reader. An idea person. Like me, you eschew the material in favor of the rarified intellectual strata afforded through your dedication to literature so, for the following scene, I do, sincerely, apologize.

Ahem.

I took a shuddering breath. I looked around. As I looked around, naturally, I turned and like a man walking on ice, lost control. My feet found no footing in the miasma on the floor. I grabbed the sink with one hand, the towel rack with the other, my feet dancing a panicked tarantula through the brand-new rug I had just delivered—then I stopped. I breathed a shallow breath, willing my body to perfect stillness, bathed in a soft, flickering, red light as I looked down before me and beheld James's remarkable work of art: the romantic bath.

The oversized tub was filled with steaming, scented water. Rose petals floated on its surface, over the edge, then out the room to, I assumed, the bed. Red candles graced every flat surface, illuminating the alcove with their rosy light. A bucket of ice was parked against the edge of the tub, cradling a nice bottle of champagne. Slivers of ice slide down its sides. Just like those martinis.

No, no, no. Don't think about the martinis. If you think about them then you'll taste them.

I could taste the martinis. I smacked my lips.

Wait, that's not martinis—

From the depths, the murky, unexplored fathoms of my inebriated self, a horrifying Netflix documentary welled up and the voice of the British swinger currently in possession of my wife, narrated as if he were a sticky David Attenborough.

Here, in the deep, a menacing predator lurks, waiting for the perfect moment to surface.

No. I thought. Please, god, no.

What had happened previously, was bad. I had power washed the floor, the sink, the underside of the sink, the toilet, two towels, and parts of the ceiling. But it was just the opening salvo. It was merely a prelude. An overture. What happened next was symphonic.

Until that moment, I had never experienced such a powerful, violent decorative fountain that lasted so long that I had time to think about it while it was happening. But this time, as I turned my head to observe the uncontrollable flume of glurk roaring forth directly into the romantic bath, splattering the walls, putting out the candles, and plastering the accoutrements and the towels and the toilet paper and the woodwork, I took a moment to reflect on my choices.

Should I have had so many martinis? Of course not. Did I save my wife from the Jet Ski mafia only to lose her to ravenous British swingers? Maybe. Maybe I did. Will I have to pay a cleaning fee for this room? Absolutely. But, I thought, as the unstoppable torrent of an all-inclusive resort waned, and I was able to breathe, I thought this will make a great story.

By the time [My Attorney] arrived, escorted by the concerned English people, I had cleaned most of it. The bath was a disaster and I had to use the ice bucket for...for other purposes. I'd thrown the candles into the trash and piled the rags and rugs and my clothes on the balcony, shut the door, then passed out on the bed in my underwear. I'd neglected to shower and frankly, how I remain married is an enduring mystery.

## GETTING NAKED WITH MICHAEL JACKSON ON THE MEXICAN RIVIERA

A few years after the Europe trip, we needed to get away, so we booked a long weekend to a resort in Mexico, and I got drunk and now we own a time share.

In my defense, I believe I mentioned being drunk. Also, this resort is fucking beautiful. It has twenty-one restaurants, a golf-cart-bus line, enormous pools, and private bungalows with semi-private swim-up bars. Our room had its own pool attached to the patio. It was swank.

We arrived in Mexico by air, which I've never done before. I was unaware of the Mexican Airport Experience which featured exotic scenarios like 'standing in line for two hours,' and 'being assaulted by resort sellers and militant taxi drivers,' which we managed to push through to a van that took us to our resort where we were greeted in an opulent great room with champagne and outstanding service like White Lotus extras.

Our representative gave us a brief overview of the services available then upgraded us from the "dirt nugget" level to "sapphire" which meant we had a private bungalow with a fully stocked bar, a whirlpool bath, an outdoor shower, and a postage stamp sized plunge pool that joined a lazy river which took one along it's slow meandering journey to the semi-private central pool where one could float up to a straw-roofed bar and order a paloma con mezcal at 11am. at ten in the morning just before nine.

She also mentioned that if we would simply endure a few minutes of time-share presentation we'd receive a free lobster dinner on the beach. She also mentioned the beach-side couples massage. I signed up for both. You know what happened during the presentation. I got drunk and talked [My Attorney] into buying a goddam time share, a move I kick myself in the ass for every month when [My Attorney] reminds me that I owe her $300 for the service fee and also when I get a birthday card from Satan which is just a picture of his naked ass and a note that says, 'wish you were here.'

After waking up to the knowledge we'd become the kind of people who own a time share, we needed to unwind. I booked the beach-side couples massage and here's where things got weird.

We were golf carted to the spa where they hustled us into stage one of our massage experience: aqua therapy. We were further hustled into a room of private showers with pebbled glass doors. We had to shower, don our bathing suits and our one-size-fits-all bathrobes, then walk on paper-thin flip flops to the hydro therapy room where we sank into a giant whirlpool to boil ourselves. But the room offered so much more than a hot tub. The pool had functional niches like the standing reverse shower, a cold plunge, a hot plunge, the flat waterfall thing, the bubbler, the rain storm, the bubble bed, and the most telling apparatus of all, the taint sploosh.

Perhaps you've been to hydro therapy before. Perhaps you're a veteran of the waters. Perhaps you are an accomplished world traveler who always takes advantage of the swishalicious spa deals, and you know all about these odd hydrotherapeutic nooks in a hydrotherapy pool. It was my first time, and I was having fun. The standing reverse shower blasted water from a perforated plate in the floor. Hilarious. The cold plunge was terrifying, and I lasted about one second before leaping into the hot plunge where I lasted a luxurious four seconds before vaulting out, lobsterishly. The big flat waterfalls were pleasant for shoulder massages, the bubbler was a ticklish dream, the rain storm was just a giant rain shower but, you know, nice, the bubble bed was stupid. Who can lay down on one of those? I kept floating away.

Finally, I arrived at the final station, the taint sploosh, a deep niche where I was advised to crouch over a perforated plate which shot a thunderous flume of warm water right up my ass. It was like trying to sit on a fire hose. It was the world's most aggressive bidet. It missed nothing. Powerful jets of water shot up into my nethers, into my unaddressable port, snaking their way up a narrow tunnel until it filled my lower cavity to sloshing, wrapping itself around my spleen before I was able to tear myself away and fall into the pool, leaking from my ears. Floating there on my back I realized the hydrotherapy wasn't designed to wash away my sorrows, but to make sure I was sufficiently abluted before baring my ass to a poorly paid massage therapist on the beach.

We were escorted back to the showers where I was trying to wash off the terror of being taint sploosed when someone kept calling "Sir". Couldn't be for me. Had to be for one of the other guys. I soaped up and leaned my forehead against the rock wall to try and purge myself of the memories of hydrotherapy when someone knocked on the door. A naked man was staring through the pebbled glass.

"Creo que ella te esta llamando"

"What?"

"¿La dama? ¿Tienes un masaje?"

"I'm naked here, man."

The naked man moves along. I rinse off. I got to get out of here.

Knock. Knock.

"I told you—" I say, turning to the glass. There is a female attendant. The glass may be pebbled for privacy, but I can practically read her name badge through it, so my privates are not so private at the moment. "Yeek!"

"Señor, necesitamos que venga."

"OK. What?"

"Please come out."

"Why?"

"Massage."

"Ok." I wait for her to go. She does not go. "Can you maybe get out so I can get out?"

"Llega tarde a su masaje, señor."

"Well, my clothes are hanging behind you so—"

She knocks on the glass again. The naked man returns.

"Senor, she wants you to come to your massage."

"Naked?"

"Is robe." He moves on, nakedly. I timidly open the door. The woman walks away briskly. I reach for the one-size-fits-all bathrobe.

Let us discuss, briefly, the phrase one-size-fits-all. This is typically true when applied to things like floppy hats, theme park rain ponchos, and lurid epithets. But I implore the designers of bathrobes please be specific and please, please stop being so fat-exclusive. My one-size-fits-all fit this one size almost. I got my arms through the sleeves, and I was able to close the flaps and tie the little belt with a knot using just the last two inches of belt. So yeah, I was enrobinated but if I so much as raised my eyebrows, it was going to fall apart and expose my august nature to the world.

We were escorted to a golf cart to take us to the beach. The driver and the massage overlord sat in front. In seats. We sat on the back, on the luggage rack, facing the throngs of well-dressed resort attendees. Rather nicely dressed. Like, formally dressed. We were driving through a wedding reception. The golf cart weaved and honked its little heart out as I hung my fat ass off the end trying to keep my robe together by sheer will power while pulling it down over my knees so I wouldn't show my wedding vows to the wedding.

The golf cart skidded to a stop, and we were asked to walk over to the massage huts which weren't there.

"Where are we going?"

"To the beach side huts."

"Which are where?"

"Over there." She pointed down the golf cart highway, past the shopping area, across a small park, over the entire Gulf of Mexico, a mountain range, the mars rover, and then out onto the beach a little where there were two wooden huts on stilts behind the advancing column of well-heeled wedding crowd who had caught up and were now swarming around us, bumping into my 'robe'.

"Could you get a little closer maybe?"

"Please," she gestured into the far distance. [My Attorney] and I stiff walked six or seven miles until we got to the huts. As we got closer, we heard the unmistakable refrain of "Don't' Stop til You get Enough," from Michael Jackson's 1979 album, Off the Wall. You know, massage music.

We climbed the stairs—slowly with a lot of glancing down to see if anyone was glancing up—to the hut proper where two women told us to disrobe. I didn't hear them because I was staring down through the wide gaps between the tarp walls into the wedding reception everyone had been walking toward. I caught the eye of the DJ who looked away. I mean, I can't blame him.

We were, as far as I was concerned, entirely exposed through these gaps. They were as wide as—you could pass a couch through them. First they have the audacity to force-clean me with firehoses to make sure I have spotless taint[1] for the massage therapists. Then they have the balls to dare me to bare my balls to a wedding reception? Did my reputation not proceed me? I can only take so much ritual embarrassment before I turn the tables and there next to the massage tables the tables turned did. The hell I'm gonna be embarrassed! I whipped off my robe, turned my flawlessly squeaky-clean backside to the bride and groom and faced my massagers.

Who were looking at me with their jaws on the floor. One of them quietly raised a sheet as a privacy screen and I slunk over to the table where she laid the sheet over my blasphemy.

For an hour, our massage therapists pummeled us with their tiny hands while we were assaulted by the DJ's insistence on spinning Michael Jackson

---

1 Which is stupid because who gives a taint massage at a Mexican coastal resort? That's strictly Tijuana shit. Also, I habitually cleanse my taint. It's already spotless. I'm a gentleman,

songs. Exclusively.

As if that weren't painful enough, I had to lay on my face and let's just unpack that for a minute. As previously discussed, I am divinely proportioned and carry the bulk of my rotundity just above my waist and just below my clavicles. Somewhere inside me is a typically sized man of 5'7" hauling a bushel sack of potatoes on wavering bowed legs and he never gets to put that spud sack down. Ever.

This presents problems. Particularly when I'm required to lie prone. My sleep position is historically known, by its common name, as 'the poor dear,' since I sleep like someone who's just been hit by a train. I lie face down, my right knee hiked up as far as it will go,[2] my right arm crooked under my chest, hand curled under my chin, my left arm under the pillow, face turned to the right. Halfway through the night I flop over to the exact opposite and blow my CPAP air into [My Attorney]'s face until she kicks me, and I flop over again. This goes on all night until I wake up, mysteriously in the supine, blanket pulled neatly under my chin, arms on top of it on either side, like I died in the night.

To lie prone is painful since there's nowhere for the sack of potatoes to go so the typical 5'7" motherfucker inside me is stretched over my stomach, like he's doing downward facing dog but not using his knees. Downward facing dolphin?

That's how it looks. How it feels is different. It feels as if I'm slumped onto the massage bed like I was thrown from a passing car, my fat face pressed down into the face-hole so I can't even talk, my naked ass trumpeting the heavens.

It is not a position of comfortable repose. I'm balancing on a medicine ball. I'm trying really hard to flex my core to keep from rolling off the bed because I'm pretty sure this massage hut is built out of palm fronds and iguana spit and if I roll off this fucking bed I'm crashing through the floor to land fully jay birded before the bride and groom. This is all made worse by a tiny Mexican woman exacting justice for being flashed hammering away on my spine. It was like being tenderized by poker chips. I'm lucky I can walk.

Or dance, and not because I was reduced to a rubbery version of myself but because the D.J. took Michael Jackson's advice to not stop until you get enough to not stop playing Michel Jackson and apparently he could not get enough. There were no other songs. He didn't even dip into the catalog of the Jackson 5. It was just MJ hit after MJ hit. We could hear it all the way to our apartment.

---

2 Not very fucking far.

We're marched stark naked seven miles back to the golf cart and whisked away to the lockers. We get dressed. We race home. We throw on our fine dining clothes then race back to the beach where they've laid out a lovely table for us.

In the sand. Eighty-seven feet from the wedding reception which has now achieved severe inebriation. The sun has set so under the party lights, forty drunken maniacs are dancing to the songs of the DJ which are still, steadfastly, unwaveringly, the number one hits of his Begloved Self.

We are led through the thick sand to our table where I sit on an aluminum chair that sinks six inches into the beach. Hidden speakers are playing Kenny G. I assume it's Kenny G. It's insipid saxophone-forward music. If beige shag carpet could sing, this is how it would sound.

They bring us champagne. They bring us a luxurious starter. The moon is rising over the ink-black waves, its argent light rippling directly toward us. A violinist arrives and despite the blare of "Billie Jean," and the muted chortle of Kenny G, he plays himself over to our table. Three strains of terrible music wash over us in a dissonant tide, but I don't care.

I manage to find a way to sit in the chair and remain above sand level though it makes me Jabbaesque. [My Attorney] has never looked so beautiful. She is radiant. She is opalescent. She is joy. She is my Princess Leia.

Suddenly, the DJ stops and the violinist moves away down the line of flapping canvas table tents and it's peaceful and I'm in the radiant presence of the woman I love, and I feel warmth rise up within me. It is a warm wave of contentment, that everything is going to be fine. I reach across the white linen for her hand as she smiles at me and the DJ lays into the Karaoke version of "Smooth Criminal," and a wildly hammered divorcé takes the mike to bellow over the music. I squeeze [My Attorney]'s hand warmly and look into her eyes and whisper "I will burn this place to the fucking ground."

### SILVER ANNIVERSARY

*[Trigger warning: remember a couple of chapters back when I warned you things were going to get gross but you were like whatevs, I'l read anyway, I ain't scared? This one's worse. The following story details massive, catastrophic, multidirectional, uncontrollable defecaction.]*

It was a spectacular day in Alabama. Blue sky as far as the eye could see. The very slightest of breezes ruffling the hair of my nephew and his bridal party frolicking in the warm waters of the Warrior River at the cabin of our family friend, The Judge.

When we say The Judge, it is spoken perfectly capitalized, and everyone is just the tiniest little bit afraid of him even though not a single member of my family has ever had so much as a traffic ticket.

I have just arrived, having driven all the way south from Chicago because this particular nephew is one of my favorites, though I despise him with all my heart. He is too perfect, too naturally accomplished, too handsome, and too wise to be related to me, and I have, for his whole life, been suspicious. He is a golden child.[1] He is perfectly Southern. He is my polar opposite.

His bride-to-be is a professional ballerina, so it should be no surprise that her bridesmaids are half the cast of the Nutcracker, all of them in bikinis splashing water at the stout manly young friends of the groom, all of them frolicking in the river like the opening scene in a feel-good movie when I lumber down the dock in my shorts.

As a courtesy, I wore a black t-shirt to "protect me from the sun," but really to cover my pendulous moobs and my massive hairy tumor of a gut. I dove in and swam out further than the youths to bide my time until lunch. I found one of those blissful and inexplicable columns of cold water one sometimes finds in deep water lakes and parked myself over it, propped on

---

1 Since this happened, he has fathered three children, all of whom are literally precious and brilliant and endlessly hilarious and wise beyond their years. My other nephew, his brother, has also married to—of course—a beautiful, accomplished woman and will no doubt soon produce children of wild capability whom I will despise.

a turquoise pool noodle, fully sunglassed, wearing a hat trying to ignore the youths, and I don't know if I've mentioned frolicking yet, but people frolicked like hell.

Up at The Judge's house, my sister and her crew were loading a table full to breaking with potato salad, Cajun pasta salad, fried chicken, Paul's slaw, Mee Maw's slaw, Grandma Whitfield's slaw, Paw Paw's slaw, fried chicken, fried crappie, hushpuppies, and look, it's a Southern wedding party. There was food.

And this scene in its full panoramic glory was like a Norman Rockwell painting if Rockwell had been born in Birmingham and wore a Bass pro cap and despite being a professional curmudgeon and generally cranky, and despite floating directly over a cold spring flume that was bathing my fat ass in sixty-five-degree water, I felt a warm feeling creep through my body. I thought, well, would you look at that: I am suffused with contentment. I am saturated with joy. I am happy.

Then I shit my pants.

I was seized suddenly by a violent shudder. It felt like I'd been stabbed and that my ass was going to explode at the same time. It was like food poisoning mixed with Legionnaire's disease mixed with dysentery mixed with a mining accident mixed with the whisky shits.

And a little got out. Just a little. A warning shot.

Floating there in the still water of a cay in the Warrior River, frozen by panic, clamping my sphincter tight against an urgent deluge of what would surely be a vile, churning, malodorous sluice of Waffle House sides, I heard the following:

"Hey, Uncle Bull."

A ballerina[2] in a bikini had floated up beside me. She'd just drifted there. She didn't mean to. She was innocent and pure and just let the current take her where it may, and the current took her into the cone of detonation for what was about to be a legendary vortex of sludge. Her pool noodle bumped up against my shoulder and I realized I had to make a decision.

I could swim violently away, further out into the lake, all the way into the main river and let nature take its dreadful course, killing off the local flora and fauna and dropping the value of the local homes by a few thousand dollars, and maybe, if there was a god, get swept away and run over by a bass

2 This ballerina was actually never a ballerina but was the best friend of the bride and has since become a steady and important member of my Alabamily along with her son who I believe is secretly a math whiz. Years later when I told this story at dinner (yes) then mentioned to her that the ballerina in question being accidentally shat on in a river quay was her, she recoiled in horror then laughed like a goddam rock star. I adore her and have adopted her as my own actual niece.

boat and drowned.

Or I could somehow make my way to shore, clench-walk up the hill in the blistering sun to the Judge's house, praying the entire way that the bathroom was free, somehow manage to get past everyone without having to narrate the Southern saga of "oh hello," and just barely make it upstairs, into the john, and onto the throne without committing involuntary ballerinacide.

I had to maintain concentration. I had to focus. Aiming my considerable bulk landward, I swam ashore. I walked slowly up the hill, taking short steps and avoiding eye contact, my glutes pressed together so tight they were cramping, one hand on my hip, the other held out before me in a fey salute like I was about to introduce a runner-up on Ru Paul. I made it into the kitchen, but the kitchen was packed four-deep with motherhood. They saw me and I could tell they were about to say hello and I didn't have that kind of time. I had to flee. The lake house was built for efficiency and space, so the halls were narrow, steep, and carpeted. I wedged myself into the chute–

"Aunt Pinky's in the toilet, Uncle Bull. Y'all got to wait."

Of course. Of course, it was Pinky; of course, it was a person known to bogart toilets and do crosswords and read romance novels and have her Goddam mail slipped under the door. My body is listening to everything and making operative decisions on deployment and when it hears Pinky is in the bathroom, it loses its goddam mind. Abort mission, release all ordnance! And I'm standing there in the narrow traileresque hallway wondering if I'll need a shovel and if they have a steam cleaner and trying to plot my escape. I'll climb out a window and steal a car and drive off a cliff.

I'm staring at the door to the bathroom, and I can hear Aunt Pinky in there humming to herself. The walls are closing in on me. My sphincter is losing its grip. It is weak. Quivering.

I'm not gonna make it, I'm–

"Just use The Judge's bathroom," somebody says.

Blessed be.

I stiff walk down the hall into the master bedroom, into their tiny camper-like toilet. I drop my pants and my turgid bowels detonate like a mine full of dynamite.

I know this is gross. I know. I know you think this is all entirely unnecessary. I know. Do you really need a story about emergency pooping? No. You've got class. Elan. You read the classics. You drink wine. You rightfully glance over at me, the spectral writer in the room, stained pages clamped in my chubby fist, pleading with you to let me tell you this story about excrement, and you wave your hands disdainfully and tell me, no, good sir, we're not interested.

But this is my job. Therefore, what follows is a painstakingly accurate, detailed, blow-by-blow description of my excre–

My ass exploded.

My bowels detonated a nuclear shit bomb so powerful, so ferocious, I had to grab the edge of the sink and hold onto a towel rack to stay upright– and I was upright, mostly, my bathing suit cutting into the skin on my knees, my—

Perhaps I should use euphemisms.

(Ahem)

The torpedo tubes were not properly aimed when the torpedoes launched.

(AHEM AHEM)

The train tunnel was not level, so the trains did not make it into the station and instead . . .

(AHEM AHEM AHEM)

The volcano fell over.

(AAAAAAAAAHHHHHEEEEEMMMMM!)

I shit everywhere.

Ever. Rhee. Where.

Staring forward, my eyes fixed onto the 1970s Avocado wallpaper swirls, paralyzed, touching both walls of the bathroom with my considerable bulk, unable to turn around, thighs trembling, knees firing off urgent requests that I sit the hell down, I tried to mentally catalog the angle of my exhaust plume and do some quick trajectorial math: of course, it hit the upturned lid, of course. That was no surprise. But I was somewhat alarmed at how it managed to hit the underside of the cabinets and the windowsill. I needed a hazmat team and blowtorch. Christ in a mop bucket I was–

Then it happened again.

And again.

And again.

I finally had the courage to turn around see what God hath wrought, and I'm just not going to go there, gentle reader, you deserve better. You deserve a story that takes you somewhere joyful and kind. Not one where you behold the newly quagmiraculous interior of a respected member of the judicial system's master bedroom lavatory and, if you are prone to detailed imaginings, the naked corpus of an excremental mancano.

But I am a grown-up. I have parented. I have cleaned up accidents that would make OSHA take a knee. I was appalled, of that there is no doubt, and I was deeply embarrassed, yes. I was facing a protracted–

And again.

–effort of cleaning and sanitizing followed by a hat-in-hand apology appeal to the bench. But I was resolute. I was undaunted. As a parent, I know there are few messes I can't handle with a roll of toilet paper and a bottle of 409.

But.

I had neither.

Not a single square of tee pee. I looked around the bathroom in a panic. Please know, gentle reader, that I was naked, besplattered, and engulfed in a palpable reek that was bringing tears to my eyes and, also, I forgot to mention this, I was blind. I don't swim with my glasses because I learned that expensive lesson a long time ago. My eyes were safely folded up on a side table on the back deck next to Mee Maw's slaw.

I'm groping around in this dimly lit bathroom trying to determine if the blurry shapes I'm seeing are toilet paper or any kind of paper, while my eyes are watering like I've been hit with mustard gas and my stomach and intestines are desperately trying to escape through my ass.

There is nothing.

Under the sink, where one normally keeps backup toilet paper, there is a bottle of hair conditioner and a bar of soap. The cabinets offer me Q-tips, tweezers, and dental wax. I'm thinking maybe I can shred the shower curtain–

Knock knock knock.

Fuck me.

"Ya'll alright?"

The Judge.

"All good."

"Alright, well..."

He's just standing there. I can see the shadow of his shoes at the bottom of the door.

"Might be a while."

The judge mumbles and the shadows walk away.

I turn back to the disaster. As my hands flap around the vanity, I find a drawer handle under the sink and pull it out. Of course, there's no toilet paper, it's just a tiny drawer. I bend down to get really close to inventory this thing when a stack of napkins snaps into focus.

Sweet baby Jesus.

I grab the stack with a triumphant whoop. I run my fingers across them, digging their luxurious heft, their surprising weight, their softness, and their delicate weave, almost like fine, soft linen.

These aren't napkins.

It should be noted the Judge in whose private bathroom I am committing a heinous act bears a last name beginning with the letter A. When I bring the linen napkins up very close to my face, I notice they are emblazoned with a large capital A in silver swooping ornate cursive. In the corner of each one it says, "40 years".

First of all, the forty-year anniversary color is Ruby, Judge, so I object. Second of all, who the fuck keeps their anniversary souvenirs in the bathroom?

I am, again, faced with a dilemma: after I use their 40th wedding anniversary keepsake napkins to wipe my waste off every flat (and vertical) surface of The Judge's private bathroom, do I jump out the window or just hang myself from the shower head?

There are fifteen napkins.

I use all of them.

## THE HALLOWEEN SKUNK WINE FIRE DIARIES AND THE MARIJUANA DOG CATASTROPHE

All Hallow's Eve was warm and clear. I'd survived my explosive trip to the Heart of Dixie and [My Attorney] and I were once again jetting off to somewhere exotic and wonderful and probably not on fire. We live in a nice neighborhood on the far, far, far north side of Chicago in an ivy-covered red brick Georgian nestled politely among glowering McMansion horror shows, stately FrankenTudorSteins, senators, doctors, Irish maniacs, and aldermen. During holidays requiring lights, our neighborhood attempts to out illume the neighborhood next door. In December, you can see us from space.

But Halloween is another monster. Our little village takes Halloween seriously. We turn our yards into dungeons; we plant rubber corpses in the dirt; we inflate massive spiders. We give out tons of candy. This reputation has trickled out into the burbs so people who live in apartment complexes, or trailer parks, or Indiana send their kids by the busload to my front door.

This invasion is second only to the Fourth of July for the sheer terror it strikes into the hearts of our dogs, who live in strict vigilance, veins popping out on their foreheads, eyes rolling in manic hysteria, muzzles speckled with foam, ready to rip the ribs out of the first pint-sized princess they can sink their fangs into.

Every October 31st, I walk them the long way around the neighborhood to tire them out. I feed them a nice fat meal laced with doggy Xanax, then tuck them into their doggy beds and for five minutes they're perfectly calm. In those five minutes, three hundred and seventy-five people ring my doorbell.

As the sun goes down we're under constant attack by witches, zombies, Frankensteins, hockey-masked mass murderers, and princesses from every realm. I shovel a good thirty barrels of candy into the scabrous claws of Chicago's ravenous spawn, even, by the tail end of the evening, giving up my secretly hoarded cache of bite-sized Reese's Buttercups, a stunningly humble act of abject selflessness for which I should receive a medal.

By 11p.m. trick-or-treating is officially over. At that hour, even the most arrogant tweens won't knock so I kill the light and let the dogs out into the backyard so we can all finally go to bed except we live next to a forest preserve so when I let the dogs out they try to murder a gang of skunks.

James Tiberius Kirk, "Ty," our neurotic border collie was raised by cats. We received him on a bright sunny day in 2004 from a Wisconsin rescue organization. He'd bonded strongly with their cats, adopting the feline opinion that all dogs suffer from irreparable brain injury and should be slid surreptitiously off the edge of a cliff when no one is looking. He tried every single day to bury his own poop, like a good cat.

Ty was the resident alpha male and endlessly abused our other mutt, Whisky Tango Foxtrot, whom we'd picked up as a balm to cover the tragic loss of a cat Ty had loved as if he had given birth to her. Whisky performed his duty with humility. Every day Ty humped him like a windmill in a hurricane while Whisky stared into space accepting his fate with a resigned, stoic aplomb. Ty ran him like a drill sergeant.

Which, on Halloween 2017, consisted of the following orders:

Ty: Private! There are skunks!

Whisky: Sir, we've been sprayed before. The bipeds lose their collective minds and make us take baths. It is unpleasant.

Ty: Yeah, but...Look at 'em.

Our neighborhood is plagued by skunks. We're just barely outside the Cook County Forest Preserve's vibrant canopy, a verdant strip of wild arboreal splendor that runs from downtown Chicago thirty-two miles northwest to the Botanical Gardens. That's seventy thousand square acres overflowing with deer, weirdos on recumbent bicycles, arrogant joggers, coyote, hobos, goth kids, and skunks.

The North Side's relationship with Mephitis Mephitis is precarious; we hate them, but we also support wildlife rights, so skunks run our streets like two-toned gangs. I am not talking about the adorable plushanimate mephitis of the Disney class that fits in the palm of your hand churbling magically. Nor am I talking about the recently cancelled Pepe le Pew, whose ribald antics finally caught up to him.

No, northside skunks are hulking aberrations the size of lawn mowers. They waddle like congressmen, eyes ablaze in the tangerine streetlight ambience, jacked-up on the caffeine they suck from spent Diet Coke cans, their confidence sky high and their minds focused like cobalt lasers from the residue of Adderall and Wellbutrin they lick out of empty amber prescription bottles. Our garbage bins are their grocery stores, their pharmacies, and their opium dens.

Also, and this might surprise you after reading such a bucolic description, they smell.

They smell like nothing else on earth except themselves times a jillion. Fat obstinate racoons scatter like roaches when the skunks swagger up our driveway, as entitled as we are and entirely absent of even the briefest gratuity they might extend to us for being such opulent hosts. They are militant. Menacing. Marching down the middle of the street at exactly 11:10 every night dragging with them a solid cubic acre of reeking, redolent, malodorous, fetid, pestilent, choking, insufferably, heinously, vaporous stank.

Ty: You smell that? That's a lack of discipline.

Whisky: Well, sir, they are uncivilized.

Ty: Kill them, smaller dog.

And so he does. Or he tries. The smaller dog charges into the gang of skunks, teeth bared, barking like an alarm. Most animals would scatter because the smaller dog is half wild and when he gets upset he's terrifying. But skunks are dangerous micro malodorous tanks. They turn as a single unit and bathe my idiot hound with their anal sac fluids. He tucks tail and howls.

Ty: ARE YOU OK!?

Whisky: SIR, NO SIR! I HAVE BEEN SPRAYED, SIR!

Ty: I'M COMING IN!

Whisky: SIR! SAVE YOURSELF!

Ty: FOR BONES AND GLORY!

At Least Fifty Skunks: [SPRAY, SPRAY, SPRAY]

Meanwhile, back at the ranch, I'm cleaning up after the Halloween hordes and unpacking. [My Attorney] and I are due to catch the redeye to San Francisco at six in the morning to visit wine country.

While it is my habit to be entirely packed and ready three days before we depart, checklist boxes neatly scored down the left-hand side of a page in my notebook, it is [My Attorney]'s habit to pack on the way to the airport using all our luggage, a box of gallon sized Ziploc bags, and undiluted adrenalin. And my suitcase because its neatness beckons to her. Our suitcases are splayed out on the living room ottoman like armoires on the half shell when our brave and stupid dogs come howling back inside the house, frothing through their teeth, rubbing themselves not only all over our incredibly expensive Persian rugs, not only all over the couches and chairs and pillows, but also leaping onto the couch, into our open luggage, to bury their revolting snouts into the warm, inviting, unpacked clamshells of our clothes.

[My Attorney] and I wrestle the dogs upstairs into the shower leaving a trail of effluvium. Our efforts only spread skunk effluviate across the carpets, the drapes, the stairs, our bath towels, and our souls.

We clean the dogs. We steam the rugs. We hustle through three rounds of laundry, and manage, somehow, to blunt the sharpest tip of the reek. We close our suitcases and survey the splendor of our domain. Which we do with our eyes closed. Because Oh My God. The stench.

The next morning our Uber driver is not amused. In line at the airport, a hip millennial smirks, says "Old School," like it's my name. I regard him with elderly disdain—as one should—but it happens again when I'm standing behind an old hippy. Then the TSA agent glares at me with the clearest really? face I've ever seen while going through our bags with an unusual attention to detail.

I mumble something about skunk, but that only makes him scowl more. Then it occurs to me that nobody thinks I smell like mephitis mephitis; they think I smell like Maui Waui.

The woman checking our boarding pass glares right into my face with a look that states with incredible precision: dude, seriously, there are kids on this plane. As we trudge down the aisle to stash our carry-ons passengers glance up at us from their seats with abject disdain—except for one guy in a suit in first class sporting a Jerry Garcia tie and an impressive mop of gray hair who silently raises his hand without even looking at me for an aisle-seat-high-five of mad respect.

All through Sonoma, at every tasting room, the twenty-something behind the counter would talk to me like we were members of a secret club. We got a refill at an expensive wine library that should have cost us $35 but the sommelier said Hey, it's four twenty somewhere, am I right?

After a few days the stink wore off. So did our brief tour as adorable fifty-something wine country dope smugglers. Back in Chicago, we adopted "skunk-protocol" when letting the dogs out and I put in a motion sensor light strong enough to show your bones through your skin at fifty feet. Skunks hate that.

I hope.

### WINE WITH FLUBBER

We arrived in California, rented a car, and headed out into the wine-soaked rolling hills of Sonoma County. We were there for the Sonoma County Wine Road Tour which happens the first weekend of November. Thousands of oenophiles pay $80 for a bracelet that gets them into wineries and vineyards where they can taste wine paired with small bites of chef-inspired crudités.

If you've never been to Sonoma County, just accept that it looks like every advertisement for wine you've ever seen. It looks like a wine-country postcard has come to life and you're driving right into it. Two-laned blacktops wind their way through lazy rolling hills. Rakish live oaks reach their branches low over the road to shade you as you zoom along[1] from one incredibly picturesque vineyard to another, discovering why California wine is so damn good.

And it is good. You may be thinking to yourself, oh come on, Garlington. You've clearly never had a decent French Bordeaux to which I will batman whisper *neither have you.*

Around 1863, French vintners noticed their vines were withering, yellowing, and dying one after the other. After having a long lunch of frog testicles and snail spleen sandwiches, they thought, hey maybe we should do something about this, but it was too late. French vineyards from Montpellier to Metz were in mortal peril. The French wine industry, the godhead of viticulture, was gasping for air. Naturally, they turned to Missouri. Or Texas. Or California. It depends on which wine association's tour you're taking.

Missouri sent an entomologist who determined the problem was an aphid, phylloxera, which was eating the vines like a Frenchman eats a baguette. By the time they figured this out, there weren't a lot of vines left. Hope was dim and thin.

But in America, in Missouri (and Texas, and California) there were vines that were resistant to phyloxxera because of course they were—

---

1 Because you're the designated driver, pal.

AMERICA! All three states sent rootstock to France who replaced their dying, hideous, flea-bitten idiotic mime-infested vineyards with thicc, swoll, American rootstock. The American grapes grew up quickly and grew up strong and grew up tall, learned to speak French, and now they don't even write anymore.

So, every time you drink a Chateau Neuf de Pape, don't say *"Dieu merci pour le vin François²;"* instead, play some Garth Brooks and yee and also haw because all French wine is American.³

[My Attorney] and I had rented a snow-white Ford Mustang convertible which required me to do ashtanga yoga before I could wedge my corpulent ass behind the wheel. I didn't care of course, because I felt like Steve Goddam McQueen and I was wearing my new Ray Bans and people could only see me from the shoulders up. I felt uncharacteristically cool. Bring on the wine.

[My Attorney] is a planner⁴ so she'd spent the last thirty days going over the tour with a jeweler's loupe and a legal pad, googling every winery to see what they're serving, gauging their Yelp reviews, and ranking them so we build our itinerary with only the highest-rated vineyards. She's proud of this. She's excited. As I drive, she passes out duplicate three-ring binders to our traveling companions and her lifelong friend, THE UKRAINIAN, both in the backseat, hair blowing in the breeze. They howl with laughter and throw her carefully annotated itineraries into the passing trees⁵.

The Ukrainian: ARE YOU CRAZY? WE DON'T NEED A PLAN! WE'RE HERE TO HAVE FUN! WE'RE HERE TO EXPLORE!

[My Attorney]: (pointing to her incredibly detailed map of the wine tour) This one has smoked duck. I really want that smoked—

The Ukrainian: DUCK SCHMUCK! WE'LL GET WHATEVER THEY HAVE AND WE'LL LOVE IT!

I round a bend and drop down an easy curve and the forest opens up, revealing a lone winery so adorable it could be sold in a Cracker Barrel gift shoppe. I pull into the lot and there on the side of the barn in big serifed capitals it says MacMurray Estate. We get out. There's no one there. We wander into the open barn plastered with giant pictures of Fred MacMurray, the 1940s film noir leading man⁶ and Hollywood star.

2 SNAILS!

3 This is fundamentally untrue. The facts of American horticulturalists saving French wine is partially true. They worked together and America wasn't the only country supplying flea-proof stock. However, all the good American vines had been grown a hundred years earlier from French roots. All the wine you drink in America is arguably French. Those bastards.

4 As we have discussed previously. See *The Full English,* "New Orleans".

5 They did not actually do this; however, they did do it metaphorically.

6 Oh, I know what you're thinking: but he was in *My Three Sons,* he's a comedian. To which I reply: you idiot,

We Oh My God and gush and scramble all over the insides of the barn, reading the promo history pictures and picking things up and generally ransacking the joint when an angry man in a golf cart skids to a stop and asks us what the hell we're doing. I hold up my bracelet.

"Dude; we're here for the wine tour."

It's my fault for using dude as an indefinite pronoun in an independent clause.

"Dude," he explained. "We're not on that stupid tour."

He followed closely behind us in his over modified golf cart until we got into our car and drove away. I rolled down the window as we passed through the gate.

"SON OF FLUBBER WAS HIS BEST WORK!"[7]

---

he was in *Double Indemnity.* He launched film noir. Get it together, man.

7  OK, he did some comedies. Whatever.

### ISN'T CALIFORNIA WINE COUNTRY BEAUTIFUL, DEAR?

The Ukrainian's captive spouse gets behind the wheel, leaving [My Attorney] and I crammed into the back seat. We head over to Coppola Estate to get some wine from the guy who made Robin Williams's worst movie. Waze tells us we're close but we're having a little trouble finding the turn when the Ukrainian receives a call.

The Ukrainian is the matriarch of a family of six. She has four kids, all of them wonderful, and they live in a broad ranch-style place out in a lonely suburb filled to overflowing with dentists, lawyers, CPAs, and—I am assuming here—future main characters in Getting-Away-With-Murder podcasts. I call it "Stepford Acres" but that makes my wife hit me.

However, as we search vainly for Coppola Estates, the Ukrainian comes to our rescue by embedding directions to the winery in the following conversation she has with her 13-year-old son and her 80-year-old father-in-law.

"WHY ARE YOU CALLING ME? WE'RE ON VACATION! GO RIGHT!" We're on Geyserville Road headed south. We turn onto Archimedes, which is the correct road but then turn left onto Fredston.

Coppola Winery is in the Sonoma Valley, which we've established is California Wine Country just slightly less famous than Napa Valley, which is a mountain over from us. We've just crossed over the Russian River which slices through Sonoma like a–

"TURN HERE. OF COURSE IT'S SET AT 66 DEGREES, IT'S WINTER! WHY THE FUCK DID YOU GO LEFT?"

[Mumble mumble mumble]

We turn onto Independence which goes nowhere looking for a place to turn around. This part of Sonoma isn't as postcardy as the Russian River, but you can see farms on both sides of the road. We're on the infamous wine trail, with Lytton, Simi, and Healdsburg just a short drive south. Vineyards fall away with–

"IF THEY'RE COLD THEY CAN PUT ON A SWEATER! TURN

THE FUCK AROUND JESUS GODDAM CHRIST WHERE THE FUCK ARE YOU GOING I TOLD YOU TO TURN WHY DIDN'T YOU WELL YOU CAN PUT ON A SWEATER TOO. I'M NOT RUNNING A RESORT OVER THERE. THIS VACATION IS COSTING ME MONEY! TURN AROUND!"

[My Attorney] and I share a look as this is the kind of easy, warm chatter we love to have on vacation with our oldest and dearest friends. Forget wine, forget the guy who made Captain EO with Michael Jackson. I'm riveted. I lean forward to find out how they are going to solve the problem of four tweens and an elderly retired salesman who are freezing to death in a bougie neighborhood outside of Chicago.

[My Attorney] and I marvel at the terraced hills just off the 101 (we're not on the 101, but we're right up against it). We figure someone is going to plant a terraced vineyard and we smile and think, gee, that will be just—

"FINE JUST TURN IT UP TO 90. FUCK IT. TURN! TURN! TURN! JESUS GODDAM CHRIST DON'T YOU KNOW HOW TO DRIVE? FUCKING TURN! YOU CAN ALL RUN AROUND IN YOUR UNDERWEAR AND SWEAT TO DEATH! WHO NEEDS A RETIREMENT PLAN!? TURN GODDAM FUCKING HERE JESUS GODDAM CHRIST!"

We turn off Independence back onto Fredson in the shadow of the Redwood Highway. Thank God the Ukrainian is there to guide us otherwise, we'd be lost.

"WHAT THE HELL DO YOU—PUT ERIC ON. FUCKING HELL. TURN! TURN! FUUUUUCK! JESUS!"

We stop at Via Archimedes and our confident pilot, the Ukrainian's indentured husband flips on his left-hand turn signal since we can see the giant sign for the wine estate owned and operated by the guy who made Tucker: the Man and his Dream. A two-laned blacktop runs between elegant brick gates under an iron arch bearing the name of the winery in yellow caps. Behind this, the vineyards rise up a—

"ERIC I TOLD YOU TO KEEP IT AT 66. WHY THE FUCK ARE YOU TURNING LEFT OH MY GODDAM GOD TURN FUCKING RIGHT! TURN RIGHT!"

Our pilot dutifully turns right out of the left-hand turn lane across traffic in an effort to kill us all and with what seems to me like a surfeit of passion. We head east on Via Archimedes, steered confidently and calmly by the Ukrainian.

You can see down the road, into the estate, down the tree-lined road.

The winery is reminiscent of a 19th century something or other. Like if Disney designed it. There are levels, and beautiful walkways, and staircases with white balustrades framed by rhododendrons and–

"I DON'T CARE WHAT YOUR GRANDFATHER SAYS. HE'S OLD. HE'S ALWAYS COLD. 66 DEGREES IS FINE. FUCKING PULL OVER JESUS FUCKING CHRIST! WHAT DO YOU MEAN YOU'RE COLD TOO? YOU'RE 14. WHAT ARE YOU WEARING? STOP!"

Our pilot takes a moment to shake the murder off then waits patiently for our guide to tell us where to go next. She is so helpful.

"WHO WEARS PAJAMAS IN THE DAYTIME? PUT YOUR GRANDFATHER ON! TURN AROUND! GO BACK!"

Our belabored driver makes a studious U-turn, waiting for a break in the sparse, yet steady traffic of grape haulers, tractor repair trucks, and the other people on the wine tour. We drive under the Redwood Highway overpass.

"IS ERIC WEARING PAJAMAS IN THE DAYTIME? FUCKING STOP RIGHT HERE! STOP! STOP!"

The captive brakes and we lurch to a stop. We're stopped just on the west side of the overpass in the dead middle of the road. "DON'T FUCKING MOVE! NO NOT YOU. GO TURN THE FUCKING THERMOSTAT BACK DOWN TO 66. I'M NOT A BANK. YOU'RE OLD ENOUGH TO KNOW HOW THIS WORKS. AND I WANT MY KIDS TO WEAR CLOTHES IN THE–"

She leaps out of the car, stopping traffic, to run around to the front of our car and lean back against the hood. She raises her huge Nikon camera up to take a series of remarkably artful photographs of the great metal sign for Coppola Estates.

"WELL, YOU'RE IN CHARGE, RAYMOND. HONESTLY I EXPECTED OH SHUT UP I'M TAKING A FUCKING PICTURE HERE!" She responds to the honking. "PUT ERIC BACK ON"

The Ukrainian gets back into the car, trailing a flurry of furious birding.

"GO! GO! GO! YOU'RE HOLDING UP TRAFFIC! ERIC PUT IT UP TO 68 BUT ONLY FOR TONIGHT AND DON'T TELL YOUR GRANDFATHER. AND PUT ON CLOTHES OH FUCK OFF, YOU KNOW WHAT YOU WANT TO HONK? HONK THIS!" She pulls her shirt up to her neck to flash her Francis Ford Coppolas at the frustrated traffic behind us[1].

1 There is some debate about this memory. I distinctly remember the Ukrainian flashing traffic. However, the Ukranian, her placid captive, and [My Attorney]vociferously deny the incident and now I am doubting myself. Did she actually free the nipple on a side road in Sonoma California? Is that like her? I may have embellished here. She may have merely wagged her chest toward waiting traffic or she may have done nothing at all or shot

I smile at my wife as we ride comfortably in the backseat. Another day of placid travel.

"Isn't wine country beautiful, dear?"

---

them the bird or said she's sorry. In any case, one must employ logic and here is where my memory gets a little fragile as she would have been wearing a brazierre and in order to flash traffic would have had to release the hounds, so to speak, and I know the incident didn't last long enough for that to happen. Also, she would have to have been wearing some kind of loose fitting shirt or sweater and when I go back and look at the pictures, she is dressed rather nicely in a buttoned blouse so how in the hell would she have deployed ordnance with any facility at all? I asked the Ukrainian if she'd prefer I remove this sketchy incident and she said, "No, embellishment is good." Which was awfully nice of her, which infuriated me.

## The French Laundry Isn't About You

The late Anthony Bourdain called the French Laundry the best restaurant in the world. It has three Michelin stars. Chef Thomas Keller is considered one of the best chefs on earth, if not the actual best chef on earth (the marker for this position enjoys vibrant mobility, but tends to bounce up and down between Keller, in California, Archatz, in Chicago (who trained under Keller), a guy in the Netherlands, and another guy in France.

Dinner at this restaurant is prohibitively expensive even if you don't get wine pairing. If you do get the wine pairing, it is insanely expensive. It is not a restaurant you run out to on a Thursday because you forgot to thaw some chicken thighs and soccer practice ran late and screw it why not. You're thinking of Applebee's.

The French Laundry the restaurant you sacrifice for. It is the menu you place in your library or in a frame on the wall. It is the experience you talk about only with your closest friends, all foodies and bartenders and chefs, who will hang on your every word. It is the culinary coup des grace of your entire gustatorial timeline and my visit, my only visit in this lifetime, was ruined–RUINED–by my wife, her loud Ukrainian[1] friend, and the Ukrainian's captive husband.

Maybe that's what you're after. Maybe you like ruining the Michelin starred meal of your lifetime. Maybe you're glad Anthony Bourdain is dead. Maybe you hate joy. If those are true, allow me to give you a step-by-step manual so that when you do ruin your evening at the French Laundry, you'll do it properly, meaning the evening will be savaged, razed, burned to the level of the earth like most of Sonoma County in 2017 in a furious inferno of rolled eyes and second guessing the sommelier. Fuck the French Laundry. Let's do this.

    **STEP ONE**–Bring your basic ass pedantic traveling companions[2]. Ok,

1 I am not positing here that she is loud because she is Ukrainian, nor am I insinuating that all Ukrainians are loud. I'm saying it to your face.

2. Because [My Attorney] is Irish, Catholic, and a powerful lawyer who listens to way WAY too many podcasts about killing one's husband and getting away with it for my comfort, and because I'd like to [she won't let me print this] with her again in the near future, I am compelled to point out that the bulk of the narrative exposition in this book and almost exactly ALL of the dialogue is absolute horse shit, prevaricated to a Satanic level, and a bald-faced lie meant to extort laughter (or a

before I go besmirching [My Attorney]'s best friend and her husband3 by labeling them pedantic and or basic-ass people, let me set the record straight: they are good people. If it weren't for them [My Attorney] would never get to play Magick, the Gathering because I am a grown-ass man and I don't play children's card games. And [My Attorney]'s loud friend is a genuinely decent human–a rare quality–who cares about her friends and family, lends them money, feeds them adequate food, and invites them to lavish dinner parties where she makes them wash dishes after every course.[4] Her husband is a dignified professional who spends his personal time listening to classical music and gardening, tending his spectacular rose patch and who apparently has a magnanimous sense of humor and mercifully bad hearing since [My Attorney]'s bellowing besty spends most of every day screaming at him. I'm saying they've got layers. She's got layers.

The four of us live in Chicago so we have access to (as of 2023) twenty-two Michelin starred restaurants and a line-up of new places that are trying to join that delectable constellation. We dine out a lot and we dine well. We think we know a thing or two about wine and The Ukrainian and I are capable home chefs who can poach an egg or throw together a half-way decent beurre blanc so it's not like our peak culinary experience was a Thursday at Outback.

**STEP TWO**–Eat at an up an coming TWO STAR Michelin restaurant before you go to the Frenchy Laundry, you *idiots*. Right before the rest of my party ruined the French Laundry, we discovered another California Wine Country gem: Madrona Manor. You may be hip and cool and maybe you're already rolling your eyes at me, thinking, oh my God, they'd never heard of Madron—Todd, come read this, but we are merely mortals, you snobbish whorebag. The Captive found it on Yelp.

Madrona Manor is a stately 19th century manor house with portcullis and covered porches and gingerbread molding and florid landscaping that teeters on the razor's edge between wild jungle and golf course. Inside, it is appointed with period antiques and happiness, and I love them. Their bartender had made up a new cocktail (which included pear liqueur and pureed pear) then allowed me to name it because I am, quote5, good at that shit.[6]

---

chuckle, or just a slightly raised eyebrow). Furthermore, I hereby and hereon swear that neither the Ukrianian, her slave, nor [My Attorney] are pedantic in any sense of the word except for how they RUINED THE GODDAM FRENCH LAUNDRY FOR ME.

3. Captive.

4. I tried.

5. Quoting myself.

6. I am. I've named various cocktails for my favorite mixologist and legendary beverage manager, Lauren "Flo" Parton. They

We were seated. We looked at the menu. We fainted. We came to and ordered the prix fix with wine and lo, the remarkably handsome sommelier, Eric Mercer, appeared so he could walk us through the wine, and we fell in love.

Our first course: Chef Jesse Malgren's extraordinary Smoked Egg which is a smoked sabayon, pureed watercress, and prosciutto-sherry syrup, served in the shell and Jesus Healdsburg Christ they need a fucking fainting couch. I swooned. I stole my wife's egg. I was possessed.

Next: Bulgarian caviar with a shitake gelee and creme fraiche paired with a 2014 Schramsberg Blanc de Blancs Brut.

Next: Onion Velouté; an egg that's sorta kinda poached because it is cooked soooo slowly, banyuls vinegar and Parm paired with Tablas Creek Patelin de Blanc Paso Robles.

[My Attorney] ordered the Wagyu beef which I knew she wouldn't finish so I stole half of it without even asking because I know her so well[7] and the fork injury to my left forearm is healing very nicely. Paired with a 2013 Jordan Cabernet Sauvignon which was just a little darker crimson that the blood pooling on the tablecloth beneath my elbow.

NEXT: Liberty Farms duck, beluga lentils, asparagus, black garlic, and a sherry vinegar paired with a 2014 Red Car Syrah.

Finally, a dessert so decadent and voluptuous I can't write it down here without threatening the integrity of my wedding vows. Paired with a 2013 Dr. Loosen Beerenauslese Riesling although I also had an after-dinner sherry and at this point, I blacked out and couldn't hear because of all the trumpets played by angels. I was having the best dinner of my life.

And so were the Pedantics. They crowed over every bite. They were enthralled at the way Mercer's pairings brought out the blue note flavors each dish seemed to leave available just for that purpose. It was a lifetime achievement culinary master stroke, and the captive was full of himself for picking it out. And what a charming bastard is Eric Mercer who captained our table and told stories about wine country and the food, and I swear to God, I just wanted him to pull up a chair and yet, yet he managed to do the exact same thing for the other eight people in the room. He's a Goddam viticultural ninja.

Afterwards, we returned to our Airbnb, warmed by the glow of a perfect meal, and sailed off to sand land with smiles on our faces and love in our hearts and I was fooled, dear reader, fooled into believing that these people,

---

are: Lost in Paris, Dead Stick Landing, and Balance Issues, which is for geriatric punks.
7. She wasn't looking.

these lovely, satiated humans who were such a big part of my life, would continue to enjoy dining.

**STEP THREE**—Go to the French Laundry.

At the French Laundry they hated every bite and here's why they were wrong.

The French Laundry is not about you. It's about the food. It's about the years and years of studied perfection Keller has put into the techniques, into the prep, into the garden from which his staff picks your salad and the mirepoix. Years and years of hiring the best people, most of whom move on to open their own Michelin starred restaurants, and every one of them making sure everyone knows they studied under Keller.

Not only are the French Laundry's sommeliers sommes at the French Laundry, which is to say they are perhaps the most capable sommes in the world; not only sommes esteemed among a mere handful of master sommeliers who can tread that sacred high terroir of talent, not only that, but every person on the wait staff is also a sommelier. Half the cooks are sommeliers. The dishwasher collects Argentinian Mourvèdres.

Dining at the French Laundry is about finally aligning your palette properly. The French Laundry is a master's education in flavor. You don't critique the French Laundry. The French Laundry critiques you.

I've been waiting since my daughter was still in diapers. I've been waiting my whole life. I know what The French Laundry is going to do to me, and I want to be in the company of people I love as I morph, from a pizza pocket pupa into a magnificent maillard effected butterfly. I will use this meal to benchmark against everything I eat from this point forward and when they lay my empty carcass in the ground, they will know, they will exclaim in hushed whispers, here, here lies a gourmand for the ages, hearken to his palette all ye who purport to know thine own tongue, ye feeble unwashed hoard.

I wanted my mind melted. I wanted it to be like taking acid for the first time.8 I wanted to cry.

First, the waiting. We dawdled in their courtyard under the leaves of apricot trees, me with my face pressed up against the glass walls of the kitchen trying to burn every nuanced skillful movement into my brain pan; the rest on their iPhones playing Words with Friends.

We are ushered in, brought upstairs, and seated at a simple white linen covered table. Our waiter talks us through everything as we smile patiently and I try very hard to memorize every word, to listen to the subtext, to see if

---

8. Every time.

even at this level of top tier culinary sport there is game.

The Ukrainian and I had sat on speaker phone together back in August, obsessively refreshing the website, our fingers poised over the keyboard, waiting for the tickets to drop for dinner at The French Laundry. They sell tickets every two months, and they sell out in eight seconds. They dropped. We slammed our digits down on a Friday evening but missed it. We scored a Sunday at 4, then plunked down $700 per couple just for the food.

Back to the restaurant and to the waiter hovering at my elbow suggesting we get the wine pairing: our esteemed companions are raising their quadruple eyebrows at the cost of an additional $150 per plate for the wine pairing so I dig out my business plastic which I have never used and spend my entire invoiced income from the previous billing cycle on wine for people I will shortly hope to murder kill.

But first, dinner.

Salmon coronets.

This is enough. I could leave and be a happy man, having tried this infamous dish which lives up to its hype without even trying. I scarf mine down in a single bite followed by a lingering guilt for not taking my time.

From me: "Gaah, herrf, lurble."

From the Pedantic Three: "I guess it's good."

Oysters and Pearls.

Again. Again, with a dish the whole world wants to eat at this table sitting in this chair. An oyster that's been trimmed and cleaned to within an inch of its life. I have no idea which oysters they used but it was November in California so I'm thinking one of the west coast jewels that already make me cry when I suck them out of their shells in Chicago, where they arrive a day or so after being abducted from the rock they'd lived their life adhered to. But these oysters had been filtering the Pacific Ocean that day. Their freshness was divine. In this dish, they are married with tapioca pearls and a sabayon and the whole dish has so many steps and effort it feels like an entire sub-staff is dedicated to just this one recipe. And thank God. I take mine in two bites, having learned from the Coronets I'd just murdered.

Wonderment. Confusion. Revelation.

The dish brings out all the flavors that make oysters so enduring. All the sexy parts are brought forward, but carefully, discreetly, quietly. Yet, the flavor punches through the fog of degustation I've been blinded by until this moment. In the second bite, the flavors from before reunite with their lost loves and somehow the bite is even better, as if the Oysters and Pearls was paired with Oysters and Pearls. Paired with a wine I can't remember which makes me want to kill myself right now because I got all snooty and extra-analog and left my pen and notebook in the car so I could experience this dinner without obsessively scribbling my thoughts down for posterity,9 for which I'd like to kick myself in the posterior. It was good wine. It worked so well with the Oysters and Pearls, I almost shouted.

Me: [straining to remain calm]

Them: I mean, it's ok.

I want to murder them. I want to exsanguinate them with a salad fork. I want to flay them alive and serve their fried rind to a stray dog, paired with rainwater and glower.

Citrus Marinated Salmon with a Confit of navel oranges, beluga caviar, and pea shoot coulis.

It was exquisite. Redolent of the ocean and all she contains. Briny, steely, pinked with salmon goodness, cooked to the perfect moment so the meat reaches its zenith of texture and doneness as the waiter is laying the plate down in front of you. Paired with the condensed breath of God, apparently, for as I followed my first nibble of salmon with the wine the sommelier had described as if he was talking about his beloved mother, this wine, with that salmon, rendered me speechless and agog. My consciousness seemed to push out the top of my head to throw its arms out wide and bellow to the nearby mountaintops: this elixir is as fine and worthy as the meniscus on the cherished lachrymatory of a small but vital deity! Music played. A shaft of argent light beamed down upon me, and I closed my eyes and—

Them: This wine is not my favorite.

Me: [Murder murder murder]

A Pork Thing

I'm sorry for the poor titles of the dishes but I can't find the menus from that day and the internet hates me. It was delicious. It was perfect. It was pork powered up. And it was paired with a Cab from the valley that Keller loved so much he made a deal with the vineyard so it will only be served at the French Laundry.

Me: [crying]

Them: I liked the cab from Madrona better. This one has a bitter nose.10

Me: [Murder murder murder]

My hands are gripping the edges of my chair so hard my elbows are cracking. I want to slap them like James Cagney slapped Joan Crawford in

---

9. Yet I had my phone and discreetly snapped shots of my empty plates just to fuck with my foodie friends.
10. I honestly don't remember exactly what G-dog said but it was along these lines. It's just the rush of blood to my head and the effort of not strangling him ruined my memory and weakened my resolve.

Whatever Happened to Baby Jane. I want to hear an imperial thwack as their heads spin around and their lips hang up over their ears.

We had dessert, which I'm not going to describe because I can't have a cigarette after we're done but I married that dessert, and we had three kids. Then they cleared our coffee and our after-dinner aperitif and then I thought my God, it's over. It's over. I'll never come back, and it was ruined by idiots.

## FISH CAMP

The next summer, I pack my truck then drive to the other side of Lake Michigan because my best friend, Biscuit, invited me to Fish Camp. Biscuit's a Chicago cop. His dad was a cop. His mom was a cop. Nearly all his friends are cops. Much of his extended family–cousins, half cousins, in-laws, etc. are either cops or southside Chicago natives, which is a lot like being a cop. For the last 30 years–since they were piss and vinegar twenty-somethings– they've been renting a resort in Ludington on the shore of Lake Hamlin the weekend before Labor Day. There are six cabins and six boats, all out in the middle of nowhere.

I'd heard about fish camp when I met Dave, and I was jealous of this men-only long weekend of fishing. We both had young sons and I was raised fishing, so I needed to teach the kid how to drop a lure but Chicago, bless its heart, makes fishing hard.

In Floribama, you can cast blind out of your backyard and 90% of the time you'll at least catch a bream. In Chicago, you have to drive fifty miles to find a place to fish that isn't wall-to-wall Jet Skis and pontoon boats. People are so desperate for open water, I had to stop a guy from putting his bass boat into my hot tub. I mean, yeah, we live on one of the largest bodies of fresh water in the world but getting out there is expensive and fishing from shore is impossible.

I could hit the river by my house, but I was walking my dog there one time and a fish walked up to me to bum a smoke so no thank you.

Fish Camp would provide me with the opportunity to get out there with ease. Every cabin comes with a boat. We're fifty feet from the water so I can just roll out of bed and take the kid to the shoreline and haul in breakfast.

And then there's the fraternal aspect of men hanging out with other men doing manly things. I saw us as a band of brothers, and I couldn't wait.

But there are aspects of my personality and my toolbox of manliness which I ought to trot out here for the purpose of full disclosure, principally, that when scored against the American punch list of macho qualities, I am barely a man and, also, I can't fish.

I should be able to fish. Like, I'm a pretty good caster. When I cast, the lure lands where I mean it to land, even if it's far away. But it's the wrong lure. Every time. I am a pointless rebel in my lure selection and a feckless obstructionist when it comes to my own success in reeling in dinner.

I choose lures based on how cool they look. I suspect I'm not the only idiot doing this, and the fishing lure industry understands us all to a tee. This is why there are top water lures that look like they were designed by pre-teen racing fans and plastic worms with loops and hooks to create a bubble trail. Not for the fish. The fish want a fucking actual worm. No, it's for me and the $16.79 I'm gonna blow on that stupid fucking useless plastic bait.

Look, fishing is not hard. You put food on a hook and drop it into a lake over a hungry fish. Wait for the bobber to make an unnatural bob, jerk the line, reel in supper. Men both qualified and entirely unqualified to perform this action have been doing so with general success for nineteen billion years. A reasonably intelligent gent from Chicago ought to be able to do it.

But I can't.

There's no good reason for my failure as a fisherman. Fish camp is loaded to the gills[1] with able anglers. Joe and Joey, who never go out in a boat but instead wait on the shoreline by the docks in comfortable chairs listening to a cubs game routinely reel in fifty fish a day. Fifty. Their technique is straight forward: worm on a hook. Bobber on the line. Pop it out fifteen to twenty feet. The environment where they fish is entirely the wrong place. It is weed-choked. It is adjacent to the docks where gasoline and oil-spewing boats cruise in and out constantly. The shore is supported by a cement wall.

Worse, they talk constantly. And they park their van longways right behind them with the doors thrown open, broadcasting a Cubs game with such poor signal it sounds more like first contact with Hinderfloovians than baseball. And Joe smokes the whole time.

Everything about this set up is wrong.

*Fifty fish a day.*

Then there's Carlos and his crew whose names I can never remember but whose skill at poker[2] is only eclipsed by their skill at netting crappie[3].

---

1 See what I did there?

2 I don't want to talk about it. One cabin is usually designated the "poker" cabin and supports a game that starts Thursday night and ends sometime Sunday morning. It never stops. It often morphs into several games or shrinks to just two guys but it's always on.

The first year I hit camp I couldn't wait to play poker and I was welcomed enthusiastically because I brought a huge wad of money which they subsequently removed from my possession while teaching me, hand by hand, just how fucking horrible I am at this game.

3 For the non-fishers, this is pronounced CROP ee, not CRAP ee.

The first day they usually bring in more than a hundred fish, all giant and meaty. This crew tends to feed everyone else.

Then there's the two old guys, again, no idea who they are or how they're related. They catch a decent string of bream every year, but their real value is their commitment to gutting all the fish. Just these two guys gut and scale something like three-hundred fish and they do it when no one is looking, and they do it fast. Inside the cleaning shack by the docks it's just a swirling tornado of scales and a constant plopping of guts as these two guys plow through most of the fish from Lake Hamlin.

Then they nap.

There's a chance my stats are related not to skill but to commitment. There are, each year, a growing list of distractions keeping me off the water.

This year it was Biscuit's new drone. Expensive. Multi-functional. Able to reach the stratosphere without losing signal. This drone was extraordinary, and Biscuit had been counting down the minutes until we landed on Lake Hamlin.

"You gonna fly it over the lake?" I dumbassed.

"I don't know, it loses signal sometimes," Bicuit says, ignoring my dubmassery.

"So yes?"

"If course I'm flying it over the lake."

"Can I fly it?"

"No."

"I want to scare the swans."

"Which is why you're not flying it."

"Fucking swans."

"Let's take it with us out on the lake and then use it to drop our lures like three-hundred yards out."

"It's not a fucking robotic fishing–what is wrong with you?"

"We can fly it over Carlos's boat and annoy him."

"He'll shoot it down."

Biscuit breaks out the drone and flies it all over camp. It takes gorgeous pictures from a thousand feet up. It's a beautiful day. Perfect for fishing. We are, naturally, on shore flying the drone over the lake and buzzing the docks. Then Biscuit decides to go live on Facebook.

He's sitting on the cabin steps staring down into the video controller for his drone. I'm lighting the grill which involves a shit ton of lighter fluid and a near-death experience. Biscuit's narrating his flight and I'm helping by singing the lead song from my new musical, GPS Superstar.

" . . . And here's the dock . . . There's Joe fishing . . . There's the a-frame cabin. . ."

"Gee pee ess, superstar!"[4]

" . . . I'm gonna come in way over the cattails, this is where all the crappie are . . ."

"Where in the hell do you think you are?"

" . . . Ok, I'm gonna come back to the cabin . . ."

"Gee pee ess . . ."

"Oh, crap. I lost signal. I can't see anything."

"Superstar!"

"Shit."

The drone is parked about eighty feet in the air just at the edge of the shoreline. It moves toward the cabins. And the giant tree by the cabins.

"Where in the hell do you think you–"

Bzzzzzzt!

I whirl around toward the sound of the drone to see falling leaves and green twigs sliced neatly from the very very, very top of the tree—sixty feet up.

"SHIT!"

Biscuit is looking down into his controller. When the signal comes back on, all he sees is green. The drone is still broadcasting live so we're looking down into it and it's just leaves bouncing in the breeze. It has a locator beacon just like in Aliens, so me and Biscuit are walking around trying to get the signal pinned.

"It's in the tree dude."

"I don't think so. It keeps saying it's right here," Biscuit's at the very edge of the weedy shore staring down into the thick grasses. "I mean, I can see leaves so it's not underwater."

"It's in the tree."

"You're an idiot. If it was in the tree, I'd be able to see it."

"I saw leaves falling."

"You see all kinds of shit. It's in the weeds."

"I bet a swan ate it."

We keep walking. We finally find it, lodged firmly at the very top of the tree, pliable green branches tangled hopelessly in the propellers.

Now there are choices Biscuit and I could make. Well, Dave. I was busy not caring and making a fire. But I tried a little. There was a huge neon green 16" softball in the grass by our cabin.

---

4 Go to www.bullgarlington.com and watch the video. I am not making this up.

"Throw this at it," I suggested.

"You're an idiot," Biscuit explained.

"Hit the branch, not the–just try."

We spend way, way too long doing this.  Biscuit's son Natrick joins us. We're at it for a solid half an hour.

"You're going to have to wait for a strong wind."

"It's tangled in branches. It'll have to be a hurricane."

"Just let the management know and they'll return it when it falls."

"Maybe I can climb the tree."

We look at the tree. A monkey couldn't climb this thing.

"We can't even climb stairs."

"I could do it."

"What's your life insurance like?"

As we're plotting Biscuit's death by tree branch, the groundsman passes by in his golf cart. We flag him down. He spends a few minutes staring at the drone.

"Might have to be patient. Wait for it to fall naturally."

"I spent $1100 on that thing."

"I could get a ladder."

He gets a ladder. It comes up just high enough so that he can barely touch the lowest climbable branch.

"I mean, a strong wind . . ." The grounds man joins  Biscuit and Natrick and I, all standing around the tree with our arms crossed looking up at the patient blinking lights of the drone, still broadcasting.

"I could ask Sylvia."

"Who's Sylvia?" We ask. We're thinking she's an arborist or maybe a tree trimmer or perhaps owns one of those construction platform truck things that pops up fifty feet off the ground.

"She's a champeen archer."

Well, of course. Why didn't we think of a champion archer first? What idiots.

He gets back into his cart. Disappears. Biscuit and I spend the time wisely throwing the softball at the drone which is not only hard but impossible to get right. Biscuit almost hits the drone once and we all cheered which made Biscuit mad because he was aiming for the branch since the softball would break the drone in half. Finally, Sylvia arrives, gray hair in a pony tail, mom jeans tucked into her leather work boots.

Biscuit's friend John is a single middle-aged man whose untreated sleep apnea will inspire me to stand in the doorway of his room at three in the morning mind-cursing at him as he snort-snore-cough-chokes three hundred times an hour. He is also a professional teller of shaggy dog tales that leave us bewildered and glaring at him after he's spent fifteen minutes interrupting himself to tell a story that has absolutely no reason to be told. Most of the story he's telling happens in his head and only the last part makes it into actual conversation, which leaves him lobbing odd bon mots like "and that's how I ended up in the produce aisle" into our conversations about Jeeps.

John joined us in the archery efforts.

Sylvia, who looked like she'd be perfectly at home in a clapboard shack in the middle of nowhere with just a kerosene lantern and her trusty Bowie knife to keep her company, threaded a fishing line through a hole in an arrow then with astonishing precision, shot the arrow up through the branches of this tree to lay that fishing line a mere inch to the left of the drone. John gasped.

She tied the line to a rope, hauled the rope over the branch, and we all spent a good twenty minutes tugging until the drone fell down through the tree, breaking its propellors on the way down, landing useless and unflyable at our feet.

Biscuit shook hands with Sylvia and the grounds man and we all went back into our shack to enjoy the crispy, coal black burgers and dogs I'd forgotten about on the grill.

We're comfortable and filled with charred burgers until our ribs crack, working on our second beers, sitting deep and napfully in the cushions of the easy chairs and the couch when John says:

"You know, that's just the kind of woman I like. A pioneer woman."

I look at Biscuit. It's hard to tell if this is the nose or the tail of a shaggy dog so we keep quiet in the hopes John will just fall asleep.

"That Sylvia. I mean, she looked like she could skin a deer, you know what I mean?"

I knew exactly what he meant but I wasn't about to say anything.

"I really like that in a woman. I think she could survive, you know? Like if she was dropped out in the middle of the tundra."

Group stare.

"John," Biscuit lights a cigar. "Never show me your porn."

**THE GIZA NECROPOLI FROM CAMP.** After fighting a camel, we find ourselves at the broken-down family camp of our camel guides, staring at this view like frikkin' lawrence of Arabia.

**KARNACK.** From the backside of the ruins, where the tourists weren't climbing all over everything and the guides weren't laughing at my giant ass.

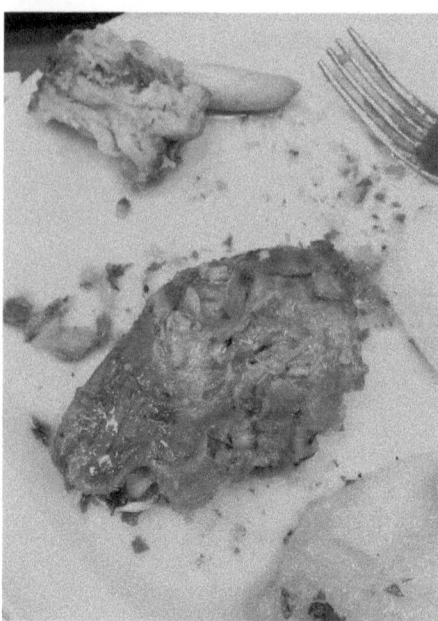 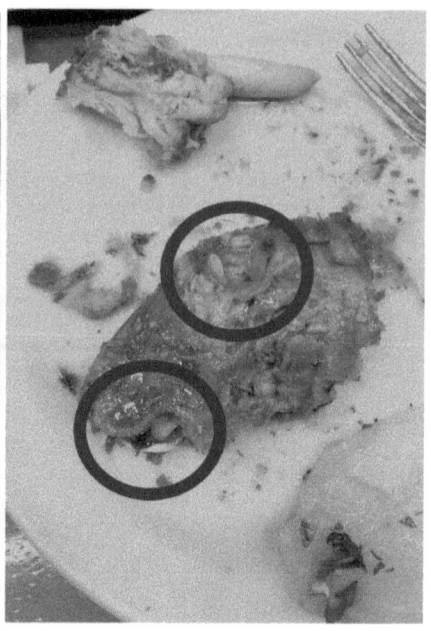

**BAR ANBALOU, MADRID.** This is the soup, called Pape de Pope, which was handed to me with no warning.

**DETAILED VIEW.** Upper circle: that's an eye socket. Lower circle: the incisors.

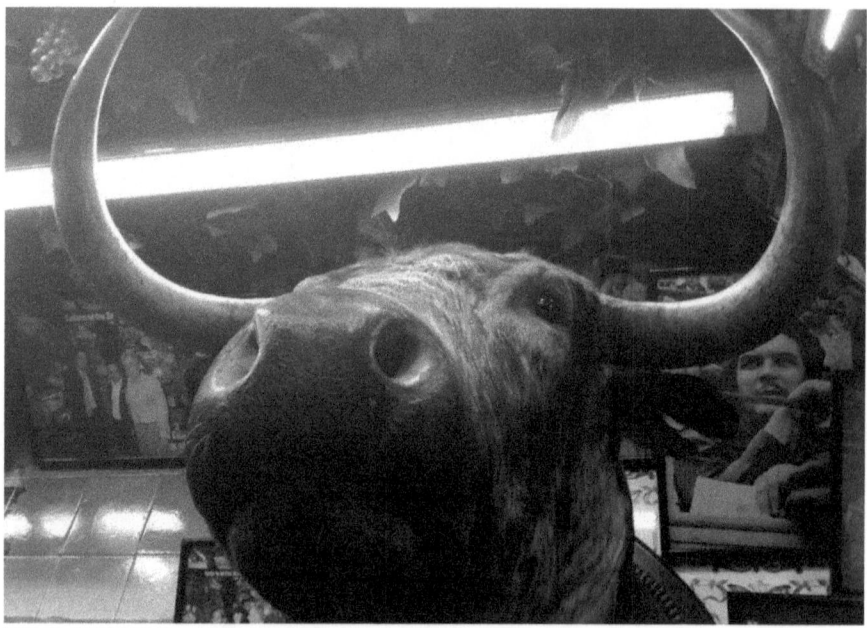

**BAR ANDALOU, MADRID.** I knew I would love this bar (regardless of their rat soup). Although I believe it's a bar ostensibly for matadors or people who identify as matadorian, which means they abuse bulls while also revering them, I enjoyed their tepid beer.

**LUXOR, EGYPT.** I felt very National Geographicky after taking this snapshot of a guy trying his best not to be photographed.

**NEAR A SUGARCANE FIELD JUST OFF THE NILE SOMEWHERE IN EGYPT.** This is the tableau I staggered past as I was dying on the way to the fishing village. Just after taking this picture, the donkey, as the harbinger of death, looked up at me and brayed: *dude, draft a will.*

**The shops at Esna, Egypt.** This was taken ten seconds before the ecstatic shopkeeper ran out of the door on the right trying to fit me with a sail. Fifteen seconds before our armed escort (bottom right, in the chair) arrived.

**The Meroe, somewhere on the Nile.** My two wives, Adelaide in front, [My Attorney]way at the back on the deck of the Nor Nil Meroe, probably in Esna.

**SAHARA, NEAR GIZA, EGYPT.** Me illustrating the distressing relative size of the camel, [My Attorney] and myself. Also, note the fear.

**CIGARETTE BOAT, NILE, EGYPT.** These guys would pull up and sell cigarettes and other sundries to our dahibaya crew.

**NEAR ASWAN, NILE, EGYPT.** If you're thinking, gee whiz that's kind of dark, just know this was our 4:30 a.m. disembarkment and I turned the exposure up as far as it would go.

**The Louvre, Paris.** The stupidest painting in the world, hating everyone in the room. My god what a let down.

**Madrid.** Drunk, wandering the tapas bars in the capable stewardship of Belgian beer grifters.

**THE LOUVRE, PARIS.** A scultptor's joke. I mean, it took this guy a year to do this and it's just basically "choking the chicken" in marble.

**NOTRE DAME, PARIS.** Behold, a goddam lobster.

**ST. GERMAIN, PARIS.** My view from the Cafe St Germain, drinking a St. Germain while listening to the DJ Saint Germain in the neighborhood of Saint Germain.

**Rue des Philosophers, Paris.** Such an iconic view of a place I didn't know existed.

**Bar Mirebella, Barthelona, Spain.** The wooden saint in the greatest dive bar in the world.

**Temple Bar, Barthelona, Spain.** About midway through a legendary drunken binge through the tourist sector of Barthelona.

**THE PRIVATE BEACH AT HANDLES, WHERE I LEFT MY TESTICLES.** This is the view from the balcony I would shortly ruin.

**SONOMA, CALIFORNIA.** The Ukrainian, Myself, [My Attorney], and the Captive Husband only a few hours before they ruined the French Laundry through relentless pedantic savagery.

**MY NOTEBOOK FROM 2017 THROUGH 2021.** It's a beautiful piece of garbage.

**THE FRENCH LAUDRY, OYSTERS AND PEARLS.** I sent my foody friends pictures of my finished courses to ruin their day.

**LUDDINGTON, MICHIGAN.** Biscuit and Bull flying the drone to attack swans.

*From the Nashville Tours itinerary for our trip. Reproduced before each chapter exactly as presented.*

## JEWELS OF EGYPT
## DAY 1
## ARRIVE CAIRO 6 NOV SAT

Transfer in Istanbul to arrive in Cairo on Saturday, November 6, 2021 on Turkish Air at 20:30. Your tour manager will meet & assist you at Cairo International Airport and then he will escort you to the hotel by exclusive air-conditioned deluxe vehicle. At the hotel the tour manager will assist with a smooth check-in and review your Spiritual holiday itinerary with you to establish and confirm pick-up times for each tour. Overnight in Cairo.

### BUSINESS CLASS

I am not business class. Not in my mind. In my mind I'm a Floribama boy from a dirt road trailer park in Ocoee, FL and in that boy's future, business class did not obtain.

But it has.

It's half past ten on a Friday night in November 2021 when I cautiously lower my ample caboose into seat G6 on the aisle in business class and a few things are immediately apparent.

First, I fit. This is a novel occurrence in my history of air travel, as I have always had to put on a brave face then shove myself into seats designed for famine victims. But this night on Turkish airlines, I slide into the seat with room to spare. I am stricken mute by the foresight and generosity of the seat designers from Boeing for perhaps being from Wisconsin and realizing most of the people who can afford business class are in the August of their years and also in the August of their pants which is to say they are old and fat so give them a bigger seat, Eugene.

Secondly, I don't have to make the universal fist-bump gesture up the aisle to the stewardess to inform her that I need an extender for my seatbelt, a moment in a fat man's life which is woefully common and woefully woeful because she brings it and then you use it and everyone is watching and it's kind of like you've dropped your pants and you're pulling them up with a sheepish grin with the hope that no one is judging you while everyone is judging you.

But not this time. This time the belt clicks into the buckle just fine because it was designed by the same Boeing engineer as the seat it's attached to and she was thinking about her tante Carol who is sensitive about her weight, so she added eighteen inches to the belt, and I want to send her a card. That click, that simple snick of the buckle closing sans extender was a true luxury.

Third, I am suddenly aware of just how much better I am than the endless river of filthy, ignorant savages streaming past me into economy class. Those poor souls. I make a note to pass them my scraps.

[My Attorney] has been pregaming this flight for months. She's as excited about flying business class as she is about seeing the great pyramids of Giza. If she were writing this book it would be called Business Class, Bitches. It would be eleven chapters detailing each and every luxurious accommodation included with our flight. There would be an entire chapter on the cheese service. Footnotes about the juice. She's also my personal in-flight announcer, smacking me in the arm and explaining what's next.

SMACK! They're bringing champagne!

SMACK! We get chicken or lamb—LAMB!

SMACK! Here comes the wine service!

But she's right. Our flight is hoity and toity. I realize this when a chef, in a chef's uniform and a big, white chef's hat steps through the curtain that shields us from the pure unalloyed glorious god-like gleam of first class to take our dinner order.

Then they bring us stuff. Each of the things they bring us raises our personal opinion of ourselves an entire level until we're banging our heads on the ceiling: first, the juice. Strawberry, mango, lemonade. Then the champagne. Then a leather toiletries kit from Versace. Then slippers. Then noise-cancelling headphones. By the time the last poverty-stricken savage had collapsed onto their rickety stool behind us, [My Attorney] and I were enjoying a cheese plate and a frigid Veuve Clicquot.

Still, I'm jumpy and self-conscious because I can't quite believe I'm in business class and let's diverge a minute here for those of you who fly business class all the damn time wondering why I'm going on and on about it, or for those of you who've never flown business class and are wondering the same damn thing: it's business class but it's Turkish Air so it's Midwest

First Class and I am both flabbered and gasted.

I knew going into this thing that I was facing eleven hours in the air at night and that our seats extended into beds, and I would probably travel most comfortably if I slept across the Atlantic. It's a cool trick if you can do it because you fall asleep in America and wake up in Istanbul like nothing happened.

But I have issues. I don't understand people who can sleep in public. It's weird. People can see you! What happens if you do something embarassing? What happens when I fart in my sleep, because I will fart in my sleep and my fart voice is a basso profundo so people will hear it.

However, this is not my worst fear. My biggest concern is that I sleep with a CPAP machine and how in the hell does that work on a plane?

Not very well, as it turns out.

I put off sleeping until everyone around me was snoring gently at 40,000 feet because setting up my sleep machine is like wrestling a vacuum cleaner. There is a hose and a mask and I kind of look like I've been attacked by an alien when I'm wearing it, which is wildly embarassing. But I've devised a strategy: I'll pull the blanket over my head like a tent. Then, hidden under the blanket, I'll put on the mask that goes over my head. That way no one will think I'm weird.

I extend the bed out a little but it's instantly alarming because I'm horribly off-balance[1] and I can't see my TV screen over my gut. I reset my chair and wait until the stewardesses are sitting in their jump seats drinking coffee and gossiping. I try it again and I get it all the way down, my head sliding backwards and seemingly under the back of my seat.[2] I shove my CPAP machine into the nook between us, throw the blanket over my head, and, half sitting up like a small child in a horror movie, try to wrangle the hoses down into the crook of the seat while putting on my mask which must appear to anyone else like a guy under a blanket fighting an octopus.3 So that I don't look weird.

Mask firmly affixed, I lie back into my little cubby hole bed, but things

1 Here's the thing: I sleep on a nice Vera Wang firm mattress that's flipped over so I actually sleep on the bottom, which is even firmer. I'd like to sleep on a 3/4-inch plywood sheet, but my wife has standards. Also, I sleep on my stomach, which is odd for a man impersonating Darth Vader every night, but I do it. Also, my mattress gives just enough so my hips sink below the waterline, and I can pretend to be normal. On this plane, the mattress is a thick sheet of stainless steel with all the give of a thin sheet of stainless steel. And I can't roll over, so I have to lie flat on my back which means my ass has me propped up like some kind of chiropractic 'before' picture. And my idea of level and the plan's idea of level are off by a full bubble. My head is shoved into the privacy space at a 45° angle, so all the blood is pooling between my ears. You know: comfort.

2 I feel like I'm on the Thunderbirds. The whole thing is ingenious but also kind of ridiculous. I'm folding down flat then sliding back into a drawer like I'm being saved for later. It should shrink wrap me.

3 And losing.

are different. I don't fit quite as nicely as I did when I was sitting. Now it's like trying to hammer the Pillsbury doughboy into a shallow Tupperware and I'm almost there when my hoses escape and shoot out across [My Attorney] who wakes up screaming because of course she does. I ram my gear down out of sight, jerk the blanket back over my head—so that I don't look weird—and somehow, against all odds, fall asleep.

## My Two Wives

Before we get started here on our visit to Egypt, I want to introduce you to my traveling companions: my first wife, [My Attorney], and my second wife, Adelaide Hunter[1].

They are besties. They met at a gigantic law firm where [My Attorney] was an attack librarian and Adelaide politely threatened people in finance. [My Attorney] got her law degree while our children were in grade school, so I've been there from the beginning and I'll be honest with you, I still don't know what she does. I can tell you how she does it, since Covid has moved her from her swank downtown office to our dining room table where she yells law. That's the best way I can describe it. This beautiful tiny woman whom I adore like she's a golden alien angelic being screams at other lawyers with the ferocity of a wounded lioness standing over her cubs. And it's not just screaming, it's professional screaming so it's smooth, velvety, corporate screaming with great respect for the person on the other end of the zoom call but also a kind of screaming loaded with the implicit threat of despleening them with a sharpened gravy boat if they don't [law thing] with the [law thing] because of the [law thing] in their [unlawful thing].

In real life, [My Attorney] is bubbly, joyful, and hilarious. I met her in the late 80s and she looked like Meg Ryan but with a sense of humor and big hair and even though she was Catholic and a fucking Notre Dame preppy white chick, I was smitten. For thirty-odd years, she has been my best friend and trash T.V. watching partner with a penchant for fine wine, dirty martinis, and insipid romcoms. She loves my cooking, laughs at my jokes, can go online and buy me shirts that fit and look great, and goes easy on me in Words with Friends. Also, and I can't overstate the importance here, she lets me touch her butt.

My second wife also works in law but not as a lawyer. I'm pretty sure she's a finance wizard but, though she has explained her work to me in

---

1 Not her real name. Adelaide enjoys her privacy and, like my first wife, though she loves me, is wary about appearing in my stories, probably with good reason.

painstaking detail using small words while gently encouraging me to keep up, I don't know what the fuck she does. Outside of work, she's does yoga, eats vegan, reads good books, listens to great music, and carries a conversation with all the wit and elan one would expect from a well-educated woman from Chicago. She loves fine wine, she is a meticulous interior designer, and her friends are like a who's who of Chicago artists, musicians, writers, and lawyers. And please understand her status as my second wife is merely honorary (one she bestowed onto me, not the other way around). If I ever touch her butt, she will deliver my soulless carcass to my first wife, who will set me on fire.

They have two great traits in common. One is their innate, pervasive classiness. They are dignified, powerful professionals, leaders in their respective fields, who can keep their cool in the middle of a boardroom where everyone else is on fire and bleeding from their ears as a million-dollar project seems to go down in flames. My wives, in that situation, would not panic, would not curse, and would not even raise their voice. They would quietly tackle the problem, breaking it down into its parts, then find solutions and ultimately put the whole shitshow back on track, put out all the fires, keep everyone employed, and save the company a billion dollars. They simply don't crack under pressure. In fact, they thrive on it.

Their other common trait is an indefatigable love of detail. They read the instructions for a game or a piece of furniture all the way through before they roll a die or pick up a wrench—and they do it with enthusiasm. Their parties are organized to the minute. I refer you to the previous chapter where [My Attorney] presented our traveling companions with a three-ring binder, tabbed, color-coded, and flagged with Post-It notes for a jaunt into wine country that only lasted two days. It brings her joy.

Adelaide took the lead planning our trip to Egypt since she is a seasoned world traveler and knows how to game touring companies. I'm pretty sure at least three people quit Nashville Tours[2] to become priests over the two-year period Adelaide worked this trip and I don't care. They are weak. The resulting itinerary was picture perfect and organized with the kind of obsessive attention to detail that brought tears to my first wife's eyes. Between the efforts of both of them, exactly fuck-all was left for me, which is fine, because as you will shortly discover, fuck-all is my wheelhouse.

---

2 Not their actual name and look, I'm married to a cautious I.P. attorney so when she reads my first drafts, she usually has to take a Xanax and lie down for a minute because of all the slander. Nobody's name in this book is correct except mine.

*"A final twist in the mountain road brings us through an arched doorway in the town wall into an open space amid Moorish shops and houses, where we alight. The Spirit irreverently remarks that if cleanliness were next to godliness, Allah must be a long way from Moulay Idris. There has been a shower of rain, and we squelch through deep yellow mud that sucks at our heels like quicksand, avoiding small heaps of garbage which have been thrown from shops and houses."*
Gordon West
*By Bus to the Sahara*
1946

## CULTURE CRASHING IN CAIRO

We are met at the Cairo airport by our tour manager, the Egyptian Liam Neeson, also known as Mustafa, which I swear did not make me laugh because I AM A MAN OF CULTURE. He hustles us through customs and gets us into the busminivan with our driver for the next five days, a man named Habibi.

Habibi is not his actual name. His nickname is Labib, but I misheard that and for the next six days, I called this body-building mountain of a man, probably a former soldier and by former soldier, I mean Egyptian ninja assassin who strangled people with his bare hands, a man with resting-action-figure face, Habibi which means "My Precious Baby."

We head toward Giza where we are booked into the Hotel Mena House which sits at the foot of the Giza Necropolis meaning you can have coffee on your balcony and enjoy an uninterrupted view of Cheops without binoculars and here is where I get the first inkling that Cairo is piled three stories deep with pure, uninterrupted, powerful madness.

I am about to say some things about a developing country that may be misconstrued as derogatory and may lead some readers to shout at me digitally and rouse angry protests against these words but I assure you they are completely accurate and I may use colorful language and literary tools to tell this story, but I don't make anything up.

Egypt is a developing country, sitting between Indonesia and South Africa on the human development index with a solid score of .696. It is below Belize, Libya, and Uzbekistan and way, way below the United States whose score is .924 (thanks Mississippi). I am relaying this information to you so that you understand that I understand that Egypt and America are different in everry way and I should not have traveled there with the expectation that I would find it only slightly foreign. I did not. Which meant I was not prepared.

I'm still not prepared. I've done a little research and I remain shocked.

So here are the easily misconstrued words: *Cairo is a rebar wigged, madcap, terrifying trash magnet.*[1]

Let us discuss the first weird thing that one can't help but notice: the rebar. Apparently, there is a tax loophole allowing homeowners to ignore property taxes if their buildings are unfinished. Every building that isn't owned by Marriot or the government sports a spiky crown of pointy metal rods. All of them. Looking out across the city, you see a rooftop forest of rusty rebar.

The second weird thing is the traffic. It is spine-chilling. Harrowing. It's thrilling in a kind of "we apologize for the parts of the roller coaster that aren't nailed down" way. But the initial impression is one of imminent

---

1 Sigh. Culture shock is real. I thought I might be cool enough to be immune to it since I read books, and I've been to other countries and I'm a democrat. But I was not immune to the extreme differences between my life and the daily life I was exposed to in Giza and Cairo. I really and truly have had a hard time understanding just what privilege means. Egypt gave me a crash course. Our Egyptologist, Ahmed Rezik, recently answered my hand-wringing questions about the litter in Giza. I told him I had to write about it, but I didn't want to sound like a white privileged dumbass. I asked "I am having a hard time writing about an aspect of Egyptian life. I feel like I'm being a jerk, but I have to ask: why is there so much garbage everywhere? Sorry if this is a stupid question." Ahmed got back to me with "It's like any country. In the big cities, in the center of the city, you can see it's clean but when you go to the borders of the city, you will see a lot of garbage. Unfortunately, most of the sites you covered in your trip were on the borders of the cities. Like pyramids, Sakkara and Memphis." Once again, I have committed the sin of Americanizing the rest of the world while committing the simultaneous sin of assuming that the tiny sampling of the 20 million people in those two cities and how they lived represented every other Egyptian. There are suburbs in Cairo. There are suburbs as pristine, quiet, and curated as any you'll find in Chicagoland. There are streets you could airlift into Naperville, and nobody would even notice. Yes, most of Cairo and Giza is poor, littered, and suffering from the same frustrating problems as any major American city. It's important to remember these are twin cities that shake hands across the Nile. Cairo has nine million people. Giza's got eight. For perspective, New York city has fewer people than Giza. In these two Egyptian cities there are twenty million people. That's more people than the five biggest American cities combined. Imagine Houston, L.A., Chicago, New York, and Philadelphia all lived in the same place. Whatever the historic name given to the area, it's been a tourist attraction for nearly five thousand years. I suppose I should chill the fuck out a keep my outrageous pearl-clutching to my damn self.

death. But you're not going to die in a traffic accident in Cairo. You can't. You'll never go fast enough to kill yourself or anyone else. You might get maimed, I'm not ruling out a good maiming, but death is unlikely.

We once reached the astonishing velocity of thirty-one miles an hour, but a donkey stepped in front of us, so we had to stop. I am not making that up. During our tour of Cairo sites, we spent a lot of time behind mules, donkeys, and flat-bed wagons pulled by mules or donkeys. There are also twenty-eight million tiny three-wheeled vehicles called Tuk Tuks which were conceived in India where they have been banned as being too likely to bury themselves in your spleen and breed. A typical moment on the expressway leading into Giza, like the section over the Nile, for instance, will find you in no lane, compressed at an angle between a bus-minivan overflowing with shift workers, two motorcycles, a mule-driven banana wagon, a flock of Tuk Tuks, and a guy just casually walking across it all.

The Tuk Tuks are a scourge on the Egyptian traffic landscape, cursed at by everyone and called every manner of dirty word but most often alfayrus which is a bad translation of Egyptian Arabic for virus. They are six deep on every street in Cairo, like some kind of infestation of beetles, following no rules, no logic, and no laws of traffic except the pressing logistics of getting their customers to where their customers want to go, not necessarily intact.

Here is an intersection in Nazlat al Batran. It's midday.

The flat front of our minivan pokes cautiously into a three-way intersection. In the absolute middle of the crossroads, three adults with two toddlers. They are not racing from one side to the other. Their car has not broken down. They're just standing there talking. Behind them, nearer to the edge of the road but still in the road, eleven locals are milling around. Coming directly toward us is a flatbed cart pulled by a tired horse. Two cars pass us and drive right through it all. We turn left, as six people shuffle toward us in the street. We stop immediately next to a giant pink bus because a teen on a horse cut us off. As a small car turns across our path, five dudes in gebellas swarm us from behind, crowd into our lane, and just keep going. They walk past a gang of six dudes walking toward us, who cut off a car which causes another group of people waking behind that car to change course and walk in front of our van then stop. We've gone six feet.

Let's try another one. A crossroads in Al Kalifa wal Moqattam. We're in a (lane?) with another minivan right next to us. Three other roads spill traffic into this convergence. There are no less than twelve people walking across traffic. We get a little further down the road and we're slowed down and I swear thirty people cross. Same town, a quarter mile further on, we turn onto a side street and drop to a snail's pace because we are riding behind an empty flatbed cart drawn by a bony mule which is barging through a couple of oncoming Tuk Tuks who are cutting off a late model Toyota which is double-parked while a scooter keeps pace with us.

Finally, and here is the worst thing I will say but it is absolutely accurate: Cairo is blanketed by trash. It's everywhere. It's worse than America in the 50s. It's worse than Philadelphia. There is trash. Every. Where. If you think I'm being insensitive or perhaps exaggerating, may I point you to MANSHIYAT NASSER, or Garbage City, a neighborhood in Cairo THAT IS TWO FLOORS DEEP WITH GARBAGE. I don't mean it's a giant dump, I mean it's block after block of apartment buildings with garbage bags spilling off third floor balconies. This is a real place.[2]

Litter is a problem all over Egypt and you will have to get used to it if you're going anywhere other than the hotel lobby. It's just a fact of the landscape. And not just Cairo. Everywhere. We drove two hours out to Sohag to see a temple and this little village was plastered with garbage. The canals that run all the way out to these villages bear flotillas of plastic bags, old chairs, cardboard, massive bundles of cane, plastic bottles, mysterious squishy packages, and random, unattended fires.

Except in Luxor. And Aswan. These two cities are hoisting the country up the humanity index. Luxor is the opposite of Cairo. Where Cairo streets are often unpaved, curbless, and choking on laneless zooming psychopaths, Luxor's streets would be right at home in any small city in the U.S.A. Perhaps even Norway, which has the U.S. beat by six slots. And I noticed there was a distinct lack of itinerant vendors on the sidewalks. Even the Tuk Tuks were sparse.

Aswan is similar. It feels familiar to Americans. You don't have to fight for lane space on the highway. There are lanes on the highway. Bus stops are marked, and on the side of the streets, not, as they are in Cairo, seemingly random and in the right-hand lane.

Of course, once every hundred years you may have to suffer through a life-threatening storm dumping a reservoir of rain water on a desert town which will cause fires, floods, cave-ins, death and release a plague of scorpions unseen since Moses lost his shit. But that's just travel, baby.

---

2 Some cultural notes: Manshiyat Nasser is populated mostly by Coptic Christians who collect garbage throughout Cairo because Cairo does not have a functioning waste management department. They are known as Zabballeen, or garbage people. The men collect the garbage, then women and children pick through it for recyclables which they presumably exchange for money. Their system is slow and manual but it's also 90 percent efficient which is four times better than anything we've achieved over here with our clean streets.

*"At last, the old man manages to grapple with the goat at close quarters. After a little in-fighting he lifts it bodily. Its forelegs are round his neck, its hind legs embrace his waist, while its head peers round the side of his turban. Thus, the old man and his captive mount the step ladder to the roof of the bus where, if we are to judge by the thumping and bumping above our heads, the struggle is continued with unabated vigour. When the bust starts again we can watch the fight in shadow thrown on the desert by the sun. It seems for a while that the goat is winning again, until at last the old man gets an effective stranglehold on his opponent, so bringing this perilous all-in wrestling to an end. He spends the rest of the journey lying on the conquered animal to keep it quiet."*

Gordon West
By Bus to the Sahara
1946

## JEWELS OF EGYPT
## DAY 2
## 4PM NOV 7 CAMEL RIDE AND BEDOUIN DINNER

Spend a free day at your hotel then you will be picked up by your tour leader at 4 pm approximate to enjoy camel riding at Giza Pyramids for 2 hours during the sunset. While experiencing the camel ride, you will enjoy the fascinating view of the pyramids of Cheops, Chephren, and Mykerinus from outside. The Great Pyramids are considered as the oldest one of the seven wonders of the Ancient World, the tallest man-made structure in the world for over 3,800 years and the most important touristic sites in Egypt. Then enjoy Bedouin dinner before getting back at your hotel.

### TEA IN THE SAHARA

Our first excursion, after landing in Cairo and settling into the Mena House hotel, is a camel trip out into the Sahara.

After I fell off his camel, my camel handler, Ahmed, walked me deep into the side streets of Nazlet el Saman. It's hard to accurately capture the vivid tableau of desolation and vibrant life tangled together in the streets of Nazlet el Saman. The history of the neighborhood is bound up in horsemanship. Legend (history?) tells us an Egyptian prince[1] was impressed by the equestrian skills of someone who lived in the area and gave them the land. Since then, it's been all about riding, with horses, camels, donkeys, and carriage rentals providing the bulk of the economy.

Ahmed[2] led me down a dirt side street into utter bewilderment. I wasn't sure if the buildings around me were homes or stables and I think the answer is yes. No glass in the windows. Just holes into dark rooms and sometimes patioesque areas with people sitting on makeshift stools smoking cigarettes and drinking coffee. Horses everywhere. Camels everywhere. Standing on the corner waiting for Ahmed to find me a carriage, no less than twelve riders on horses, six or seven carriages, and ten camels pounded past me kicking up dust and debris and causing me to flatten myself against the wall in terror.

I peered down another side street. Bored camels and horses poked their heads out of windows chewing cud. Children rode past at a gallop, bareback, yelling at me, at Ahmed, and at everyone else. Young men thundered by, bareback, headed off into the desert. The streets were deep sand strewn with hay and piles of manure. Trash everywhere. I had a moment of doubt where I thought, you know, I could just disappear into one of these stables and they could definitely avoid a lawsuit, but my better angels stepped up and tweeted "@bullgarlington racist much? Oh no, your privilege is showing!" so I muscled up a little courage and kept walking deeper into this neighborhood of horses.

I had read reports of animal abuse by the camel drivers at the pyramids and was confident that getting our camels in Nazlet el Saman meant the beasts were treated more humanely. But after Ahmed found me a carriage (I sat on a buckboard with my feet knee-deep in fresh greens for the camels) and hauled me past the cemetery out into the Sahara uphill toward the Giza plateau, I realized it wasn't Ahmed or his fellow drivers who were the problem, it was me. We stopped every twenty yards so the horse could rest,

---

1  Look, this book is not exactly burdened by scholarship. I've done a halfway decent Google search for "Nazlet el Saman+prince+legend" and not much comes up in the realm of details. The story is related by tourists and visiting authors, most notably in *The Mena House: A Short History of a Remarkable Hotel* by Nina Nelson, 1997. Nelson relates a story told to her by a local of Nazlet el Saman, but her story is light on details and bereft of names. Getting a copy of this book would require me to spend almost $50 which would eat up 187% of the profit I'm going to make from my sales. I'll make some calls but I'm not promising anything.
2  We are going to meet a lot of Ahmeds in this book as you will meet a lot of Ahmeds in Egypt, along with Mohammed's and Mamouts. Calling out Ahmed anywhere in Egypt is like yelling "Nick!" in Greektown. thirty guys turn their head.

and I thought for a minute it was because we were the same weight but then a carriage overflowing with an entire Wisconsin family drove past us on their return trip and they outweighed me by a nine-year-old. So for once, it wasn't my obesity causing a problem.

The sand was ten inches deep and dry as hell and again, we were on a slope. The horse, breathing heavily, seems to pause. His shoulders twitch and he drops his haunches, digs his hooves into the dry sand, drops his head, and surges forward five whole inches.

Animal cruelty might have a different meaning in Giza. Surely this culture of animal dressage was wildly different from what I've encountered in America. In Chicago, the horse and carriages in the city are (despite many arguments against the notion) treated well. They are swapped out often, don't have to haul people uphill through sand, and as far as I know, aren't whipped furiously by their driver.

As our horse pulled us up the hill of sand, Ahmed used a braided lash tied to a stick to whip the horse. His whipping never corresponded to any behavior of the horse; it was more like an afterthought. A trio of riders raced past us. One of them leaned far out of his saddle to whip the horse running next to him. He whipped someone else's horse. It was a wild, senseless desert opera of bareback screaming business slacks and dress shoes-wearing horse abusers.

I read all those articles about animal abuse and investigations into Egypt's tourism trade of horses and buggies without really putting myself into the equation. Clambering onto the bench in my buggy I didn't think I was adding to the dilemma of animal abuse, but I sure as hell was. Our horse was exhausted, and its path was difficult, if not unsafe, and finally, the whipping. So much whipping.

A respectable man would have stopped Ahmed, tipped him handsomely, then walked the rest of the way. I like to think of myself as a respectable man, but I'd just fallen off a camel and the sand was deep, and I didn't know where the hell we were going. I remained on my bench, gripping the sides like I was going to fly off, legs knee-deep in a pile of horseweed, hating every second.

We arrive at the Bedouin camp which is an actual Bedouin camp because Ahmed and his cousins and brothers who own the horses and buggies and camels and donkeys they're savaging are Bedouin and this was their camp. It was a weathered frame of driftwood covered by tattered tarps and a lot of windswept desert sand on a high plateau with some old couches and armchairs that made my inner Bohemian feel right at home. Ahmed offered me refreshment as I flopped down into a shredded armchair to gaze in amazement at the distant pyramids and take stock.

I couldn't help but hear the Police's beguiling sonic oddity, "Tea in the Sahara" in my mind and as the sun sank fully over the horizon, we were left in a pool of bottle glass green electric light drinking mint tea.

I couldn't muster the existential dread and sense of dilemma Paul Bowles suffered so many decades previously as an expat in Tangiers. I wanted to. I saw myself, in the planning and desperate online shopping phase of this trip, in my white shirts and khaki pants and Stetson, as the desert traveler: literary kinsman of Bowles, Burroughs, Hemingway and all the great writers who've meant so much to me over the years, all of them having spent time in this very desert doing this very thing I'm doing then turning out a venerable, historic book.

I don't know what their days were like. I know Burroughs was high out of his mind on hard rock dope candy. I assume the others were too. I know he cranked out page after page of Naked Lunch on a manual typewriter, flinging them over his head as Jack Kerouac and Allen Ginsberg plucked them out of the air then tried their level best to make sense of the genius and baffling narrative of his work.

But we don't know much about their moment-to-moment lives. Who knows? Maybe they had plenty of incidents where they ceased for a split second to be so literary and cool and instead yelled at a scarf peddler or sat in resolute silence wishing for a viciously frigid Arnold Palmer. I hope to God they did because that's probably my only point of purchase with the top of the paper mountain.[3]

Ahmed's brother turned on a portable radio. As I sipped mint tea and gazed at Cheops waiting for a literary moment to bloom in my life, the rusted truck tones of Morgan Wallen's insipid faux-country glurge of twang-vomit "Whiskey Glasses," blasted over the sands and I whirled in my chair, involuntarily, I swear, in a voice with the authority of a thousand Karens, growled "Absolutely not," and made them turn it off. I may be in pain. I may be passing through as a pathetic bougie tourist and I might not be a literary giant but by God I'm not letting my moment of ennui in the Sahara be infected by bad country music.

Because I'd so graciously declined my camel transport and because it had taken so long to find me a carriage full of weeds, we almost missed the actual Saharan sunset, which was the point of the day's excursion. We arrived at the Bedouin camp rattled and thirsty about ten minutes before the sun dropped over the edge of the world, just long enough for us to take

---

3 Or maybe not. See Appendix: Gordon West.

stupid camel pictures with the sun battered pyramids behind us. And then the tattered chair and the tea and I thought perhaps we'd missed our moment but as I sank back into that dreadfully bohemian trash-picked Barcalounger I had an existential moment.

We think of the existentialists as Van Dyked sourpusses who never spoke but instead intoned on and on about how we are born without purpose into a world that makes no sense. Brother Bowles languished in Tangiers writing his existential masterwork, The Sheltering Sky, and soaking in his overarching literary message: Everything gets worse.

And for Bowles, that concept came to pass. Paul Theroux interviewed Bowles in his apartment when the author was 83. Here's Theroux's description of his first glimpse of the famed novelist:

"I found him sitting on the floor of a back room in a large chilly apartment in a gray building on a back street in Tangier. It was October and clammy cold. To drive the dampness away Bowles had a sort of superior blowtorch going, a fizzing blue flame heating the curtained-off cubicle, where he was seated like a hawker in a bazaar, on a mat, back straight, legs out, because of a leg infection. Around him was a litter of small objects: notebooks, pens, medicine bottles—everything within reach—a teapot, a cup, spoons, matches, and shelves with books and papers, some of them musical scores. A metronome sat on a low table nearby, among bottles of capsules and tubes of ointment, and cassette tapes and a tin of Nesquik and cough drops and a partly eaten candy bar and a note folded and jammed into an envelope scribbled Paul Bowles, Tangier, Maroc, a vague address but it had obviously found him, as I had, with little more information than that."[4]

Reading this as a fifty-seven-year-old man from the comfort of a backroom office with a nice in-the-wall heater and a well-appointed desk and a dog nuzzling my elbow for a scratch, I feel for Bowles. If I had read that same passage in my youth, I would have packed my bags, as there is something exotic and louche about living low in an unmarked apartment with a blowtorch and a half-eaten candy bar.

Bowles was a traveler, not a tourist. This is a distinction I wished to make through my actions as a newly minted global journeyman and part of me secretly hoped I'd come down with a mild case of Covid so my wives would have to leave me in a ratty apartment in Cairo where I'd live off of mint tea and dried dates and shisha, a feeling linked directly to the kind of idiotic passions of a literary teenager reading this kind of thing in The

---

4 Theroux, P. (2018, May 11). Paul Bowles: 'Here's My Message. Everything Gets Worse' LitHub.com https://lithub.com/paul-bowles-heres-my-message-everything-gets-worse/

Sheltering Sky:

"He did not think of himself as a tourist; he was a traveler. The difference is partly one of time, he would explain. Whereas the tourist generally hurries back home at the end of a few weeks or months, the traveler, belonging no more to one place than to the next, moves slowly, over periods of years, from one part of the earth to another."[5]

Sitting in that ratty-ass chair, however, I had a brief moment of timelessness, a feeling of being suspended, just existing there in the vast blank of the Sahara with the Giza Necropolis in the distance and some camels and nothing calling me away, nothing nudging me out of my reverie.

This is what I believe appealed to all those expats, to Jean Genet, Gertrude Stein, Bowles and Aaron Copland from the first wave as much as it did to Kerouac, Tennessee Williams, Burroughs, Gysin, and Truman Capote in the second wave. There's a suspicious lack of urgency. In Western Europe and America, we can always hear the ticking clock, we always know exactly how much time we have left, how much we've spent on project X, and what's next on our agenda. Even independent weirdos like me, writers who spend an inordinate chunk of each day staring into space, even we can hear the knock-knock-knock of the metronome of the 21st century propelling us helplessly forward.

It's that constant ticking we're trying to escape from when we take a jet eight hours into the future to jump on a camel and speed out into the desert. Tourism is an effort to escape. A failed effort, since one glance at our itinerary would show we brought that metronome with us. That's why we're tourists, not travelers. That's why I'm just some guy drinking tea and not Paul Fucking Bowles, because even my travel journal was a kind of clock, the scritch scratch scritch of my pen being nothing more than the tick tock tick of the minutes disappearing out from under me.

But here in the high desert I couldn't hear a goddam thing except the occasional dromedarian belch and the snick of a lighter as Ahmed lit a cigarette and didn't say anything to me at all. We were there for maybe a half an hour, just us and our Bedouin companions, the camels, and the noble remains of ancient Egypt, but that ticking faded out and in the pink and golden dusk I experienced the very briefest moments of timelessness, lost in that golden moment as if I were lost in a beautiful song. I detached from the maelstrom of the western mind. I floated there for what seemed like hours and hours thinking nothing, worrying about nothing—wanting nothing and perfectly content.

5 Bowles, *Sheltering Sky*

Which is a grand serenity.

Which is all anyone ever really wants.

I stood up from the trash-picked divan and tried to look cool and expatriotic and tried to soak it all in before we had to leave and at this moment, at this exact moment, a sound erupted in the East.

It was the roar of the evening call to prayer, where every minaret of every Mosque and the voices of most of the twenty million people living there howled into the open sky. It started quiet as not every minaret is synched, but it built to its middle and it became a titanic wave of sound, a somewhat harmonious, flat cacophony of spirit and longing and resignation and hope and it washed over me and blew out my literary preening and reminded me I am one of many, a speck of sand in a vast desert, alone in an alien world, and nobody cares about my fucking Stetson and nobody cares about my notebook and all this useless beauty is there for the taking you imperialistic, colonizing, culture-appropriating mildly existential white privileged dickhead.

We mounted and headed back toward Giza in the dark and I want to be clear about this, it was desert dark, not downtown dark so our exhausted horse looked like a ghost. But the moonlight seemed to catch on his haunches, and on the edges of the seemingly invisible paths and the tops of low dunes to outline everything in silver. As my carriage skidded to a stop at what I swear was a cliff, Ahmed jumped out and pointed at the distant lights of Giza and Cairo and said "Titanic," like eight times. I have no idea what he meant.

He was definitely saying Titanic[6] and he thought it would mean something to me. I know there is a remake of the film, a frame by frame reshoot with an Egyptian analog of Leonard DiCaprio, titled Titanic bel Araby which was supposed to be a spoof but was so stunningly unhumorous it spoofed itself. I know the Egyptian translator, Hamad Hassab Bureik survived the actual Titanic, though his sanity didn't.[7] Apparently this was

6 Yes and no. According to our Egyptologist, Ahmed Rezik, Ahmed the camel driver was saying "titanik." This is an Egyptian idiomatic phrase which is used like we use the word 'fuck,' as an epithet or an expression of flabbergastedness. It also means, much like it does in English, very big. So Achmed was openign his arms to embrace the ocean of twinkling lights where he lived, an image of great power, great antiquity, and just deeply, deeply moving, and expressing his wonderment that something so spectacularly old and beautiful exists. He was saying "Look at Giza! It's fucking enormous!"

7 Hamad was a close friend of Mira and Henry Harper of the publishing house Harpers. Hamad was a translator and hotel manager who Harper asked to travel with him to America on the Titanic. Hamad's First-Class ticket would have cost $100K today. Hamad spent most of the time in the company of the Harpers and spoke rarely—if at all—to other passengers. When passengers abandoned ship, Hamad ended up in a lifeboat with Mira though Henry didn't. They were rescued and Hamad disappeared for three years before finally returning to his family where he spent his days abjectly refusing to ever travel again and not ever talking about the night the Titanic

a special moment in the desert tour as he kept me there for several minutes and here's where I had a little lesson in cultural differences.

Ahmed grabbed a thick handful of the green watercress from around my feet and fed it to his horse, whom he'd named Casanova, and hugged the horse's long shaggy head, cradling his nuzzle lovingly against his narrow chest and whispering quiet encouraging words to Casanova and stroking his ears and his chin and under the harness. He told me what a good horse he was and how proud he was of his horse, and I had trouble balancing that love with the savage whipping he served Casanova earlier.

I can't give Ahmed any credit in this by claiming it's cultural differences or he's from a developing country or any of the other excuses one may levy on a horse wrangler from Nazlet el Saman. If you love your horse, don't whip it. Maybe use ATVs to haul fat tourists out into the sand and leave the horses for the flat parts. Maybe just dial back the horses all together.[8] I also know that won't happen. You think of Egypt as wall-to-wall camels but there are just as many horses and equestrianism is as deeply embedded in the cultural landscape as the garbage they gallop through.

While we waiteed there on the top of that dune, the sharp disembodied cries of local horseman floated past us as they were somehwere out in the dark hauling ass across the sand. They were howling with joy, racing each other through impenetrable blackness, their rides pounding through the gravel and the sand. None of them were in a saddle. It was all bareback, all wild, all slightly reckless and unhinged. But there was joy in their speed, in their release after a long day at work, gripping a big horse with their knees and rocketing along under the moon. Sitting in that carriage behind Casanova, I sure as hell wasn't in any position to judge.

---

sank. Survivor stories were popular and lucrative—yet Hamad never went to the media. He discarded any memorabilia related to the ship, never spoke to Mira again, and quit his job as a translator.
Said, Y. (2018, August 3) "The Mysterious Story of Hammad Hassab". Encyclopedia-Titanica. https://www.encyclopedia-titanica.org/hammad-hassab-egyptian-titanic-survivor.html
8  Ha. This will never happen. If I had traveled further into Nazelt el-Samaan, I'd have discovered the underground subculture of drag racing horse carts as described in Max Siegelbaum's Roads & Kingdom's story, The Drag Racing Horse Carts of Cairo which is exactly the kind of trouble I should have been getting into. (Roads & Kingdoms, March 19, 2014)

**JEWELS OF EGYPT**
**DAY 3**
**NOV 8 DAY TOUR TO SAKKARA, MEMPHIS AND DAHSHOUR**

Your private tour guide will pick you up from your hotel in Giza and drive you to the south to start your Great Pyramid Tour of Red Pyramid and Bent Pyramid at Dahshur, Dahshur is a famous royal necropolis in Egypt holds many famous Pyramids of king snefru. The site is about 40 km from Cairo. Move on to visit the Step Pyramid of Zoser, the world's oldest major stone structure. It was built in the 3rd Dynasty (around 2630 BC) for King Djoser. Lunch will be served at a local restaurant, before moving on to enjoy visiting Memphis City. Later you will be transferred back to your hotel in Giza.

### WHO WORKS AT THE PYRAMIDS?

We drove out of Giza through farmland to the desert to see the original pyramids. As I've mentioned, Adelaide put this trip together. She studied archeology in college so she rearranged Nashville Tours' usual itinerary to show the pyramids in chronological order starting with the Steppe Pyramid of Djoser, which is something like 4,700 years old, and ending with the Giza Necropolis, which, comparatively speaking, is brand spanking new.

We headed out into rural Egypt which looks a lot like East Texas west of Galveston or West Florida just south of Sarasota. It's all tiny plots of corn, hibiscus, sugar cane, rice, clover, and cotton. We drove miles and miles westward along a canal filled intermittently with garbage, kids fishing, old tires, and fire.

When we finally turned off the road, we drove north through more farms. We were now more on their level. Farmers were digging micro-canals to divert streams onto their property. We snaked through the farmland of Saqqara, all palm trees and hibiscus and jasmine until it ended abruptly at a guard shack, beyond which was just the desert, punctuated by ancient ruins.

I don't know what the guards were for. They asked My Precious Baby a few questions, with the phrase "American" thrown back at them; they recorded the name of the tour company and the tag number, all in pencil in a massive floppy notebook which I am certain no one ever looks at.

Another guard took cash from Ahmed and gave us tickets to the pyramids, and we were off. The guards were clearly employed by the government, but there's no gift shop or groundskeeper. There aren't any grounds to keep, or more accurately, there's nothing but ground and it won't keep a damn thing alive except spider wasps and scarab beetles.

Who works at the pyramids? Just peddlers and the weirdo on the donkey asking me if I need a taxi. But nobody with a fucking name tag. No one with a job description. Or expectations.

**Dahshur: The Bent Pyramid–2600 B.C. (4621 years ago)**

The weird thing about the pyramids, in fact, about nearly all the ancient monuments of Egypt, is they're just there. Dahshur is just out there in the middle of nowhere, plopped down in the sand. No fence, no gate, no commerce whatsoever. As an American, I find this confusing. If the pyramids were in Florida, there would be an enormous parking lot, a brace of gates with a stylized King Tut waving at the line of cars streaming into the park because it would be a theme park and it would cost money. That's what makes it real.

The necropolis at Dahshur cost money, but the entrance gates need some work. First of all, the soldiers made me nervous. They had machine guns and grimaced a lot and were smoking cigarettes and my biggest concern was not my own safety, but that Disney might see this and get ideas.

But you don't have to go through the gate. You can just trek across the Sahara and walk right up to Dahshur and crawl all over it if you want to.[1] You can easily hike between the clover farms lining the desert by the pyramids. I mean, if the soldiers see some lone dude walking out in the desert, I get the impression they would shrug and say, Crazy tourists.[2]

**The Red Pyramid 2551 B.C. (4572 years ago)**

Like us. There weren't any officials at the sites. No park attendants. No

---

1 Guarantee you'll find a bunch of Russian tourists at the top, smoking cheap cigarettes and wearing the wrong clothes.

2 Please don't test this theory. I might be wrong. Hell, I probably am. You'll get shot. Please don't.

one wearing ancient Egyptian kilts or robes or even a gallabiyah. Just rickety steps leading up to a landing where two local guys sat on a wooden bench smoking cigarettes[3] next to an unguarded hole where, if you were nimble, you could duck-walk down into a pyramid and say to yourself, oh, cool, rocks then duck walk back up the slippery incline then down the rickety steps to find yourself alone, somewhere in the desert.

**The Step Pyramid of Djoser** 2700 B.C. (4721 years ago)

Which is weird because, again, there was a nagging sensation that something was missing. Like, where were the gift shops? Where were the rides? At least have an information kiosk where I could buy a cartoon map and maybe drop a dollar into a Mold-a-Rama that would spit out a fist-sized hot wax version of the necropolis.

**Another Pyramid / Temple thing**

But there's zilch. Zip. Nada. At the next temple, pyramid, thing we walk through a phalanx of peddlers. These guys are on the tail end of the worst economic disaster to Egyptian tourism since the plagues, so they're pretty happy to see us. Here's where I learned a one thing about globe hopping: American humor does not necessarily travel well.

I fight off the scarf peddlers and the coin man and decline the guy selling t-shirts. A book peddler comes up and offers me a guidebook to the Pyramids (In English!).

"Sorry, I can't read."

"It is in Eeng Lesh, my friend."

"I don't speak English."

The peddler just stops in his tracks staring at my fat ass as I drag my companions away. Our guide hangs back and chats with him. There's a lot of nodding. I get the distinct impression Ahmed is agreeing with the vendor that yes, the exceedingly large American is fucking nuts. We shuffle along the edge of the great plaza, past a line of vendors.

One of them says "Man with two wives, very lucky."[4]

I come back with "It's a Mormon thing," and all fifteen of these vendors laugh. All of them. Which just proves thing number two I learned which is even in the middle of goddam nowhere among a group of scarf peddlers who earn three dollars a day, Mormons are weird.

Who works at the Pyramids? Mormon-hating scarf peddlers.

**The Tomb of Tetties** (Sixth Dynasty, 2300 BC)

Also armed guards. There are a lot of people with machine guns in Egypt.

---

3 Cleopatras. I was fairly disappointed they weren't smoking Camels. But they're on brand so I can't complain.
4 This is the moment Adelaide became my second wife. We've been married for two years.

Frankly, there are a lot of people with machine guns all over the world but in Egypt the sense of casual threat is most obvious. In Spain and France, the machine guns felt like they were almost emblematic. Despite having them pointed in my face a little bit in Spain, I never felt like anyone was going to use them whenever I was around. But in Egypt, I kind of felt like the guys with machine guns and sidearms were looking for a reason to pop a couple of tourists in the dome. And it was never clear who was in which service. Was the guy with a pistol a military guard? Was he a policeman? Is there a special branch of the Egyptian police just for the pyramids?

I quickly got used to being in the presence of men with guns, finding myself so often standing next to an ambiguously aligned dude who could take out a battalion.

In the funerary complex of Teti, we strolled through rooms with well preserved wall-to-wall floor-to-ceiling hieroglyphs. They were in full color, still vivid in many spots. We walked the grounds, trying hard to avoid the vendors which was impossible. Adelaide wanted to go down into the actual tomb.

Here's how you get into a tomb. There is a pyramidic structure with a gaping hole in its side. A rickety wooden ramp leads up to the hole, then a rickety wooden ramp leads down into the dark at something like a thirty-five-degree angle, which is terrifying on the way down and impossible on the way back up. Because you're not striding confidently down that ramp, you are crab-walking like you're doing CrossFit. Adelaide does yoga so she just dropped into a crouch and waddled down the ramp to disappear into the dark like it was nothing.

WHERE SHE WAS SHAKEN DOWN BY A COP. Because there are men in uniform everywhere in Egypt it was not entirely odd to find a dude in the dim belly of a tomb the size of a luxurious broom closet. Adelaide is an amateur archeologist who wanted to see the sarcophagus of Teti, accessible by crawling through a short hole near the floor on the wall like an old school handball court.

Adelaide gets to the bottom of the ramp, wanders into the complex and is sort of, kind of, guided by a mustachioed official. He doesn't explain anything, and he doesn't answer any questions and he's essentially useless and the choices in the dim tomb are right or left so his curation was entirely unnecessary.

Then in the room with the infamous casket this official, working in a four-thousand-year-old international treasure, encouraged our amateur archeologist to run her hands along the stone. And not just goaded her. He insisted. Finally, because this walking mustache was making her nervous, Adelaide did something no archeologist would admit to: she touched an ancient artifact, adding to the endless decades of people wearing it down with their finger oils. I can tell you; she was not happy about it.

Adelaide abused the black sarcophagus then turned to leave only to find her path blocked by the guard with his hand out. The guard made motions that clearly translated to "give me money, lady". But Adelaide didn't have any money. He made more motions, these were a little more aggressively suggesting, "I'm not kidding, you have to tip me, dammit" to which Adelaide turned her pockets inside out and the guard was pissed because he thought he should get a tip for the tour Adelaide did not ask for or require and that he wasn't supposed to give her which included her touching a sacred artifact that should never be touched.

When she came out, she was clearly upset. More about touching the tomb than Egyptian Tom Selleck's behavior but as soon as she told me, I duckwalked down into that tomb and punched him right in the nose.[5]

### Ramses II, God of Branding

This is my western privileged dialed up to eleven. You can't really, truly appreciate how cush we live in America until you visit a developing country.

Egypt is trying. The entire Arab world seems to be trying and they have been for the last ten years since the Arab Spring when thousands of Arabs in Tunisia, Libya, Yemen, Syria, Bahrain, and Egypt filled the streets of their cities in protest of authoritarian rulers and eventually overthrew their autocratic governments in favor of democracy.

Which is why nothing works.

Democracy is just not as efficient as authoritarianism. In a Democracy, someone posits an idea and everyone else argues about it for six months to find out if they should talk about it officially then there's another six months when they talk about it and finally there's a vote and the damn thing fails because Shannon in Parks and Rec wants more money for a perennial garden which nobody else wants so she abstained and the whole thing went down the tubes. In authoritarian governments, the Supreme Leader says "Yo, clean this shit up." Next day, there are fifteen million volunteers, thankfully protected by soldiers pointing their AK-47s, picking up trash.

Egypt's revolution blew up in 2011 and in 2013 the people finally overthrew the government of Mohamed Morsi to install Abdel Fattah el-Sisi and put a true democratic government in place. Since 2011, Egypt's

---

5 No, I did not.

economy has struggled terribly, a problem that wasn't helped at all by the Covid crisis. Tourism is one of the top economic drivers for Egypt with millions of people visiting every year. Until 2020. During the Covid restrictions imposed on pretty much the entire world, Egypt's roaring torrent of tourism dwindled to a trickle.

The other two pillars of the Egyptian economy are energy and transportation. But transport is about tourism. Egypt Air and the Egyptian National Railway from Aswan to Alexandria haul a lot of visitors so when tourism is down so are their ticket sales.

Egypt is trying hard. When we drove to Abu Simbel, we passed brand new cities being built from the ground up with contemporary infrastructure and fields of green farmland.

Despite the wall-to-wall garbage and poverty of Cairo and Sohag and points in between would lead me to believe, Egypt is booming. Instead of fixing places like Giza and Cairo, Egypt is just building brand new cities. They're like, screw it. New city, who dis?

Cairo is one of the most congested cities on earth, with the population of nearly 10 million expected to double by 2041. To meet the future growth of his country, housing minister Mostafa Madbouly drew up plans to just relocate the capital to a mostly undeveloped region 50 kilometers east of Cairo, near the Suez Canal. Instead of a city literally as old as the pyramids where the roads were worn into existence by camels and horse drawn carts over eons, a $45 billion city is rising up out of the sand as if by magic.

And it is one hell of a city with a planned 700-square-mile footprint, administrative buildings, hotels—you know, city stuff. Brand spanking new, logical, organized, and, one assumes, litter free.

They join thirty other countries who've recently relocated their capitals by building new cities from scratch (Nigeria, Kazakhstan, Brazil, Myanmar, and more) and I'm just wondering if America might give it a shot. I say we build our new capital just outside Orlando and don't tell Congress. Just elect all new people and leave the old ones arguing in D.C.

Egypt isn't just building a new capital. They're pregaming the future with Galala City, Mostakbal City, New Almein City, New Ismailia City, new Damietta City, New Mansoura City, and New Aswan, the city I saw as we zoomed south toward Abu Simbel. All of these projects were started prior to 2020 so they're behind schedule so I'll be in my late 60s before I can go to New Diametta and fall off a camel again.

There is money coming into the country and tourism is returning and I'm saying all this to ameliorate my American privilege and the wide-eyed reaction I had to the severe difference between these two economies and to say that culture shock is real.

### SAQQARA CARPET SCHOOL

One of the ways the Egyptian government invests in tourism is to sponsor new tourist destinations featuring contemporary Egyptian culture and industry, one of which is the Carpet Factory and School of Carpet Making in Saqqara.

Nashville Tours knows their market and their market is wide-eyed American tourists with deep pockets who are terrified of Egyptian toilets. Each long tour is punctuated by rest stops at local museums featuring classic pedestal commodes instead of the squat toilets you'd see in most public bathrooms.

When you combine a pedestal toilet with government sponsored cultural shopping, you get a perfect retail opportunity. In Saqqara, after visiting the statue of Ramses II in Memphis, we raced into the carpet factory to make use of their facilities which left us much relieved, standing there observing all the young people whipping colored fibers through cotton strands to make drop-dead gorgeous rugs. We were then shuttled into a show room, given comfortable seats and mint tea and a brief education on why the carpets made in Saqqara were the real deal. It was almost impossible not to buy a carpet after that. We'd used their bathroom and drank their tea. We'd sat on their couch.

The prices were the only prices we encountered during our two weeks in Egypt that were on par with normal American retail. A 10x8 Egyptian cotton carpet ran about 23,000 dollars American. That's not much different than what I'd pay for one in Schaumburg if I were insane enough to lay down twenty-grand on a rug.

I assumed my wives, who are not cheap but are frugal and wise with their money, would smile at the nice man then race back to the bus but I was wrong. While I had to haggle with my first wife for a man-dress that cost slightly more than a latte, she picked up a silk rug for the cost of a used Kia Soul, a rug now splayed out in the room she swears will be her office, when she's done painting, which will never happen, where I now do sweaty yoga on her expensive Saqqaran rug.

### A Local Lunch with Traditional Music

If I were to lob a complaint against Nashville Tours it would be their definition of "lunch at a local establishment" in Saqqara because it should read, instead, "lunch-at-a-blatant-tourist-trap-with-terrible-music-and-busloads-of-Spaniards" which is far more accurate.

And again, with the tourism-vs-travel argument, I know, I really know, we were tourists. Despite booking a very private tour managed by Achmed who is an actual Egyptologist, we were hitting the same stops as the massive coaches filled to overflowing with gawping Europeans. And look, I know these people. I grew up outside Orlando. My people made careers building the hotels and attractions that would one day house and entertain millions of idiots hitting the Disneyversalworld[1] triangle. I know the route of theme park attraction architecture:

Thematic music

emblematic architecture outside the attraction

then the attraction

then exit into an even more entertaining gift shop

next to a thematic restaurant.

This is what we got in Saqqara. We walked into this place through a gauntlet of authentic Egyptian musicians in golden robes playing authentic Egyptian instruments, a classic composition I believe is entitled "please-tip-us-these-costumes-cost-a-week's-pay-and-we-haven't-had-any-business-for-18-months-my-children-are-starving-thank-you."

I don't want to be a complete dickhead about the quality of traditional Egyptian music. After all, I'm on a tour where I paid to learn about ancient Egypt, so the music is part of it, but the music is also fucking terrible. Almost all traditional music is terrible. If you're a traditional musician or a music nerd whose particular milieu is traditional music, then of course you love this stuff. But if you're a regular joe like me it's very, very similar to the dulcet tones of a wombat being fire roasted by a Learjet and frankly, that's hard to dance to.

And these guys never finished a song. I assume. I don't know anything about the traditional compositions they were playing but they seemed to only play them when a bus showed up. I think they played snippets of

---

1 Walt Disney World, Universal Studios, and Sea World. Although I maintain Gatorland should be included, but no one takes me seriously at the meetings.

longer pieces, which were probably nicknamed for the sake of time so their band leader could call out "three-bars-of-caterwauling-that-really-gets-to-the-Slavs" when three-hundred Russian tourists fall out of a Greyhound, or "make-it-sound-like-banjos" when they saw me dragging my starving carcass to lunch.

Which was the same lunch I'd gotten, in fact the same meal I'd gotten, everywhere. Meals were included in our tour package, a point of contention for me since I regard such tours with a permanent sense of "that's-how-they-get-you." Like breakfast is included, yay. But breakfast is already included at the hotels we stayed at and that's the breakfast they meant so Nashville Tours didn't provide us with a breakfast, they just charged us for it and put us up in a hotel that already serves free meals.

Lunches were mixed grill with little bowls of baba ghanoush, tahini, and various pickles lined up next to the naan. The mixed grill was a meat kabab, green peppers, eggplant, and onions over a small brass firebox placed on the table. The first time, it was great. Woo hoo! Fire! I loved it. And it was still great the next five times it was on the menu. But at some point, I began to wonder if Egypt served anything else. I know they had pancakes at the Mena House so they must be able to put flour and milk together in a bowl and they sure as hell had sausage so how they never discovered biscuits and gravy is a mystery.

### JEWELS OF EGYPT
### DAY 4
### NOV 9 GIZA PYRAMIDS HALF DAY TOUR

After breakfast, Your tour manager from Memphis Tours will pick you up from your hotel in Cairo, starting your Pyramid Tours visiting the Pyramids of Cheops, Chephren, and Mykerinus. Then proceed to visit the Great Sphinx, the head of a pharaoh with a lions body, dates from the time of Chephren. The tour also includes a visit to the Valley Temple which belongs to the Pyramids of Chephren. This temple served definitely two functions: First, it was used for the purification of the mummy of the king before its burial. Second, it was used for making the Mummification process of the king.

#### CHEOPS: THE ONE YOU SEE ON STAMPS

I had already glimpsed Cheops from my patio balcony. I stood in stunned stillness at sunset in the wide Sahara staring across the salmon sand at Cheops. It had already moved me.

But up close.

Wow.

Also, wow.

*Jesus, fucking wow!*[1]

We've seen pictures of this structure our entire life. It is scattered throughout literature, art, and media since Bernard von Breydenbach mentioned it in his 1486 book, Peregrinatio in Terram Sanctam.[2]

But to be there. To stand in the shadow of the Great Pyramid of Giza is

---

1 actual quotes from my journal of that day.

2 *Peregrinatio in Terram Sanctam* (Pilgrimage to the Holy Land) is the first illustrated travel book. It was published in 1486 and sold through 12 editions, remaining a bestseller through 1522. If it was an LP it would be *Dark Side of the Moon.* The author, Bernhard von Breydenbach (1440-1497), was an unordained Dean of Mainz Cathedral (St. Martin's Cathedral), Mainz, Germany. Breydenbach's pilgrimage took him and his companions to Corfu, Modon, Rhodes, Jerusalem, Bethlehem, Mount Sinai, Rosetta, and Cairo. Breydenbach delivered the first published and widely read descriptions of the pyramids and his illustrator, Erhard Reuwich, was the first to illustrate them, though the only surviving images are tiny representations on a map of their trip up the Nile.

'Peregrinatio in Terram Sanctam' by Bernhard von Breydenbach; National Library of Scotland; nls.uk https://www.nls.uk/collections/rare-books/collections/breydenbach/

to be wonderstruck. My moment in the Bedouin camp was just a prelude. This was the real thing, up close, literally beneath my hand, under my foot, the first wonder of the world.

First of all, the Great Pyramid of Giza is not as big as you imagine it. However, at the same time, it is fucking enormous. I didn't grow up around skyscrapers, but as a kid I visited the VLB at NASA where they roll the rockets out, a completely open building so high that when you stand inside of it, you can see clouds formed against the ceiling. It has its own sky. I live in Chicago, and I've stood in the glass cubicles affixed to the sides of the observation deck at SEARS tower and looked out over the entirety of the Midwest. Big buildings are not foreign to me.

But this was different. This was big and old. For more than 3,800 years it was the tallest structure on earth. Until 1311 when the Lincoln cathedral in Lincoln, England, finished the great spire which rose to 520 feet, 39 feet higher than Giza's 481.

There are a lot of facts about the Great Pyramid of Giza and our personal tour guide, Ahmed, who is an Egyptologist and knows a thing or two about pyramids, was getting them all out there, loading us down with data which began to kind of wash over me as white noise because I have the attention span of a highly caffeinated squirrel which is why I found my mind wandering to ask myself questions like:

How many discarded bottle caps are there around the Great Pyramid of Giza? If I did a detailed search of the surface grounds, would I find antique bottle caps? How much are they worth? When was the last stupid graffiti carved into the Great Pyramid of Giza? Who was it? What did they write? Where is all the camel shit? I count at least twenty-five camels and not one guy with a shovel, yet I don't see a single pile of camel poop. What is camel poop like? Is it more horse apple or more cow pie?[3]

My mind ran down these rabbit holes, which is PART OF MY JOB, OK? when Ahmed said something that popped me right out of my ADHD space out. He held up his clipboard where he'd drawn a pyramid shape with some kind of lozenge drawn beneath it and he was pointing emphatically at the lozenge.

"Say what?" I asked.

Ahmed ahemmed and started over. "I was explaining how the shape of a pyramid has strange effects on physical objects. If you leave a dull razor under a small pyramid, after 24 hours you will find it is sharp again."

---

3 Turns out camel poop is closer to horse poop in that camels form golf ball-sized round nuggets of poop and it's the same color as the sand which may explain why I didn't see any.

"…," I stared. "What is your degree in?"

"Four years at university for Egyptology, then 15 years as a tour guide."

"And you're telling me I can sharpen a dull razor with a pyramid?"

"Not a real pyramid."

"Well good because we have a small bathroom."

"It is what people say." He replied, slightly apologetically.

Oh Ahmed, you had me firmly in your grasp until that moment. Such a brilliant, patient explainer of ancient Egyptian customs and architecture, able to mostly hold my attention with what amounted to a live National Geographic episode all day every day for three days straight only to derail the whole thing with essential-oils-level bullshit. I was so disappointed.

But this was really Ahmed's only low moment. He was an astute guide. He listened to us. He operated like we were a band, listening to our rhythms, adjusting his delivery to match our attention, our questions, and our labored humor. I mean my labored humor. He will always have high marks for how he shut me down when I was showing how funny I am during his lectures. Like when he mentioned Imhotep and I interjected.

"Of course, I'm familiar with his work."

"You know Imhotep?"

Adelaide looked at me with mild surprise because she knows my previous familiarity with Egyptian history was mainly culled from YouTube and mainly occurred while we were waiting on our plane in Chicago. [My Attorney] looks away because she knows what's coming and she knows she can't stop it.

"Actually, yes. I've seen the Mummy movies starring Brendan Frasier, so I know all about Imhotep."

"You've—movies?"

"The Mummy, in 1999, The Mummy Returns in 2001, and of course Mummy: Return of the Dragon Emperor, 2008."

"Imhotep was–"

"Featured prominently. I know. I know everything about him. He could control scarab beetles with his mind…"

In retrospect, it wasn't that funny. But I was dehydrated and nursing an old camel-riding injury so maybe I deserved a little bit of a break. Ahmed did not give me one.

"Mr. Bull…I am an Egyptologist[4]. I study Imhotep and…" He stared at me with the kind of deadly patience Liam Neeson gives to someone he's

4 He says this with the same exasperated indignity of a man who's played Sweet Home Alabama, on the piano, for the eleventh time in the song bar of an all-inclusive resort whose name rhymes with candles, rising from his bench with a flourish of his swallow tail coat and growling I went to Julliard! Same. Same.

choking to death. "You know, Mr. Bull," and here he paused to let me know that he knew what he was about to say was common knowledge and that he knows I was just joking but Jesus Dadjoke Christ I am a career Egyptologist and I'm working here you twat so show some damn respect then said, slowly, laboriously, as if talking to a five-year-old with a head injury, "movies are not real."[5]

Well neither are pyramidical razor sharpeners, Mr. Egyptologist, because if they worked we'd all have a tiny little pyramid on our bathroom sink and we'd only buy one razor in our entire lives and Gillette would be making paint sticks.

---

5 I didn't even bring up the rest of my expertise, like my dissertation on the portrayal of Imhotep in the seminal documentary on ancient Egypt, *Bubba Ho-Tep,* starring the renowned Egyptologist, Bruce Campbell.

## THE SPHINX

The view from the very short steps leading you up to the viewing of the Sphinx and its background of famous pyramids is impressive. Laid out before you in its most glorious full panorama are the great wonders of the ancient world and it would make for a great picture if it weren't for the German dude who walks in front of us to get a better view. Skinny and tousle haired, he's wearing yellow shorts and a blue safari shirt, and he just stands there, right in the peak of the clearly defined picture-taking area, just looking.

This happens constantly. Earlier that day, we drove out to the new "Panorama" viewing plateau where there is a wide flat space at the perfect distance to get all the pyramids in one glorious selfie if it weren't for the fifteen Spanish tourists who climbed over the wall to stand directly in front of us to take their picture.

Ahmed is furious because this spot is where his trick photography skills really shine and though we all hate ironically posed photos at historic landmarks, I bow to pressure and he and I are working on our "Man Holding Giza in his Palm" series when the Spaniards swarm over the wall and Ahmed, who up until now has demonstrated remarkable restraint, loses his shit. Ahmed dropped his forehead into his hand and massaged the bridge of his nose, which was crinkled tight enough to restrict blood flow, and mumbled in Arabic before taking a quick breath to steady himself and give himself the strength to not slaughter a handfull of tourists.

"Hey," Ahmed leans over the wall. The Spaniards are literally up against it on the other side of us. I could reach out and punch them. "Hey—we're taking a picture."

The Spaniards demonstrate frank European disdain and continue posing in our photograph. Ahmed addresses them in Spanish. I don't speak Spanish, but I'm pretty sure this is an accurate translation of their brief conversation.

Ahmed: You idiots need to get back behind the wall and wait your turn.

Spaniards: We don't speak English.

Ahmed: I'm speaking Spanish, idiotas. Get out of the way. (Waves them aside.) I don't know how you were raised, but obviously you aren't of the same caliber and quality as my wards here—especially the fat one, who is a prince among men—so please do everyone a favor and remove your sad, ravaged Eurotrash skeletons so we can take our pictures according to the posted rules.

Spaniards: (they move fourteen inches to the left) How's this?

Ahmed: I have a machine gun in the van.

Spaniards: (they move eleven feet to the left which is enough)

Like the pyramids, the Sphinx is smaller than you imagine it. Unlike the pyramids, that doesn't change. When you get a glimpse of Cheops from far away, you think, well, it's not so big. As you get close, however, its enormity swells until you lay your hand on it and realize how hard it must have been to supervise all those workers. That doesn't happen with the Sphinx. It actually got smaller as we got closer. The Sphinx would fit comfortably in your average Texan double-wide with only its head popping out the top.

If you've seen pictures of the sphinx you may think it is out in the middle of nowhere, popping up out of the sand like a mirage. But if you just turn your back on the German for a minute, you can practically reach out and touch the neighborhoods of Giza heaped up against the edges of the necropolis. You could, if you were so disposed, jog over to the garishly colored Kentucky Fried Chicken and order lunch.

Much like you can reach down and pet the wild dogs sleeping under the odd legumish sculpture. It's kind of like Chicago's Cloud Gate which everyone in Chicago calls The Bean. This one is only about ten feet long and urine yellow. At least twelve wild dogs are sleeping in its thin shadow when some tourist kid walks up to pet one of them and the entire pack goes after him with the clear intent to rip him open.

Ahmed grabs the kid and yells at the dogs as if they were Spanish photo bombers and the dogs back down. They slink back to their hot shade and Ahmed lectures the kid about the dogs. No parents. Anywhere. The kid toddles off into the dust, sporting a new phobia and wiping away tears.

We hike over to the Sphinx complex and waited for a group of Egyptian teenagers to finish their instagramming and once again, Ahmed's veneer of Canadian-level serenity seems to lose a little luster as the teens were in no hurry and all five of them had to take the same picture then a group photo then another group photo with a different guy taking it then three more single poses, all in the main room. Adelaide wanted a picture without people in it, but these guys did not care, and Ahmed growled something at them, and I didn't catch all of it and my Arabic is sub-par, but I think he mentioned liver, fava beans, and a nice chianti.

A few minutes later we emerged onto the viewing ramp of the Sphinx and Ahmed finally lost it. People were crawling over every surface even though there were poorly painted signs in various languages clearly telling tourists to stay the fuck off the priceless national treasures. Ahmed talked sternly to every tourist, one at a time, while we stared at the giant statue trying to feel something other than heatstroke.

## CAIRO'S GOVERNMENT-SANCTIONED PAPYRUS MUSEUM AND
## VELVET ELVIS PAINTING BLACK-LIGHT GIFT EMPORIUM

Our itinerary lists an official papyrus museum as our final afternoon stop, one very conveniently furnished with Western-style commodes. Their timing could not be better. After spending the day fending off rude Spanish tourists, a sartorially challenged German, and wild dogs in the Giza necropolis after a breakfast of three Turkish coffees and juice, I need to get western on a commode.

Our busminivan hurtled off the expressway[1] onto a sideroad, passed by two rather solid looking papyrus museums with boring tan columns and Helvetica caps proclaiming their official papyrusness before parking at a somewhat dilapidated, half-sunken shop that I immediately assumed sold neon-colored bongs and pocket pipes.

It was worse.

I thought papyrus artifacts would be staid and historic. I figured they would trend toward hieroglyphics and finely wrought line drawings of the Sphinx. We were, instead, confronted by wall after wall and column after column of vividly colored renderings of unicorns, stoned camels, shadowy dramatic selfies of Nefertiti, and painting after painting of Mohamed Salah Hamed Mahrous Ghaly, the Egyptian soccer sensation. There were also poorly rendered paintings in bright, pale colors on black backgrounds.

I looked for anything indicating a museum but the best I could find were ornately illustrated quotes from the Quran and given their price tags, I didn't think they were treasured artifacts. We weren't in a papyrus museum; we were in a gift shop for rolling paper.

After hurriedly unhydrating, we were refilled with hibiscus tea and Turkish coffee as the "museum" guide showed us how papyrus paper is made. Then he showed us around. Then he gave us a conspiratorial wink,

---

1 I don't know how they can actually call it an expressway and in fact, perhaps they don't. Our original tour manager, Mustafa "Please Don't Interrupt Me" Osama, was very proud of this highway as we hurtled its length on our way back from the airport that first night. But I don't see much express occurring. They should rename it the stop-start-never-more-than-25-mph-look-out-DONKEY!-way instead.

said "Let me show you something really cool," and opened a hidden door in the wall of black velvet papyrus paintings, hustling us into a narrow room, also covered in black velvet papyrus paintings. He closed the door behind us, gathered us together, then said, "Watch this," then turned off the lights.

I was tempted at this juncture to goose [My Attorney] in her necropolis but I realized I wasn't sure which of my wives I was actually standing next to, and Adelaide knows krav maga. Instead, I beheld the darkness until our guide flipped a second switch that turned on a blacklight and there, where there were originally paintings of pyramids and Mohamad Salah in bright vibrant colors, there were now . . . Ghostly images of pyramids and Mohamed Salah Hamed Mahrous Ghaly glowing in the dark.

I was a child of the 70s, so I know all about black-light art. I had a 'keep on trucking,' poster in the back of my bedroom door. It was flocked with velvet and showed a bearded cartoon hippie in fourteen frames walking ever closer to the viewer. It was painted in vivid blue and red but when the blacklight was on, it was, well, it was still blue and red, but they glowed in the dark. Blacklight paintings are idiotic. It was as stupid trend that died on time, buried in the same mass grave as lava lamps and platform shoes.

I glanced over at my two wives to register the shock and dread and baffling disappointment on their faces. Then I walked out.

To be clear, this was not the Hassan Ragab Papyrus Institute of Cairo which is rightly famous for its extraordinary collection of ancient papyrus documents. No, we were in the Egypt Papyrus Museum which is a tourist trap.

I understand. I get it. Egypt's tourism economy is in the crapper. Nashville Tours is sophisticated and data-based, so they probably chart how many of their clients want to buy papyrus and maybe have opted to take people to the Egypt Papyrus Museum instead of Egypt's papyrus museum. And look, maybe there's a sizable demographic of customers who liked it better and were really, really satisfied to drop a couple of hundred on a shitty black-light papyrus painting of Mohamed Salah Hamed Mahrous Ghaly with a glow-in-the-dark halo. We were not in that demographic.

I was genuinely happy for the bathroom break, even though I barely fit through the phalanx of toilet paper salesmen. But the toilet was narrow and small, with a hose attachment because that's how Egyptians do it and the paper was all wrong and there were eight guys standing just outside the door talking in Arabic and laughing and how the FUCK are you supposed to pee in that situation? I pee in perfect silence. I don't pee for the sake of others; I pee for myself, and I didn't need an audience. I didn't want an audience. But there they were, expensive single sheets of paper held out like a bouquet of flowers. It was the nail in the coffin for me. I stormed out of my upright pee casket to take a seat in the area designated for tour drivers, ignoring their raised eyebrows and sluice of Arabic indignations, ordered a cup of shitty coffee and endured the protracted performance of my two wives pretending to be interested in the papyrus pictures of soccer stars.

From deep in my furious meditation, a nagging question finally surfaced. Why are we here?

What are we looking for? Why push ourselves to walk through thick sand and get ass blisters and sweat. So. Much?

My first thought, and this is based solely on observing my two wives, is we're here for selfies. We're here for the likes. But when I dig deeper I realize a selfie is just a part of a story and so we're here for the story and that story can be summed up as: we can afford a hyper luxurious trip to Egypt and here's a picture to make you jealous. The pictures are not illustrations. They are vital emblems of status. They are plumage. Our trip is just a giant fuck you to all our broke ass friends. Cause it ain't educational. I mean, I just spent the day with a motherfucking Egyptologist personally telling me the history of each pyramid and I didn't hear a fucking thing he said.

I felt bad for Adelaide. For two years she'd sent me articles about Egypt, kept me up to date on her endless negotiations with Nashville Tours, and chatted about Egypt and Egyptology and Pyramids and the magnificent splendor of ancient Egyptian sandstone pillars, their upper pedestals disappearing in the shadows of temple ceilings stained black with eons of smoke. For Addy, the importance of this trip was deep—and personal. Her grandfather was a professor in the Agriculture School at University of Arizona from 1918 until 1968. He'd traveled to Baghdad to study cotton and teach. She grew up hearing his stories of rural Egypt and the amazing ruins. She'd studied Egypt and Archeology in college. She spent her two-year run-up diving deep into the history and lore. She'd learned the language. She'd read the books. In the temples, Adelaide was giddy with excitement, asked incredibly astute questions that made Ahmed grin with delight and in general exuded pure uninterrupted intellectual joy.

Adelaide was here to connect her intellectual understanding and appreciation of Egypt with the real by laying her hands on 4000-year-old temples and walking on the same sands as the people who built them.

[My Attorney] was there for, ostensibly, the same reason. But she was mostly there to luxuriate and bide her time between business class flights.

We all read The Alchemist, by Paulo Coelho because the main character goes to Egypt and Death on the Nile was too on the nose. We were trying to hit all the best notes of a great trip: history, resonance, fine dining, intellectual fare, and cushions. My first wife and my other wife were taking full advantage of each trip, engaging Ahmed, and even taking notes. They were imprinting this trip with rigor and energy. They were here to bring Egypt back home with them. They were here to etch their trip with a laser into their memory.

I was not. In the first temple we visited I tripped over an open hole that was at least feet feet wide and three hundred feet deep[2] and fell face first onto a pile of sharp rocks[3] and almost died.[4] I'd looked forward to this trip with the same rigor as a five-year-old. I was really excited to go, and I couldn't wait to get inside a pyramid and dance with the mummies, but when I got there it was a class on ancient history that made you do laps.

Apparently, I was in Egypt to discover my nascent vapidity. My attention had the sticking power of smoke in a breeze. I couldn't keep up with Ahmed because there was too much stuff going on and also there wasn't enough stuff going on. Inside a temple, it's all stone pillars and hieroglyphs and great stone slabs and light shafts and other people and carvings and bats and Russians and graffiti and sand. And while I'm in the middle of all this stimuli, Ahmed is giving a lecture on Nefertiti with a voice like Ray Romano which is surprisingly hypnotic. I'm sweating into the air and sliding into heatstroke and my ankles itch and why aren't there any spiders? Are there spiders in Egypt?

I politely disengaged from class to drop into an on-premises coffee shop to write an imaginary apology to my second wife.

Adelaide, my dear, I could not stay focused. I could not rouse an abiding interest in these magnificent ruins. As much as I am a man of culture at home, I am a man of coffee shops abroad. I failed at culture on this trip. I could not sustain interest in people who'd been dead for six thousand years while I was being served coffee by a dude who was alive right now and being hustled by a stray cat with its eyes on my lunch.

The sad truth is I was bored. My appreciation for the temples and the tombs was entirely superficial. I took pictures. I liked them because they looked cool. I didn't need a guide. I needed a beer.

---

2 Four inches wide, half an inch deep.
3 Staggered briefly.
4 Was mildly embarrassed.

### JEWELS OF EGYPT
### DAY 5
### NOV 10 CITY OF THE DEAD, CITADEL, OLD CAIRO
### TOUR, AND ISLAMIC CAIRO TOUR

Pick up after breakfast then enjoy your visit to The City of the Dead (Al-Arafa) comprises two 4 miles (6 km) long cemeteries - a north and south cemetery - dating from Mamluk times (the 1200s - 1500s) and is still in use today. Proceed to visit the Famous Cave Church of St. Simon, passing by the Garbage City in Cairo. Lunch will be served in a local restaurant. Then proceed to visit Salauldeen Citadel and The Mosque-Madrassa of Sultan Hassan is a monumental mosque and madrassa located in the historic district of Cairo, Egypt. It was built between 1356 and 1363 during the Bahri Mamluk period, commissioned by Sultan an-Nasir Hasan

### CALL TO PRAYER

I grew up in a religious household. My mother took her religion seriously and took my attendance at Sunday services even seriouser. I was never particularly impressed with my mother's brand of religion,[1] which was the holy rolling variety born from the tent revivals of the 1900s and its various hands-in-the-air ecstatic iterations of Christianity popular with Pentecostals, evangelicals, some protestants, some Methodists, and absolutely no—not even one—Baptist.

And just to set your rising fears at ease, I'm not about to launch into a diatribe against religion—I shook all that nonsense out in my late teens and have made peace with institutional dogma under the agreement that we can

---

1 Sorry, Mom.

have the occasional coffee together at a nice cafe downtown, but I'm not expected to warm up a pew any time soon.

Yet I am preoccupied with theology and cosmology. I almost never stop thinking about God and how deity meddles in daily affairs.[2] Or how people truly believe deity is meddling when really deity is busy not even knowing we exist, as deity is indifferent as cold space itself which is an important differential in any argument about a deterministic universe.

Of the various distillations of faith available off the shelf for your average armchair cosmologist, I generally employ cataphatic[3] and apophatic[4] tendencies with a layman's Hallmark Movie understanding of divine providence.

I don't—*ever*—claim to know a Goddam thing about theology at a quotable level. True theologians are as argumentative as hipster music nerds—and about as much fun at parties. Endless religious one-upmanship and claims of "well, I think Anselm of Canterbury's work in the early eleven hundreds is oh kay, but I prefer his earlier stuff—before he knew how good he was," which could be applied to Minor Threat as easily as it's applied to Rev. Horton Heat.

I'm a happy speculator which means I don't have to back up my opinions with research nor do I have to maintain a consistent belief, which comes in handy since I'm about 98% atheist and the rest of me is locked in a vicious spit-flinging scream fest about when to covert.

To nutshell my belief, I do, despite my limited intellectual capabilities and despite a personal library where the shelves groan under the weight of books to the contrary, and despite a genuine allergy to organized religion, and despite adoring the work of atheistic philosophers and writers, despite all that, I do believe in a divine something or other.

My belief, however, is generously speckled with absolute madness, ornamented by indefensible positions, and married to an incomprehensible belief in the nature of reality that poured its jiggling foundation from a bucket of Baudrillard, Erich von Daniken, and Sir Terry Pratchett in a three-part slurry that will never harden. I can't explain it and if you were to catch me praying then subsequently asked the obvious question of "who the fuck are you praying to?" the answer is as likely to be Om the Conqueror as it is my favorite Barcalounger.

All of which is savagely defenestrated when I reflect on my life as a

---

2 Hello, atheists. How are you? Don't worry, it's not that bad. Keep reading.
3 Knowledge of God obtained through affirmation.
4 Knowledge of God through negation.

world traveler and just in general walking around on this planet in abject fear of finding myself in another situation where it is evident I am being pranked by the divine.

I was talking to a dear friend recently, the imminent Safety Professional and Misinterpretive Dance Choreographer, Timatheen "Ocoee" Barnhardy,[5] when he finally stopped going on and on about how the purity of his Grand Jete is only eclipsed by the beauty of his tour en lair to take a breath and I jumped in to fire off a few words about this trip to Egypt and when I got through two minor episodes, Timatheen asked, dead serious: "Dude, is any of this true?"[6]

Which is a fair question. Actually, you could ask this from nearly any moment of my life wherein I was left to my own devices, unsupervised, or even slightly bored. I tend to experiment with being alive. But the stupid antics of a semi-rural childhood wherein I was left alone with snakes, power boats, spare cars, barn animals, alligators, explosive model rockets, spiders, power tools, snakes, fire, and snakes should remain in childhood. That sort of lucky-to-be-with-us-today foundation should have withered as I grew into a mostly beige boring corporate nobody adulthood wherein the vicious humor of the divine should have taken no notice of me. That didn't happen. God likes me and I wish it would stop.

As much as I believe in an indifferent deity (faceless, stoic, doesn't know we're talking to it) I am constantly reminded—by that deity—that this is an erroneous belief, that deity is very much involved and though it allows us all the freedom to disbelieve in it, will sometimes prank us mercilessly, as if cruelly causing us cosmic embarrassment while nodding its head, saying, "No, you're probably right, I probably don't exist. Enjoy the plague."

Divine intervention isn't always about deity stepping in at the last minute with undeniable evidence of innocence just as a hooded figure is flipping a big Frankenstein switch to roast another heretic. Sometimes it isn't even about us; it's about God being bored. Which is a blasphemous thought and I'll probably get struck by lightning before I finish this sent—

**Mosques**

---

5 Most definitely his real name.
6 He was also concerned about the camel, which I assume is an artifact of his profession and not a misapplication of our bromance.

And it's not always God taking a malicious interest in us. Sometimes memorable deific moments happen entirely by accident.

When we visited the Mosques of Cairo, I dropped into humble mode, which is just me being quiet and contemplative and not desperately seeking attention with ceaseless Dad jokes. There are moments when human ingenuity and art kick my fat ass into reverence and though the pyramids did not achieve this,[7] a Muezzin singing the call to prayer in the Mosque of the Sultan of Hussein did.

The mosques we visited were beautiful. Stunning, really. If you think your favorite cathedral corners the market on religious architecture and hallelujah ornamentation, you might want to step inside a mosque for perspective. The Mosque of Mohammed Ali[8] shushed me into placid observance. It was cool, with the shadows of the far round walls punctuated by sepia sunlight streaming in through arching windows and tall, heavy doors half open for the religiously curious. We stood staring at the painted ceiling and domes, quiet in a room full of whispering tourists.

At the much smaller Mosque of the Sultan of Hussan, we sat like locals on carpeted floors in a courtyard with high fortified walls and a lot of pigeons. Where the Mohamed Ali Mosque swarmed with tourists, this one held just us, two locals praying, and a muezzin.

Our Egyptologist very respectfully and quietly lectured on the history of the mosque and a little about the practices of Islam. While we sat in the cool shade of the prayer courtyard, the muezzin spoke quietly to Ahmed who stopped lecturing us and ushered us to a row of chairs in the back. As we sat down, the Muezzin disappeared into the Mosque to sing the midmorning call to prayer and I disappeared into the pure music of his voice.

In 2021, Spotify reported that I had spent more than 66,000 minutes listening to music. That's more than a thousand hours, or forty-five days of non-stop music through a worn-down pair of Bose noise-cancelling headphones that eventually broke in half. And that doesn't count the music I listened to on the other apps I use, including Radio France and NPR and just my own collection which probably add up to another 5,000 minutes. Music is the air that I breathe. I am deeply affected by it, absolutely without bias[9], capable of enjoying everything except pop-country, bagpipes, drum-

---

7 Sorry, Second Wife

8 Not Mohammed Ali Mohammed Ali; the historical Mohammed Ali.

9 Which has proven surprising. In the late 80s I picked up an EP by Jah Wobble and Bono Vox. Like all Eps it was the same size as an LP and I was an idiot, so I played it at 33 1/3 RPM on my turntable for something like six months. It was an instrumental, hauntingly beautiful, completely brilliant and kind of odd and woggly, which I loved. I was already listening to nonstop ambient, so the music tracked. Finally, a friend came over and I put

circles, and, apparently, traditional Egyptian folk songs.[10] Music moves me.

So did the muezzin. His voice was enormous. Powerful but not bombastic. It didn't thunder through the Mosque. His voice filled the space like water, and I sunk beneath it and was lost in its beauty, humbled by its dignity. As religious experiences go, it was mild. But then, that is the wonderful thing about such moments. They aren't cinematic. In fact, most of the time a religious experience is just a sudden realization that you've been having a mild religious experience for the last couple of hours. Sometimes, it's about just how beautiful the world can be. How beautiful people can be. And in this case, how the enduring substructure of the divine can be revealed when you are struck by beauty, when you are possessed by the simple power of a man singing to anyone who will listen "come to prayer, come to prayer, come to prayer".

---

the thing on, and he jumps up to switch it to 45 RPM as it is meant to be played. I hated it.

Later, after having kids and a good job and car payments and a mortgage (all paid for by [My Attorney]) I found myself alone in my ubiquitous green Dodge Minivan stopped at a train crossing (my neighborhood has five roads intersected by three train crossings and a bus station all in the same tiny space so it's nearly impossible to get through without stopping for a bus or a train). It's late summer and I have the windows down and some kind of ambient piece comes on and I sit there as the endless train cars roll past, digging the long ululation of the piece, the odd lack of time signature, the low metallic drag of it. I glance down to see what's playing only to find out my radio isn't on. I was listening to a train brake sheering off. It was beautiful.

10 And pan pipes. Goddam pan pipes.

## JEWELS OF EGYPT
## DAY 5
## NOV 11 CAIRO SIGHTSEEING TOURS—AHMAD IBN TULUN MOSQUE - FLY TO LUXOR

Start your day visiting the Egyptian Museum, where you will admire the splendid collection of Tutankhamun alongside many other fascinating artifacts. There is an extra ticket (not included) for the Mummies Room at the Museum Transfer to visit El-Darb El-Ahmar and see the mosque of Ahmad Ibn Tulun Mosque. Lunch will be served in a local restaurant. Then we move on to Coptic Cairo to visit the Hanging Church and Ben Ezra Synagogue. Finally, you will be transferred to Cairo International Airport to fly to Luxor. overnight in Luxor.

### LUXOR

Where Cairo was uninterrupted traffic madness, Luxor is orderly and clean. I walked four goddam miles today and it's only a half day. Tomorrow we do a "big" day so I suppose I should make out my will. The arid air of Egypt is no fucking joke. It will wick the fucking moisture out of you like its wringing a rag. I pissed pure dust and bits of gravel earlier, but now I'm at the Lebanese Restaurant with a Stella and enough water to drown in. Hopefully I'll make it.

We did, perhaps, over prepare for this trip. We had printed the literature for every prescription and packed a Covid's worth of toilet paper; we exchanged money; we made copies of our vital documents and look, if someone with a machine gun hanging off his shoulder doesn't corner me and demand the documents for my ALLOPURINOL I'm going to consider the entire trip a bust.

Last night we went to Luxor's Winter Palace[1] after a brief interlude

---

1 This is where Dame Judy Dench stayed when she wrote "Murder on the Nile".

with suspicious taxi callers. We were told the trip would be 40EP—$2.54 for three people. The driver had the infuriating nerve to ask for $100 EP—$6.36—but we stood our ground.[2]

We had dubonnet cocktails in the Royal Bar then moved to a small table in Restaurant 1886 where we enjoyed fine French food while being serenaded by PAN PIPE INSPIRATIONS[3] (1995, Polygram) which drove me to paroxysms of fury. Why not Satie? Why not Truffaz? Hell, Miles Davis' Ascenseur Pour L'èhafaud in a pinch. Fuck, even Egyptian chill would've worked. At least it would have been on brand. But pan pipes? Of Simon & Garfunkel?! Jesus Hathor Christ, no.

The dining room of 1886 is gorgeous—fuck, the entire Winter Palace is a goddam jewel box—with an appreciable wine list and a decent menu at good prices but the real value is the ambience and our ambience included a cocktail waiter who was a little person, an aging British rock star (we don't know which one but trust us, that guy had a hit song in the early '90s), and a man who appeared to be a French auteur, reading a French book on Egyptology in a French restaurant entirely alone, occasionally chuckling to himself, while wearing a salmon and gold lamé sarong.

*I want to be this guy.*

I want to grow my hair out and let my beard come in and read French poetry alone with the ghost of Agatha Christie and Dinis Roche and use my severely outdated cell phone even though the front of the menu clearly says no goddam cell phones[4] and we rigidly observed that rule even when I was served lobster medallions in a morel sauce that looked like a wedding ring for Elton John. Even then I restrained myself from taking a picture and texting it to my Alabamily (who would have woken up at three in the morning to curse me in their most florid "bless your heart's").

So, despite all our preparation, I wasn't ready to be confronted by a portly French auteur who could have been Gerard Depardieu's third cousin. It took all my will power not to stare at him as he ate daintily between turning pages in his trade paperback about Egyptian archeology WHICH

---

2 In Chicago, I'll drop $30 to Uber three miles to my friend's house for a beer.

3 What the hell is it with pan pipes? They're everywhere. Once you get out of the United States, you hear pan pipes in hotels, airports, grocery stores, and I am assuming Moe's Pan Pipe Emporium and Rustic Flute Discount Warehouse.

When we landed in Istanbul for a coffee-break layover, the overhead music was panpipes. When we stood in the lobby of the Mena House, the overhead music was panpipes. When we were waiting to board in Aswan, the airport was playing panpipes. When we landed in Cairo the airport was playing panpipes. I heard them in Paris, in Barthelona, and in the trinket shop in the airport in Berlin. What the hell is wrong with the rest of the world? Panpipes are horrible!

4 In French *(pas de putain de téléphones portables!)*

WAS MAKING HIM LAUGH and just being goddam amazing in the most expensive restaurant in Luxor BY HIS GODDAM SELF!

I was not feeling particularly elegant that evening, being on my fifth day of walking five miles in hot sand and also being incredibly out of shape and also being remarkably fat and also wearing clothes that had not been hemmed because I forgot so I look like a hillbilly teen who'd borrowed a blazer from my dad. I'd managed to sneak a sample vial of Creed's Irish Tweed on the trip to surprise my wife and impress my other wife but I'm so damaged from falling off the camel and all the trudging that I was essentially an invalid with the charisma of an exasperated Cairo mule. And then this fucker is there hogging all the panache in the room while [My Attorney] is trying to discreetly figure out what he was reading while Adelaide's absolutely convinced he's a film director. That son of a bitch. [My Attorney] checked my liberally perfumed wrist which was supposed to send her into some kind of state wherein she'd agree, finally, to get me an actual bottle of Irish Tweed[5] but she hardly noticed it because she was furiously googling OLD FRENCH ACTOR and eating cheese.

---

5 The preferred cologne of Cary Grant, David Bowie, and countless members of the royal family. Priced accordingly. Some guys dream about owning a boat. I just want a three ounce bottle of this magnificent cologne.

**JEWELS OF EGYPT**
**DAY 7**
**NOV 12 WEST BANK TOUR AND DER EL MADINA**
Breakfast box, then you will Start Luxor City Tour through transferring to the west bank where you will visit the Valley of the Kings, the magnificence of the grandeur of architecture, which was used for burial, there are many kings buried in this valley. The most known tombs are King Tutmosis I, Tutmosis III, Tut-Ankh-Amon, King Ramssess VI, King Mrenptah and AmonhotepII. Move on to visit the Temple of Queen Hatshepsut, which was built by Queen Hatshepsut, daughter of Thutmosis I, who ruled Egypt about 20 years during the 18th Dynasty (approximately 1490-1469 B.C), the only pharaonic woman who reigned ancient Egypt. You will pass by the colossi of Memnon which are remains of the mortuary temple of Amenhotep III. Later you will be driven back to your hotel in Luxor

### FAT IN KARNACK

And it happened again. I was ridiculed for my rotundity in the Temple of Karnack as I rested on a bench next to some young tour guides. They unabashedly leaned back to take in the sheer, well, monumental scope of my ass then grinned openly at each other and laughed, and I took it like a pro because fuck those guys, but I was also tired and sore and really, I'm a fucking professional. Don't look your gift horse in the ass.

If you are booking a tour of Egyptian temples, don't skip Karnack. It is the most gloriously ruined ruin in all of Egypt. So picturesque. So accessible. So strollable. It's enormous, porous with footpaths, loaded with hieroglyphs unprotected at face level, and absolutely lurid with photogenic vistas. You can take pictures with your eyes closed and they'll turn out perfect. Also, there is a coffee shop. It's on the back side, near the lagoon, and it's a trash pit and I fucking loved it. Finally, I could vacation my way: to sit in a dilapidated desert café among the ruins overpopulated with stray cats and manned by a disinterested Mullah and his nephew who served me strong coffee and nuts for too much money but otherwise left me to my reverie as I gazed placidly out at the back of Karnack and the idiot Russians skittering along trying to get it all in before their bus leaves. My pictures from Karnack are absolutely glorious. My time enjoying coffee there remains a luxurious vacationary zenith.

Which brings us to bathrooms

So far, I have yet to encounter the dreaded squat toilet I have fearfully obsessed over since we planned this excursion.[1] I thought as I hauled my mutilated cadaver into the water closet at Luxor temple, well this is it. Finally, I will have to piss like an Egyptian but no, it was an astonishingly spotless, flawless, granite and cedar stall that smelled amazing and was, all in all, a delightful place to urinate.

The next day I declined to visit the Valley of the Kings in order to take the waters and smoke a cigar and generally heal up since I could barely walk.

I had tried to train for this trip at my pricey ass gym, but my family levied a fear on me, and I obliged them and, for Covid, stopped going. I tried to walk a few miles every day, but it was hot and humid, and I walk in Chicago's lengthy forest preserves, so I was ravaged by mosquitoes (more training for Egypt) and gave up. So here I am now like an 80-year-old fat bastard carefully and, to be honest, fearfully lowering myself out of our van and taking steps one at a time. I have short legs so the ancient time-worn steps of East Bank monuments would put me out on a good day, but now? After the Incident d'la Dromedary? I creak and groan like an old tugboat.

I know there are seasoned travelers who can drop into a squat and piss into a hole in the floor like the locals and sneer about it when those of us who can barely bend down into a golf swing rear back in horror at the idea of third-world water closets, but fuck those guys. I don't have to justify my lavatorial customs. They're all like 'it's a different culture, don't be judgy,' and I'm all 'I can't bend down that far, people will suffer,' but it doesn't matter. Egyptians don't care. If we shit into a box at home they'd find a way

---

1 Ha! I didn't plan diddly squat. Adelaide did it all.

to accommodate us because, as I have mentioned, their economy is tourism based and if those tourists need Western commode accommodation then that's what they'll get.

## JEWELS OF EGYPT
## DAY 10
## ESNA

Breakfast box then you will be driven to Esna to embark your dahabiya cruise then start a tour in Esna. A thriving merchant town, Esna is best known for the small ancient Temple of Khnum, which sits 9 meters below street level. Your trip will begin with a brief walk to the temple and a stroll through streets filled with beautiful textiles and other exotic goods. Overnight in Esna on board your Nile boat.

### DRIVING TO ESNA

I wake at the unholy hour of 5:30 in the morning to gather my debris from around my bed and from under the bathroom sink and from over the back of the chair and from under the dresser and from the hallway and every other goddam place I've debrised.

This drives [My Attorney] completely batshit as she likes to unpack everything into drawers and onto hangers. I don't understand it. I live out of a suitcase and by living out of a suitcase, I mean I live out of a small tornado.

We arrive in the lobby of the Steiglefloofer Hotel[1] at 6:50 am, bags herded into a holding pattern by the divan, my two wives pressed up against reception begging for small bills. We didn't have breakfast because Ahmed said to be there at 7am and he'd provide breakfast. So there we are at 7:15 and Ahmed is nowhere to be seen. I'm infuriated by this insubordination because being infuriated is my hobby. He finally shows up and we load into the van and shoot off to Esna.

Breakfast is juice boxes, bread, a boiled egg, cheese, and fruit. The vegan's breakfast is juice, bread, and fruit. No nuts. No nothing. My second wife is dejected and starving for protein. I watch in horror as she eats a piece of cheese through vegan tears.

And so there we are out in the Goddam desert headed to Esna, and we

---

1 Steigenberger Nile Palace right on the river. It's gorgeous and equipped with cafes, bars, stores, and more. Very nice. I just can't ever remember the name.

get stuck behind a truck hauling sand. Not hauling sand to be discarded, not used sand, not excess sand, but just a massive load of ungraded sand. Sand someone paid for. In the desert.

You can reach out the window of pretty much any house in Egypt and scoop up a bucket of sand. Why in the hell is this guy trucking dirt? I realize that somewhere out in the desert is a little shop in front of a big pile of sand with a smiling Bedouin offering anyone who pulls up the finest sand he can shovel into their swaybacked 89 Buick Skylark.

Like there's a subculture for it. Like snobs arguing about music, there are sand punks out there bitching to each other about granularity and grit. There are silicaphiles hanging out in sandbars talking about how they're really into pea gravel, but your interest in oceanic granules is cute. They'll have T-shirts with ironic monosyllabic sand types in a retro font like "Flake," and "Shale," and "Loam."

The drive to Esna gives me the opportunity to observe early morning Egypt and I must say, Egyptians hate it as much as anyone else. The look of resigned fuck-it-let's-do-this on the faces of the people we passed was as familiar to me as my own visage in the mirror on a Monday morning. I feel for them as I roll out of bed at the crack of 10:30 to commute through the kitchen and the living room to the verb mines where I hammer away hoping to hit the motherlode.

When we'd landed in Luxor, we'd switched tour guides and were now under the watchful Yul Brynner gaze of Ahmed[2] whom we, with the full imagination of highly literate beige Americans, dubbed Ahmed 2. Ahmed 2 was slightly less engaged than Ahmed Prime. Not that he talked to us any less, nor did he slack in his explanations of Egyptian esoterica. But when Ahmed Prime talked to us, we felt like he'd known us for years. There was a kind of familiarity to his discourse, a fraternal warmth to every word, to every explanation. We felt like he'd invited us into his inner circle of avid Egyptologists. We felt like family. Ahmed 2[3] got the job done. But we felt, we knew really, that we were tourists in his office. He was at work. We were his customers. It was ok, it just wasn't Ahmed 1.[4]

We were fascinated by Yul's daily routine, which to us seemed extraordinarily abusive—we'd never stand for it back home. Yul was our guide for the second half of our trip as we sailed up the Nile. He stayed

---

2 The proliferation of Ahmeds in Egypt is endless.
3 I'm calling him Yul henceforth.
4 We still talk. He sends us holiday greetings and I ask him stupid questions and I can hear him smiling when he texts me over WhatsApp "No, Mr. Bull, camels aren't reptiles," "No Mr. Bull, ancient Egyptian temples weren't 'essentially rap video orgies 24/7."

in Luxor but met us each morning wherever our dahabiya had moored to whisk us off into a new adventure. This meant he drove three hours before dawn then back again every day. I know how much we paid for our trip[5] which seemed exorbitant when it was dragged kicking and screaming out of my wallet[6] but when balanced against the imaginary spreadsheet of salaries, fuel, hotel rooms, tips, and various sundries I just couldn't figure out how Nashville Tours made any money. But Yul and Ahmed Prime had been doing this for years. They were both in their early 40s with families and homes. Obviously the job paid well enough, or they wouldn't do it. But my God, getting up at four in the morning to meet a trio of sleepy Americans to drive them out into the desert to, essentially, stare at rocks just seemed pointless.

Yet there we were, Yul kicked back in his passenger seat texting madly, our driver staring steely eyed into the middle distance, my two wives lost in the passing view, and myself worried about how much to tip Yul Brynner.

---

5 A lot.
6 Out of [My Attorney]'s wallet. I'm a writer. My wallet is full of crisp, folded exposure.

*Trigger warning: more luridly described bodily function humor ahead.*

## GLOCK AND SPIEL

Regarding me being a man of adventure: no, I am not. If this trip and the last couple of days has proven anything, it's that I'm barely even a man of leisure. I've walked six miles a day, every day, since we arrived in the Goddam Egyptian frying pan desert, and though it might be November, it's still hot as hell and there is nothing between us and the sun but heat waves, and it burns. My downfall started earlier at Abydos after a two-hour drive, punctuated by a stop at a nameless gas station for a piss and some coffee. It was hot as hell at the temple, and I may have stood my fat ass in the light a little too long trying to frame a lone sycamore because I AM A PHOTOGRAPHER, then walked the MILE LONG hike through a phalanx of savage Russians to get back in the van.

It may have been shorter. I'm only guaging the distance on the likelihood of fainting. It was pretty damn far and I parked my amplitude on whatever availble architecture or what I presume were priceless ancient artifacts (sorry, Ahmed Prime) I could find. It had been like this for days. Every morning we're up at the crack of dawn to get into a tiny bus that bounces us out into the Saharah where I slog through ankle deep sand. Where I trudge up ancient stone steps. Where I stand with my group, marvelking at all the new places on my corpud from which I was sweating for the first time (elbows, earlobes, right nostril) and trying like hell to catch my breath, pay attention, and perhaps not die.

We drove 100 kilometers to Dendera, and it is there, in Dendera, that my body informed me it had suffered enough by sending a hot river of liquid shit to the well-known terminus while giving my horrified mind a minute or two to prepare for the inevitable.

I sat on an 8000-year-old abutment while Yul Brynner educated my wives about Hathor. I couldn't focus. I was slightly bent over, my guts in retreat. A freezing sensation ant-walked up and down my legs while a white-hot sensation lashed at my terminus. I felt faint. My second wife stepped over.

"You don't look so good," she said.

I was fading out. I mentally built a damn in my ass and turned my rheumy eyes to Adelaide. My stomach made a noise, a kind of dark, purling chortle. Adelaide looked at my abdomen.

"Oh wow. Did you eat something—"

"I need your wet wipes."

One thing about my wives, they are preppers. Their purses and go-bags are magical cornucopias of necessity. Adelaide produced two foil wrapped wet wipes out of thin air. I looked at these inadequate soggy napkins, snatched them from her delicate hands, then aimed myself at the distant gift shop and lurched off.

"I'll meet you at the van," I said in my manliest screech.

I stiff-walked a half a mile back to the tourist center where some skinny ragamuffin Egyptian men formed a gauntlet, their hands held out with wads of butt napkins. I handed the first guy I saw ten Egyptian pounds, grabbed the entire role out of his hand and headed for the loo. But I'd paid too much. I'd revealed myself. The whole gang of them leapt into action, dousing the bathroom floor and walls with chemicals and water, wiping everything down, plowing squeegees across the tiles while I danced in place. They hand detailed my stall until I finally growled "You might want to take a break!" hauled my enflamed corpse through them, slammed the door shut and grabbed hold wherever I could for a barely controlled explosion accompanied by involuntary grunts of effort and shuddering sighs of horror followed by the multi-sploosh rhythmic paroxysms of sweet, sweet relief.

Sweat sheathed down my back and sides. My Stetson hanging on the back of the door swam in my vision, its saw-toothed woven straw blurring indistinctly. I should have realized this is not normal behavior for common evacuation, or even for routine terror shits. Something was afoot in my abutt.

The next day in the temple of Esna it happened again, and I suppose I shouldn't be surprised. I am an immoderately overweight 4X-shirtted short man with dainty feet and a genetic predisposition to hypertension who's only real exercise is getting up from my desk and walking into the living room to play video games or binge on cooking videos the way other guys watch baseball. Coming to Egypt was like drifting a gas-filled balloon into an open flame.

We descended rickety wooden stairs into a pit to the temple of Esna.[1]
As we hit the bottom, we slipped into a reservoir of super-heated humid air

1 If you're going to only see one temple other than Abu Simbel, it should be Esna. It is gorgeous, brilliantly preserved, and currently being detailed by a flock of archeologists lying flat on their backs thirty feet up on trembling scaffolds.

that hadn't moved in twenty years. I broke into another full body sweat. My vision faded into a vignette. [My Attorney] and Adelaide's voices drifted further away until they sounded like they were talking through a transistor radio on a boat in the middle of a lake and I thought, Oh great, this is just like Florida.

I'd suffered heatstroke in my youth when I lived in the Sunshine State where fat white retirees regularly burst into flame. Standing in the temple of Esna, I felt fire rising up within me and I panicked[2]. I fought my way up the rickety stairs. Suddenly the air was cool again. Breezes from the Nile swept through the tin-roofed bazaar. I leaned forward gulping the cool air, my hands on my knees.

I resigned myself to stand next to the guard armed with a machine gun and wait for my wives, or death, but I was accosted by a shopkeeper who's been sitting on a 4X Egyptian cotton shirt for twenty years waiting for a Hindenburgian American to show up. When he saw me his eyes bulged with dollar signs, and he would. Not. Leave. Me. Alone.

"My friend," he says to me, laying a sail's worth of puke-colored cotton onto me. "Look at this jabella!"

"La chagrin, la chagrin[3]." My eyes are barely open. I'm drenched in sweat. My second wife pulls up next to me and we aim ourselves for the distant open mouth of the bazaar where our taxi waits.

"Sir, please, this shirt is for you!"

Adelaide slips her arm through mine because she thinks I might fall over.[4]

I can't blame the guy. He probably bought this shirt in 1985 and he's been staring at it every day since, silently bitching out his cousin Ahmed who talked him into buying it because Americans are fat and then finally, FINALLY, the mythical creature, a hyper corpulent American man practically walks into his shop. I'm sure he acted involuntarily. I get it. It was, in his eyes, a sign from Allah.

"My friend, look it is big—like you!"

He presses the shirt onto me, and I can't take it anymore. In my delicate condition, and as he presses this shirt against me for the third time, ignoring my pleas of le chagrin, I yell "FUCK ALL THE WAY OFF!" in fluent American.

---

2 Except, ok, no I didn't. What I felt were white-hot chills. It's hard to explain. I was hot cold. I was chill fired. I was fainting.

3 This is the polite way of saying, 'no, absolutely not, best of luck, I'm not buying anything ever.'

4 Because I might fall over. God bless her, she's brave. If I did fall over, I'd just break through the crust of the earth and drag her down with me until we hit magma.

It should be noted that on any given day, my regular speaking voice is like a cannon so while I was dying of heatstroke as this fucktard wouldn't stop trying to sell me his fat shirt, my voice erupted at a level that can only be described as Vesuvian. People heard me. In Jersey.

Well now shit changes. Suddenly, a man in civilian clothing appears beside us. He is the Egyptian Charles Bronson. As Adelaide and my first wife drag me away, Bronson walks with us. He never looks at us. He never says a Bronsonian word. He never even indicates we're there; yet the feeling of being escorted is palpable.

An eager alabaster salesman leaps out of his store directly into our path, but the silent man walking silently beside us wags a silent finger—one tiny wag, just a quarter inch—which propels the alabasterian back into his cave like he was mind-thrown by goddam Professor X. That's when I notice Charles Bronson is strapped with a fat Glock on his hip.

The bazaar by the temple of Esna is a conglomeration of buildings, tin shacks, and odd scaffolding all covered in a corrugated metal roof. The street we're walking down is under this roof so it's weird, like we're outside but inside and I'm still suffering so it's like I'm in a tunnel and there's light at the end of it and I'm not happy with the symbology. I can barely make out our van parked across the street way at the end of the corridor. I know it's poorly air-conditioned, but any port in a storm and—MY FRIEND!

Godammit, another one. This guy is draped with scarves and dances out of his shop like Steve Tyler, almost into my lap, but Silent Guy lifts a single hair on a single eyebrow and scarf guy snaps his own spine whipping himself out of our way.

In the wavering distance, our driver hops out and I mentally command him to shut his damn door to conserve the AC, which works. He opens the back of the van and is filling his arms with arctic bottles of water—MY FRIEND!

Son of a BITCH! A trinketeer swoops in front of us with a tiny glass pyramid held out to shove into my paw but Sir Glock's a Lot dilates, by a millimeter, one nostril and Trinketey McTrinkface disappears in a cloud of dust.

The driver is loaded with water bottles. Condensation is forming a pool in the dirt. I can read the labels—oh man, they are FIJI, the rarest of bottled water, the kind of—MY FRIEND!

This guy is sneaky, as he comes around Glockenspiel with an armload of coin books, placing one in my hand, outstretched toward the Fiji bottles in desperation. Obviously, he doesn't see the gun.

"Mother FUCK!" I explain.

It has, over recent years, been brought to my attention, discreetly, delicately, that I may, possibly, perhaps employ the F-word with alarming regularity. The F-Bomb, the S-Bomb—the length and breadth of the lexicon of highly explosive no-nos. I have mostly disregarded these fucking incursions into my vocabulary because I am a Goddam wordsmith and I will use whichever words the world requires according to my professional assessment of a given goddam situation. However, my two wives warned me about Egypt, that they don't curse. More, that if I were to curse, the average Egyptian would be deeply offended and the above average Egyptian would likely punch me in the face. I'd been trying to curtail my cussing but Jesus fucking Christ, this guy with his coins!

Bronson leaves us blinking in the sunlight. He sits in a chair positioned just inside the great open gob of the bazaar—just a regular old kitchen chair. Silently. I nod to him, and he nods back with the kind of stoic aplomb that would make Bruce Willis shit his pants. We get into a dirty white van. I pour a half-liter of nearly frozen water into my body then loll my head to stare out the window at the deep blue Nile as we scuttle off, lurching through Esnanian traffic, around donkeys, camels, Tuk Tuks, toward our final destination.

## ME, MY WIFE, MY OTHER WIFE, A LOVELY FRENCH COUPLE, A PLAGUE OF SCORPIONS, AND THE MORMON TABERNACLE CHOIR[1]

We finally get to our vessel, the Meroe of the Nour il Nil fleet of dahabiyas. I've been waiting for this. I come from a long line of people who dream of owning a yacht and this was as close as I'd ever get. A bunch of skinny Arab dudes in djabellas haul our luggage across the deck of the wide, brilliantly white dahabiya moored closest to us, onto the deck of the next one. My second wife, Adelaide, leapt adroitly across the gap between the boat and the dock. She was a competitive sailor for most of her life and knew her way around a couple of sails. But [My Attorney] and I come from a long line of people who spent their lives in easy chairs so planting our tiny feet on the wildly swaying gangplank, a rope bridge without rails of any kind, was unnerving. Finally, the skinny Arab guys pretty much reached out and dragged us all eighteen inches across the water onto the deck of the boat, then hoisted us again over the next gap and then there we were in our room and, if you'll allow me an emotional moment, oh my fucking God.

What luxury. We had reserved the panoramic room on the back of the Nour el Nil's flagship boat, the Meroe. Fifty-two feet of luxurious, old-world sailing vessel. The ship was propelled by two giant red and white striped sails that would carry it slong at a stately pace, silently and steadily making its way south which, against my Western sensibilities, is UP the Nile.

All the Nour el Nil boats were built by hand in Egypt and there aren't any other boats like them. They have deeply varnished wooden floors with thickly painted white walls and ceilings and red and white striped upholstery and pillows. They have huge windows, low couches, low tables, and pillows, pillows, pillows. The crew are Egyptian to a man, the food is perfectly authentic, often picked up in whichever village we dock at, and cooked by the crew. It is an extraordinary experience, and boasts of having the longest sailing time between Luxor and Aswan, a trip these boats take at nearly walking speed as the waters of the Nile lap at the hull and the palm

---

1 Not the Mormon Tabernacle Choir

trees and sugar cane fields of rural Egypt pass silently by.

We booked the Panoramic Room. It is enormous—essentially one side of the entire back of the boat. It's got a bathroom at one end, a king-sized bed, then a sitting area facing three great windows hanging off the stern. It has a chandelier, an air conditioner that forms ice on the bed posts, some shelves with books on them and not much else. No TV No touch screens. Just pure gaslight-era amenities. It was heaven. I was, yet again, stunned and speechless by the sheer luxury of our accommodations.

I changed into my boating clothes, skipped up on deck to enjoy our departure only to find it had been delayed by fourteen remaining fellow passengers who were late because (choose your answer):

A) their tour guide had been arrested

B) there had been a once-in-a-century-level rainstorm in Aswan where they were bivouacked

C) a plague of scorpions.

The answer is D) all of the above because oh hell yes it was. You can look this up and I will add a link[2] in the footnotes to prove to you that I am not making things up here. On Nov 12, while my two wives were enjoying the Valley of the Kings and I was considering paying $60 for a shot of drug store whiskey at the Shoopenflurfle hotel, one-hundred-fifty miles upriver the people of Aswan were pounded by three days of deadly thunderstorms, rain, lightning, and flooding. Aswan is one of the world's driest cities, averaging just .12 inches of rain annually which wouldn't fill up a bottle cap. The rains that hit over the weekend were terrifying. The winds topped 40mph. Roofs were swept into the air. More than sixty families were driven from their homes. Power was shut down. The city's fresh water supply was cut off.

While this was happening, somewhere in that town, the Mogrom Stabernacle Squire[3] was shut up in their hotel room—and I am assuming here—prostrate and praying because outside their semi-modern haven of safety the Old Testament was on replay. The rains, the wind, the lightning, and the floods were bad. But as the city imploded from all the disaster, it was as if God looked down and thought I can do better, waggled its spectral fingers over the soggy desert and cried RELEASE THE SCORPIONS!

Billions of them boiled out of the ground. And I am choosing my words carefully here. Click the link I've provided here.[4] That's boiling. That's the right word. And they were not happy. More than five-hundred people were

2 Please visit bullgarlington.com where the author will direct you to a video to prove the veracity of this ludicrousness.
3 NOT the Mormon Tabernacle Choir.
4 https://youtu.be/a_TPcHX5dPY

stung, many of them were hospitalized, and several of them died.

While our boats were docked in Aswan they thrashed against each other. Lines snapped. Urgent nautical problems obtained. They had to be rehabbed a little on their way to pick us up at Esna. Each boat was descorpioned then got a new coat of paint.

I don't think it's an accident the Doorman Block & Tackle Buyer[5] were in Aswan during a Biblical-level plague of scorpions. I think it was their fault because I was stuck on a boat with them and damn, they are the worst.

**They're Mostly Teeth**

The Fourman Crabby Grackle Liar[6] group were business delegates scheduled to meet with Egyptian notables, and they were, no doubt, the whitest people I have ever met. That's coming from me, the whitest guy I know. I had to shield my sensitive eyes from the lactescent glare of their Osmondian smiles. I should maybe refrain from shit-talking the Norman Flapper Mackle Cryer[7], since they are the Utah branch of the Christian Mafia but as I write this, sitting at the back of the dahabiya, they're at their table, all of them on their phones, loudly facetiming and cackling like high school mean girls.

Pour yourself a whiskey and kick off your shoes and get comfortable while I recount the joy of traveling with the Moron Taverncackle Briar[8].

Incident 1: the deck of the Meroe easily accommodates twenty guests with plenty of room. But not everyone is on deck all the time. When we're docked, most everyone is on an excursion or garbage swimming, so the deck is pretty free. Once everyone got back from their trip, they tended to disappear into their rooms to shower and iron their magical underwear before coming to supper.

The deck was divided into snugs, with a u-shaped settee, a low table, and seventeen million cushions. Each group sort of adopted a snug for the trip. There were also low couches and benches that were unclaimed where anyone could sit and enjoy a little alone time away from the crowd.

[My Attorney] was lounging in our snug in the early evening by herself on the deck when Mr. Toupee arrived, took the snug directly next to her, then fired up his iPad to watch a 20-minute TED talk without headphones. I hope you are properly horrified by this. He had the whole boat. He could

5 NOT the Mormon Tabernacle Choir.
6 NOT the Mormon Tabernacle Choir.
7 NOT the Mormon Tabernacle Choir.
8 NOT the Mormon Tabernacle Choir.

have sat anywhere. HE COULD HAVE USED HEADPHONES.

Incidents 4–11: Every night one couple facetimed their daughter on deck, loudly, with the entire choir[9] joining in. You may think to yourself, well come on, man, that's not that bad. They're just being a good family. But you didn't hate them like I did so you just don't know. It was maddening.

Incident 34: Being friendly. On several occasions, various members of the Morton Saltine Cracker Choir[10] tried to engage members of my party, including the lovely French couple we had befriended, in friendly chatter which infuriated me (and the French). What is wrong with people? CAN'T YOU SEE I'M LOUNGING? Once we leave this dingy, we will never see each other again so let's just fast forward to that and never talk now. I am curmudgeoning. I don't want to talk to you. Your teeth are blinding. Your cackling is piercing. Return to your cabin and pray.

Incident 65: One of them was an accidental member. He's not in the choir. He's a last-minute addition whom we will call BOB and he spent much of the trip trying to become my new BFF, but I saw though his grade school machinations. His real goal was to get next to our traveling companion and my second wife, Adelaide, who hardly paid attention to him which only made him try harder. Which was too bad because Bob had no game.

Witness how he complimented her dress at dinner. You have to know, this is a garment Addy purchased specifically for its abject modesty, its plain style, and its utter lack of come hitherness. It's a dress that would make a 19th century Amish school marm say, "Girl, loosen up."

Bob says "Well, we'll only know how nice it is if you stand up and—" then, as my eyes overclocked the diameter of our dinner plates he says, "—give us a twirl."

That fucker. That's my fake second wife you're talking to there bud, and if a Mormon should know anything it's to not talk smack to another man's second wife. This comment launched his career as my personal bitch for the remainder of the trip, whereby I will tell him at least three dozen times, "Nice shirt, BOB, give us a twirl."

To their credit, the teeth-firstian trophy wives in his party glared at him and yelled, "You're a married man, BOB!" but he never caught on and they're all still pale faced Utah prudes and sister wives and no one takes them seriously, least of all Bob.

Our French companion, Marie, who sat to my left at meals as my cultural advisor, had their fucking number. Every time they burst into cackling she

9 NOT the Mormon Tabernacle Choir.
10 NOT the Mormon Tabernacle Choir.

glanced at me and made a face in French that judged them as Américains blancs stupides and sent me into fits.

Besides our alabaster companions, our delicate and quiet reverie is disturbed only by the four-story floating castles of Russians powering past like Q-Anon stickered 4x4s rolling coal and blaring their idiotic 'melody' horns—as if we needed their nautical obesity announced. Every time it happened, Marie tugged an invisible trucker's horn. She was my hero.

We are here to answer the question I posed earlier: can we, relatively solvent middle-class professionals with fiber optic WIFI and three college degrees between us,[11] put together and execute the perfect vacation? Can we obtain a flawless respite from our endless grinds (of course I'm talking about my two wives, who work sixty hours a week, at actual offices, not me)?

On the silent deck of the dahabiya, alone in my cushioned comfort I fade into the susurrus of the river lapping at our hull, glance out across the water at exactly fuck-all occurring, quietly thank Ahmed for pouring me another copper cup of gritty brown coffee, and think we have, perhaps, come close.

After trying so hard all these years. After Paris, Barthelona, Madrid, New Orleans, Sonoma, England, Mexico, Belize and everywhere else, after all those trips fraught with stress and worry and mania, after all that, here I am with my beautiful wife who is finally sitting in the crook of a low couch reading a novel and drinking hibiscus tea and enjoying the sunlight and not doing a goddam thing.

Bliss.

Drifting serenely on this legendary waterway, we at last obtain brief serenity. Just the creak of the steering ropes and the low babble of our capable sailing crew; there is the muted clinking of glassware from Alleh who is setting our table for lunch; a quarter mile away one of our tugboats tugs along but I can barely hear its put put put. We are moving so slowly, so barely. Our red and white sails belly in the breeze and the air is fragrant with smells from the kitchen, a distant cigarette, and the river. We are—I am—utterly content, perfectly relaxed, and quietly, gently, finally delighted. This is perfect.

And no other holiday will ever measure up. After the drama and horror and isolation of Covid, we hit Egypt like a champagne cork shot into a velvet pillow. All previous excursions were trial runs. And I'll never get [My

11 None of them mine.

Attorney] to drop this kind of cash on a trip again so this might be peak vacation for me. For us.

Alleh stopped by our nook of cushions to tell me he is preparing a shishka for me and so my pampering deepens. I've already been assigned (stole) the seat at the head of the table so the staff calls me El Presidente. I am 'sirred' all day and hosptalitied to within an inch of my life.

I am wallowing in whiteness. I am, if anything, worse than the ashen, pallid members of the Whoreman Crapper Cackle Buyer[12] because I am aware of my privilege and instead of finding some way to mitigate this entitlement, I am gaming it for everything it's worth. Everything in my personal list of shit that will make me laugh later, I mean. Like when Bob tells me he sails, I tell him there's twenty foot of shoreline right there by the railing if he wants to practice his knots. He looks for it. I'm still laughing.

---

12 NOT the Mormon Tabernacle Choir.

### JEWELS OF EGYPT
### DAY 11
### NOV 16 EL KAB & EDFU

Whilst sleeping, we gently sail en-route to El Kab, on the East bank of the Nile, was once the capital of Upper Egypt and is still home to the temple of Nekhbet, as well as a row of fascinating decorated tombs carved into the slope of the mountains. Upon docking, you will embark on a beautiful walk through a small fishermen village to visit the necropolis. In the afternoon, the boat will arrive at Edfu, home to the Greco-Roman temple dedicated to the god Horus. This is among the best-preserved of all Egyptian temples. Horse and carriage will take you to the temple through the busy city streets. After returning to the boat, you will set sail for a beautiful island.

#### FISHING VILLAGE FAT BOY BLUES

Our itinerary lists the evening's excursion as "a short walk-through authentic fishing village." Their idea of a short walk and my idea of a short walk are maddeningly divergent. I figured we'd tie off at the village dock, amble through rugged fishermen to pick up a few trinkets at their shoppes then step back onto our boat which would have been in full view the entire time.

Instead, we walked hesitantly down a wobbly gangplank onto the rocky bank, then walked for forty-five minutes along a palm frond paved pathway dotted with donkey shit, then finally turned into the interior, walking another fifty miles through sugar cane fields.

I am not a superstitious person, but if you will take a moment to look at the picture of a mule in the inserts, you will see what I saw as we hurled ourselves deep into the Egyptian farmland. On my left, a biblical tableau of a grotto, mango trees, sugar cane and there, perched meaningfully, a white ass who turned his heavy old head to follow me as we walked by, braying once, quietly, to remind me of how perfectly he was a harbinger and omen of death.

I'd not had a good day. I'd nearly died of heat stroke then I'd had a dramatic fight with a savage shopkeeper before being marched away under armed guard. I hadn't eaten much and before I fled the sunken bucket of humidity and death at the temple of Esna I'd sweat out a magnum of perspiration. This, on top of just not paying any attention at all to the fact that I was excursioning in a desert meant I was dehydrated as hell. That donkey knew something.

Twenty tourists marched around a bend in the road then down a gravel path and into a village at dusk. They said it was a fishing village, so I had expectations. For two years I had imagined this moment, had imagined us stepping off the boat, off the Nile, onto the docks, the sound of gulls, quiet men mending nets, strange cargo hauled aloft, and fish. Boxes and boxes of fish.

We walked into a village where there were some people who probably fished. They didn't seem overjoyed to see us. The village was maybe ten or fifteen squat buildings, a single narrow lane dropping away from the middle of the square. A bare electric light shone from the corner of a building, casting sharp shadows. An open door showed the mysterious interior of a home bathed in the blue glow of an unseen television. An old man stood in the middle of everything watching us. We took pictures because of course we did but this village didn't seem to be in on the whole "visit an authentic fishing village" agenda. They didn't seem to care that we were there. There was nothing to buy. Nothing special going on, just villagers in their village villaging when a parade of Americans—each of us wearing clothes that cost more than a month's salary for them—mosied our bougie asses through, snapping selfies and whispering and pointing.

On the long walk back, I was reeling from heat exhaustion and dehydration. I struggled climbing down the rocks to the gangplank and swayed enough that one of my djebella-clad helpers grabbed me in a panic thinking I was going to fall into the Nile because I was about to fall into the Nile (except it was all rocks, so I'd be fine. I'd be dead.)

[My Attorney] held onto me with an iron grip because I married well and though she is absolutely terrified of the gangplank, rocks, rivers, donkeys, and the entire terrifying process of planking a gang, she loves me and turns into a fierce five-foot-nothing superhero and drags me over like she's leading me across our own living room floor. All the fear she'd shown in previous gangplanking evaporated when she saw me almost faint. I love her so much.

When I fell into the beautifully appointed bed in our egregiously beautiful room I was done. Exhausted. Shaking and timid. I tried to tell [My Attorney] that I wasn't up to dinner, but my voice was a mere creak. Not only was I overheated from walking an hour in an Egyptian heat farm, I was dehydrated. My heart was pumping dust.

I pounded a half a liter of water, took a fistful of Advil, and tried to sleep as [My Attorney] went above deck. I lolled fully clothed on our gorgeously swaddled bed linens as frigid air washed over me. The water rehydrated me like a desert rose. Everything would be ok. I was fine.

Then the air conditioner turned off.[1] My room, which—being on the west side with the windows and uncurtained—had been storing heat in the glass and the walls turned into an oven and I laid there on the brink of immolation and took stock.

I'd been in therapy for more than a year to figure out why I eat the way I do. After many sessions, I had a breakthrough. It was, surprise, something from my childhood. Not something weird or gross or traumatic. Instead, it was no more than the attention I received for eating all the Krystal burgers[2] thrown at me (a considerable amount) when I was five. I swelled with pride whenever my dad would brag about how much I could eat, or when, on one of our weekly excursions to Red Lobster, I'd order the patently gigantic Captain's Platter[3]—me, a marginally portly-but-still-has-a-chance child—and finish it.

Which became a thing. I was a performative eater—I ate for the entertainment of others. As I grew older, those others disappeared but I still loaded my plate as if they were applauding.

Now, if you're wondering why there is such an interlude in the middle of a travel book, it's because as I laid on that bed in the kiln of my room, I felt claustrophobic. I felt small inside my body. I felt trapped in it. Trapped in layers of fat that were heating up like bacon in a cast iron pan. Fear hit me like a bomb. I was going to die trapped inside this enormous bag of fat.

My therapist has been trying to convince me size is no big deal. I get

---

1 They did this each evening during supper and in the wee hours of the morning to conserve fuel as the AC is powered separately from other parts of the boat and I don't know, maybe it would explode or something. I know I was about to.

2 If you're from the south, you already know about Krystal. If you're north of Indiana, think White Castle, but better.

3 Currently. The Ultimate Feast, which after adding a baked potato, mac & cheese, and enough butter to drown in, is a whopping 1,950 calories. I was eight years old.

what she's trying to teach, and I feel kind of like I briefly entertained the view that I'm just fat, with no caveat nor addendum. Just blunt recognition of fact.

I lost that constant nag, the ever-present thwart fat people (fat guys) live with, the belief that we are wrong, that we are aberrant and perved, monstrous, malignant, and grotesque. That we are scary anomalies. I had managed, with the help of my therapist, to dispose myself of a constant lifelong guilt of eating.

I'd suffered from a daily obsession over what was wrong with what I ate. If you think guys—and I mean white cis privileged males—aren't constantly talking about their diets and weight loss, think again. Every MAGA hat wearing pickup driving country music tobacco chewing redneck fatass you know sits in the cab of a Ford Bronco with another guy just like him talking about their waistline.

Which is idiotic. For a lot of reasons, some that are psychological and legit. The biggest reason is that life is too short to spend so much of it focused on your own ass.

Also, diets don't work. Most weight loss programs only give temporary results because they are focused on limiting, on punishing, and most of all, on denial.

But your desires—your hungers—are real and valid. You have every right to want to eat a goddam New York strip with garlic butter, mashed potatoes, and a beer. It's ok. That shit is delicious. If you deny yourself that steak and instead eat a fucking salad with lemon juice and water you are eating your fear with each sad mastication—and you're starving.

There is a medical movement afoot revealing new data which show— when all things are equal between a person who is "skinny" and a person who is "obese"—that their morbidity rates are the same[4]. This study indicated that one's morbidity hinges less on one's diet or morphology, and instead is all about how much you move.[5]

I recently took a heart test and my heart, buried as it is inside a barrel of pork fat and biscuits, is strong as hell. It's not limping along under some undue burden. Which boils down to me not walking around being horrified by my rotundity[6].

---

4 More than two years after dumping that therapist, I am now wondering where all the 300-pound octogenarians live because I don't know any.

5 Still not good news for me…

6 It's more than a year since we got back from Egypt, and I've revised my opinion about being a fat man. Although I retain my opinion that diets are stupid, and that being fat is partially just a thing about you as an individual you may not be able to change, I simultaneously don't believe that. Body positivity is important—maybe

And I did. Until Esna and the authentic fishing village and the overbearing heat of an Egyptian dusk. I experienced my own personal global warming. Then I laid there in the bed in endless, mortal terror: I was trapped in a fleshy bag that was about to explode. I closed my eyes and tried to regain my composure but all I could see was that goddam alabaster ass watching my goddam alabaster ass walk by, braying his dreadful omen of my impending demise.

Then the air came back on, and I returned to watching Karen videos on Reddit.

---

even vital—for the well-being of most people in the U.S. because we are abused by advertising and media campaigns to get us to buy awful food. We also live in environments designed for cars instead of people, so we don't walk much. Parisians walk about seven thousand steps a day, every day. Americans might walk five thousand steps, but only at Disney. We're culturally predisposed to being overweight and we should not be ugly to ourselves or abusive to ourselves if we are. However, at 59 years old and 320 pounds I can tell you that it does not get better. My knees are shot. I'm out of breath just tying my shoes. One flight of stairs leaves me breathless and concerned. I fight a secret fight every day to walk out of my house to go to the store, to go to a meeting, to hang out with friends. I fight the idea, every day, that I am scary and gross and appearing in public is harmful to others. That's fucked up. But being fat sucks. It just sucks. There's no way around it, and it weighs on you to move less, to exercise less because your body obeys and supports your unconscious habits. I realized this year that if I want to enjoy life as an old man, I need to change my life so that I move more. I need to embrace the discomfort of cardio and I need to push myself to endure the painful boredom of exercising. Not to lose weight, though I may. But to make sure that when I'm older, I can move. That I can keep going, because I expect to live a while and I want to have fun when I'm doing it. Also, this Egyptian trip may sound funny now, but at the time, I did not have a good time. That fear I talk about was real fear. It was terror. I was worried I would die, and I was terrified and claustrophobic because I could feel my smaller self enveloped in my actual corpus. I'm taking up Yoga. I'm training to walk the Camino de Santiago. Exercise is no longer the point, it's training for a fuller life.

## JEWELS OF EGYPT
## DAY 14
## NOV 19 KOM OMBO

After a night on the water and beneath the stars, the morning trip will take you to the town and temple of Kom Ombo. The temple was built during the Ptolemaic period on the site of an older temple and at one of the most beautiful locations, on a bend on the river. The temple was dedicated to Sobek, the crocodile-headed god. After enjoying the temple, you will visit the new Crocodile Museum, which contains many mummified crocodiles, attesting to the importance the creature played in this region in ancient times.

### SCARF HAGGLING IN KOM OMBO

We dock at Kom Ombo and a guy on shore whom I later learn is named Adam, is going through his entire stock of djebellas showing me he has some in my size. He's holding them up like sails in the breeze yelling "I have big ones!" So of course, I am giggling. I steadfastly ignore him while we wait on our nasal swabs[1] so we can visit the crocodile temple which was not worth it. I had finally gotten off the boat after taking a few days of rest to regulate my tempers and vapors and humors and my knees. For some reason, I thought the crocodile museum was going to be an Egyptian Gatorland and it was not, and I was disappointed.[2]

---

1 required so we can fly out later that day.

2 Gatorland is a venerable Central Florida theme park predating Disney by decades. Its theme is alligators, and it is loaded with them. There are more than 3,000 of these murderous suitcases at Gatorland and yeah, Disney is nice and all, but at Gatorland you can stare at way too many alligators in muted terror then go for lunch and eat them. Try that, Disney. Put your money where our mouse is.

     The thing is, they have a couple of shows where large gators are lured into rising up to snatch a raw chicken off a pole, a feat that is mortifying when you realize alligators can rise up and snatch a raw chicken off a pole. Because you are subsequently released into the nature walk, an INADEQUATELY PROTECTED wooden path meandering through the swamp behind Gatorland where most of their alligators lie in warm torpid waters after being trained to snatch raw chickens off a pole and so when you poke your fool head over the rail it looks, to a gator, a lot like a raw chicken and so they will RISE UP TO TRY AND SNATCH YOUR RAW HEAD OFF YOUR RAW SHOULDERS AND IT IS LEGITIMATELY SCARY, NOT THEME PARK SCARY, AND YES IT HAPPENED TO ME AND THAT IS WHY I AM TYPING IN ALL CAPS, ALSO, THEY SHOULD SELL PANTS.

My knee gave out about ten minutes into the tour, which is a very short walk from the boat, so I sat on a bench while the local guys in the gayebelas and turbans admired the goat-footed walking stick I'd borrowed from the crew.

Obo Booboo was the first temple where no one bothered us. No beggars, no hagglers, no scarfers—in the temple. On the way to the temple, and therefore on the way back, there were twenty-eight million of them. Hordes of insane urgent Egyptians jiggling our elbows and hitting us up for scarfs sales like pushy West-Side meth dealers.

On the temple grounds, no one said a damn thing to me until I sat down and twirled my kick-ass walking stick supplied to me by our captain. Suddenly the local guys came over and asked me a lot of questions in Arabic. They borrowed the stick and gave full-on lectures to each other, pointing to how the wooden shaft was sheathed at the bottom with the skin and hoof of an actual goat. They were clearly asking me where I got it and I was clearly telling them I wrenched the goat out of the jaws of a crocodile and made it myself.

The men and I shook hands then I rejoined my wives. We descended into the bazaar which was fairly antiseptic and had the stench of tourist traps and [My Attorney] lost her damn mind haggling over a scarf. To be clear, I mean she took that poor scarf seller for everything he was worth. I joined in occasionally from my low wall seat, yelling at her that I was growing a beard. We made it through the aggressive gauntlet of vendors until we got to Adam's shop where Adam discovered why I travel with a contracts attorney after he basically paid us to take this grubby gayabela off his hands for less than $30. This is a giant garment made from fine Egyptian cotton which I'd probably pay $200 for in America but I, a privileged upper middle-class American, haggled him down[3] for pennies because it was fun. Meanwhile, those poor bastards have been living on old bread and cigarette butts for the last two years as their main source of income stayed at home and died because they didn't want Bill Gates to track them through their vaccination. These hagglers used to see ten thousand tourists a day. They'd sell out by 3 o'clock in the afternoon. Now it's just a lone humor writer looking for material and the Mordor Stanky Ankle Choir[4].

---

The crocodile museum in Obu BooBoo didn't have a single living example. Our entire trip on the Nile was sans crocodile which was wildly disappointing. In fact, there are a host of animals listed in the brochure (which exists entirely in my imagination) who did not show up: hippopotami, lions, tigers, bears, hyenas, Timon, Poomba—they were all off the clock during our trip.

3 I mean she did.

4 NOT the Mormon Tabernacle Choir.

Adam held out a vast djebella which I really liked and asked for 1000EP which is a little over sixty bucks, an amount I'd easily spend on a cheap bottle of restaurant wine, but I grumped and scoffed and hustled out. I yelled "I may have just got off the boat," which he could see, and which I was pointing at "But I didn't just get off the boat!"

I felt bad a little for haggling for pocket change, but traditions are what keeps a culture alive, so we ought to respect them. I got back on board, tossed it to my Mormon BFF, and said "Give us a twirl, Bob!"

**JEWELS OF EGYPT**
**DAY 15**
**ABU SIMBEL**

Breakfast on board your Dahabiya Nile boat, then you will be transferred to Abu Simbel (around 3 hours and a half one way) by a modern air-conditioned coach to enjoy a small group tour to Abu Simbel. The two Temples of Abu Simbel, with their unique style, are considered to be the masterpieces of ancient Egypt. They reflect the glory and grandeur of the new Kingdom. The Egyptian government and UNESCO decided to co-operate in order to save these temples from the flood. The Temple of Ramsses II was dedicated to the four universal gods Ptah, Re-Her-Akhtey, Amun-Re, and to Ramsses II himself. The great Abu Simbel temple is also called The Sun Temple of Ramssess II. The Temple of Queen Nefertari is also Called Temple of Hathor who was the wife of the Sun God so in a symbolic way, the two Temples, that of Ramsses II and that of Nefertari, bring Ramesses II, Nefertari, Hathor, and the Sun God together as one. Later on, you will be escorted back from Abu Simbel to Aswan Airport to fly back to Cairo.

## DONKEYS AT DAWN

We were scheduled to leave at 4:30am for our three-hour minivan excursion from Aswan to Abu Simbel. I was not looking forward to this trip for a few reasons.

First, not looking forward to road trips is my other hobby. Secondly, it meant I would have to use a rest-stop toilet and there's no way a roadside men's room in the middle of the Sahara was going to meet my standards for roadside men's rooms in Egypt or even my roadside men's room standards for mid Louisiana in the middle of June during an economic slowdown. I knew exactly what I was facing.

As a man of a certain age, I have come to grips with pee certainty. I had recently been diagnosed with one of the many prostate problems for men in their fifties[1]. The symptoms are peeing three-hundred times a day. Even with meds I was way above normal pee frequency for any adult man and a trip through the desert with only two stops meant I was going to spend a considerable time wincing. And groaning. And squirming. All followed by an uncomfortable couple of minutes peeing in staccato into an alien coffee urn.

But first, donkeys.

I had encountered more donkeys on my trip to Egypt than I'd seen in my entire life. As a man who's lived in rural Alabama, rural Florida, and visited the Illinois state capital, I'd seen a lot of jackasses. But I was seeing more ass in Egypt than anywhere. I saw them first just passing me in the street, pulling wagons, bearing riders, and sometimes just standing around. No one with them. Just a mule on the sidewalk.

But on the cruise, I was really getting a lot of ass. First, there was Donkey Island, a term applied loosely. Not because it wasn't an island. It was. But because it was loose. Muddy. They should have called it Donkey Slurry. We were docked there in the afternoon to stay overrnight. The first day was all about swimming. Our captain encourged us to slip on our trunks and wade into the Nile which I don't know if you've looked it up, but I've seen a lot of Tarzan movies and the Nile is wall-to-wall crocodiles, except in those places where it's wall-to-wall hippopotamuses who will suck the flesh off your bones like you're an overcooked chicken wing.

Also, the Nile is a garbage pit. It's like swimming in a ditch off a county road in New Jersey in 1972. Back on the second day of the cruise, I was still suffering from being enormous in Africa. Fortunately, my second wife was so overly prepared we could have bivouacked in a cave for a year living entirely from the contents of her purse. She made me add powdered electrolytes to my water and slowly I came back to human. But at sunrise, I was still dazed and sitting in a chair staring out the window at the river. I'd have drooled but I was still too dehydrated to work up a nice sliver of spit, so I just stared, pounded my vaguely lemon-lime electrolyzed water and hoped I'd live.

Docked close to the shore as we were, the eddies of the Nile swirled around us, its gentle currents capturing discarded coke bottles and used

---

1 It's not cancer, settle down.

diapers in little whirlpools just outside my window. I followed various flotsam and jetsam as they sailed by. Obviously, science was required. It was clear different parts of the river move at different speeds. If you followed the half-submerged Styrofoam cooler in the near middle of the Nile, you could see that it was traveling at three knots, where the Ziploc bag filled with an unidentifiable shaggy liquid bobbed past at a crisp six, showing a clear difference of Oh my Jeebus Crass.

I calculated the speed of the garbage, tried to stay alive as the sun rose behind us, casting its golden rays over the spent candy wrappers, cracked two-by-fours, and other decorative river jetsam when someone's grandma swam past my window. Through the garbage.

She had a serious but contented look on her face. She was wearing a blue and white one-piece that made her look a little like an animated Chinoiserie teacup. She got about halfway past, saw me, waved at my corpse then kept going.

It turns out this was Eleanor, the owner of the dahabiyas. She cut through the garbage like it was nothing, pushing floating fruit jars and strange diaphanous strands of plastic out of her way with an elegant, detached elan.

I was near death and still had the wherewithal to tsk tsk and whisper hoarsely through cracked lips, girl, serious? Then Bob and Bob's handler swam into view behind her.

When we docked at Donkey Island for a swim party, I disembarked fully clothed and fully opposed to swimming unless it was in a pool that was 80% chlorine. I followed [My Attorney] across the rickety plank bridge with its decorative safety ropes that wouldn't fool an OSHA inspector if she was blind and in Florida. I say we were docked at the island, but this is perhaps a misuse of this word. The boat had pulled alongside the spit and let's just paint a picture here of the splendor that is Donkey Island.

Donkey Island was about two Ikeas square, with a long shallow ditch in the middle and a pubescent copse of low trees at the far end. There were cows, cranes, several of those ubiquitous white birds that eat the ticks off cattle, and donkeys.

A lot of donkeys.

Like, unless you're a donkey farmer, this was more donkeys than you'd see in your lifetime.

I stepped onto the grass, which the donkeys had clipped to a nice par four and stabbed my walking stick into the dirt triumphantly sans bathing suit then was assaulted by a tiny burro.

Look, I don't blame the animal. Any poorly educated creature looking at that disembarking crowd would have zeroed in on me as the one mostly like to have a tuber in my pants. I named him Eddy. Eddy named me potato. He nosed up to me, sniffing me up and down to find food. I patted him on his snout and walked away as [My Attorney] was trying her daintiest to tiptoe between mounds of charcoal-briquet mule turds. But Eddy followed me no matter how many people poured off the dahabiya, their hands full of fresh carrots and sugar cubes. Didn't matter. Eddy was a one-potato donkey and shadowed me for the excursion, which lasted about eight minutes as I got an eye full of Donkey Island and trash-swimming Mormons[2]. I got back on board and had a gritty cup of coffee.

We left Donkey Island. We had dinner then went to bed early. As we slept, our boat sailed slowly up the river toward Aswan where we were the only passengers scheduled to disembark. At 4:30 in the morning. I didn't mind that much. As a functioning adult, I was able to adapt to one early morning so we could get back on our trusted busminivan which would take us on the six-hour drive to Abu Simbel while the Morgan Freeman Tackalacka Choir, hopefully, fell off the boat and drowned.

I had envisioned this morning for two years, as I had gone over the itinerary fifty-seven-thousand times with [My Attorney] and my second wife, Adelaide. In my mind, it was a no big-deal disembarkation. The Meroe would dock quietly at a rustic but trustworthy and brightly illuminated pier where our bus would sit idling in the early morning river mist. We'd quietly gather our luggage, say goodbye to our luxurious digs, then walk easily off the boat, onto the dock, and into the van.

But that last day, at 4:30 in the morning, as sleepy crew members collected me and my two wives and our luggage, dragging it all to the front of the boat, we emerged from the quiet cabins behind them into perfect darkness.

"Where's the dock?" I asked the captain.

"Yes."

"Where do you think we are?"

"Of course, my friend."

"Where is our car?"

"Is there," the captain indicates the wall of absolute blackness.

"Are those cows?"

My second wife stares out into the night as ghostly shapes loom. They are snow white skinny cows and several donkeys. We've docked at a field. And not close to the field. The rickety, terrifying gang plank is spanning

2 NOT the Mormon Tabernacle Choir

a good thirty feet and worse, it ends against a wall of sharp boulders. She spots our car.

"There's Ahmed 2. We're going to have to cross this field."

Far across the field and up a steep slope, you can just make out the taillights of our van. I turn to the captain and his sleepy crew. They are staring.

"Was good trip," the captain says. None of them move. We have seventy-seven bags of luggage each. Lady Gaga tours with less.

"Yeah, well I don't think it's over yet," I say, sweeping my hand toward the baggage suggestively. They all groan and grab our suitcases and dance across the death plank.

"Wait," [My Attorney] yells. "There's poo!"

"Of course there's poo, look at all the donkeys."

"I don't want to step in it."

"Just follow the guys," I say. The guys have disappeared into the darkness with our bags.

"They just left us here?" My second wife says, clearly writing a Yelp review in her mind. Adelaide is a hardened global traveler, the kind of person who books hardship into her itinerary and even she's miffed.

"I'm sure it's fine," I lie. My second wife clicks on her phone light which illuminates a pile of donkey shit taller than [My Attorney]. She leads us through a gauntlet of poop pyramids. Here is Darfur, here's the Steppe Pyramid, here's the great poopamid of Giza...until we scramble up the hill like refugees, out of breath and slightly scuffed. Ahmed is on his phone. The driver is smoking a cigarette and staring off into the stars. We tip the crew FOR ABANDONING US and they disappear down the slope. Off in the darkness, miles and mile downriver, Eddy cries Potato? in his native language.

Abu Simbel was the closest thing to a properly organized tourist site we'd seen. There was a gate. You had to provide a ticket to a ticket taker. There was parking. There was a rest area with proper restrooms and, of course, you exit through a gift shop.

But first, you walk from the conclave of official buildings around the back of the mound of Abu Simbel and find yourself walking along the cliffs of Lake Nasser which is odd because we're in the desert. It's just sand and mountains. Yet there is this insanely enormous can-see-it-from-space deep sapphire sea.

Then you round the bend and there they are, Ramses II and his wife, Nefertiti, sixty-six feet high. Impressive. Stunning. Impassionate. Mysterious. Not underwater.

In 1967, these statues and the temples they guard were moved piece by piece two-hundred-odd feet up and several hundred feet back because Egypt was building a dam and the damn things would drown. The project began in 1964 when they carved the colossi into chunks. By 1968, they'd moved the whole shebang to its new site, which includes a huge viewing park with comfortable benches and stray dogs.

Our tour guide whips out a laminated guidebook of the temples[3] and points to all the stuff we're supposed to look at because he's not allowed to go inside and/or the company won't pay for a ticket. At the doorway, we are greeted by two Egyptian men in jebellahs bearing ankhs and other ancient Nubian paraphernalia offering themselves for super official-looking selfies then asking for enormous tips for just standing there because it's a Tuesday and there's no work in the village of Abu Simbel. I declined, followed my second wife into the temple and enjoyed a sudden, debilitating, overwhelming, butt clenching onslaught of claustrophobia.

Oh yeah.

I have a wee bit of claustrophobia. I learned of this way back a million years ago when I was a fourteen-year-old in California. We visited a ghost town—an actual ghost town, not a theme park—and I trotted off to explore one of their mines. This mine was drilled into a mountain horizontally, like a deep walk-in closet. I just walked in. I got about 30 feet before overwhelming dread and danger and doom washed through me. I could feel the weight of the mountain. I thought I'd never make it out of there. I ran in semi darkness toward the light at the mouth of the cave and shot out into the desert.

The temple at Abu Simbel is basically a cave and even in the off-season of November, it was packed with Russians and Russians don't like wasted space so no matter where I turned, I was pressed up against fifty or sixty sweaty Russkies all jabbering away and taking pictures and ignoring the splendor of the walls which were closing in fast.

I shot out of there into the desert. I picked a bench and stared at the colossi, holding my hat on tight, and keeping an eye on the stray dog sleeping nearby.

I'd had it.

I'd had enough of Egypt. I'd had enough of temples, and tombs, and Russians. I wanted my chair. I wanted to sit at the corner of the bar at the Welcome Back Inn in Logan Square and drink weird beers and slowly finish

---

3 One for Ramses, one for Nefertiti.

a heavy pour of an expensive whiskey and listen to the dive bar playlist and talk to Chris the owner about punk rock and listen in fascination as my buddy Pie Hole Willie manages to have an entire conversation exclusively in 1980s pop lyrics. I wanted to watch funny pet videos on YouTube with [My Attorney] and binge the worst episodes of Intervention while drinking expensive wine. I wanted to pet my dog.

I was done with Egypt.

My two wives emerged from the temples. We took the long meandering curve to the back of the mound and then up the little hill to the exit where I learned that Egypt had more to give.

Abu Simbel is the second biggest draw after the ecropolis of Giza. Their gift shop area is an enormous gauntlet of scarf peddlers, coin book costermongers, jebellah duffers, hat hawkers, and shop after shop after shop. We were accosted and while [My Attorney] and Adelaide were modestly pleading le chagrin le chagrin to move them on and our guide, Ahmed was doing his best to shoo them out of our way, I decided to employ humor. One of the djebellah hucksters laid a sail-like shirt across me and said, "my friend, your size!" and I yelled, "ARE YOU CALLING ME FAT?!"

A few words about the Egyptian sense of humor.

Despite the assurance of experts[4], vendors at ancient temples and tombs do not have one. My comedic timing is expertly honed. I went to stand-up classes at Second City. I've won awards. When I dropped my all-cap self-referential anti-joke I did so based on my experience in America where a joke like that would kill. I mean it would produce howls of laughter.

Maybe a few laughs.

Perhaps a chuckle.

But there in the gift shop, the subtlety of delivery did not translate. Americans would have immediately noted the tone of my voice as ironic and self-deprecating. They would have realized, oh, he's really joking about the absurdity of the situation and it's actually pretty funny, ha and, additionally, ha.

The very large vendor holding the shirt against me shut the hell up. His sudden silence spread to the vendors around him and the shop keepers and the scarf scalpers until I was standing in a sudden well of silent, glaring Egyptians who did not know that I was joking and were trying to figure out if they had insulted me or I had insulted them or if I was maybe German.

4 "Ancient Egyptians sanctified humor, to the extent that they even consigned a humor goddess and married her to the deity of wisdom. This is the closest explanation to the relationship between Egyptians and their sense of humor, showing their attitude to life. It is said that ancient Egyptians believed the world was created out of laughter." —Dr. ABDELLATIF EL-MENAWY, Arab News, 9/21/2017

Ahmed stepped back and took me by the arm and drug me out of there.

I was done with Egypt and Egypt, bless its heart, was done with me.

### Epilogue
January 17th, 2023

We never found the perfect vacation, but that's because the perfect vacation's a Macguffin. Our desperate search for a righteous holiday was stupid. Our vacations are perfect already. Not because they unfold seamlessly from the brochure that inspired us to the actual place we visited; as you have just witnessed, that's highly unlikely. They are perfect because we are together and we are en route and that, for [My Attorney] and I, is bliss.

As I write this, I am in Alabama sitting on a couch in my sister's pied-d-terre (basement guest room) because actual calamity has befallen various family members. My sister is on point, and I've come down into the land of my birth to help out and eat biscuits.

During the calamity, as the family members were convalescing, their post-operative status being 'remarkable,' and 'better than we could ask for' and their enduring futures being assured, they contracted covid and are now shut up in their little home out in the woods where I visit them to drop off Bojangles and fried catfish from the gas station at the bottom of the hill. They greet me at their glass door as if they are slow moving fish in a murky aquarium and I am trying, trying very hard, to not lose my shit.

Covid put a hurt on a lot of people. Even if you didn't get it, even if you lived through it, even if you suffered in a hospital room, the effects of Covid stretched out beyond the individual to society and to the precisely fitted cogs and wheels of our former normal. Everything is still up in the air, three years after the pandemic hit. Nothing is completely stable. Nothing is resting solidly. We're all looking around to see what will happen next.

Of all the problems caused by our virulent passenger, I think its injuries to hope may be the worst. Hope matters. It's one of those intangible traits, a philosophical ornament, we tend to forget about. Just like we quit noticing the tip of our nose or the quiet hum of the refrigerator that fills up the silence of our house. We notice it when it's gone, and hope took a hit in the last three years. Maybe in the last five.

Yet.

Yet, even at an age when I'm totally allowed to peter out, an age when my friends are retiring, I'm excited about my life's new season. Part of this comes from an enduring, persistent, almost naïve optimism matched with a newfound and quiet confidence and that's what I want to talk about.

I've never been confident. I didn't realize this. I thought the bluster and bombastic humor and sheer gall were confidence, but I was wrong. You can't fake confidence. You can't hack it. It comes from truth. From fact. From evidence. My self-deprecating wit and so much of my barrel-chested former self were not talents. They were symptoms of deep insecurity. Even my desire to travel was just as often merely a way to run a flank and get out in front of my insecurity. A useless gambit.

Somehow in the last five or six years, I've matured. A little. Enough to find myself looking at my former insecurities and abrasive traits in the rearview mirror. I attribute much of this to therapy and just a little bit of it to my own efforts to grow the hell up.

Therapy, specifically traditional psychoanalysis, is not what I expected. I still don't know how it works and when I asked my therapist, he shrugged and said, "Hell if I know," while taking my Zelle payment.

Here's what I think: picture your mind as a giant pile of debris. Somewhere underneath that debris, somewhere deep, are the better versions of yourself you'd like take with you out of the therapist's office. To get to them, you have to remove the big pile of debris piece by piece. The debris is words because words are thoughts and thoughts are fucking awful. Therapy is you saying many, many words in order to clear them from the giant pile of suck until the pile is all gone and all you're left with is a truth.

I've told a couple of friends about my therapy and one of them said, "If it doesn't hurt, your therapist isn't doing her job." My friend is wrong. Therapy isn't necessarily constant pain. Of course, if you're in therapy because of trauma, that's going to be there. But I went to therapy because my doctor told me I was suffering from anxiety. I told him he was crazy.

Doctor: Actually, that's you.

Me: Look at my life, Doc. I sit and stare for a living. I get up at 10:30 and take a two-hour nap at three. Where's the anxiety?

Doctor: Anxiety isn't just about what's happening. For a lot of people, it's got nothing to do with what's going on in their life. You need a therapist.

Me: Ridiculous.

Doctor: You know I've read your books, right?

He was right. As I've worked through psychoanalysis, I've begun clearing the debris, the big steamy pile of stupid words circulating in my conscious mind, and what I'm discovering is a version of myself that works. Like, this was the me I was aiming for all along.

This new me looked at my obese body and said, oh no, this will not do.

He (I, me) has booked me for yoga classes, makes me walk an ungodly number of steps every day, and has changed how I eat. I'm losing weight for real, finally, and I'm getting into some kind of shape that's trending away from weak and ovate.

Now I know there are some large folks reading this book, so let me get real here: if you are a large person , you might be thinking *Well, learn to love yourself, embrace your self image.* You may be thinking maybe you should put this book down and find on Instagram and cancel the shit out of me for betraying my people. You may think I'm crossing over to the other side, to become (gulp) *outdoorsy,* but you are wrong.

I made a lot of jokes aout being fat in this book. I will continue to make jokes about being fat. But I'm not shaming anyone. Not even myself; not really.

I'm not fat. I'm obese and there is a difference. Being a little overweight is inevitable in this country. We hate walking and we love Cheetos. We live in food deserts bordered by fast-food restaurants. We are blasted with advertisements for food that will kill us in our fifties. Of course we're gonna put on a few pounds.

But obesity is different. For me, it was a symptom of my insecurities and my innate sense of being the weirdo in the room. Of not being right. I felt this way all my life. My anxiety was constant and I would eat to calm down. To find comfort. Food was a drug. Psychoanalysis has allowed me to clear the mental garbage away and that's cleared a path for some rather positive and welcome traits to surface.

Look, I still weigh a lot. It's a long, long road to healthy. But I don't wake up at 3:30 every morning like I used to, roiling in awful memories presented in stunning 4K with surround sound. I do sometimes, but now my new self (which is really my old self that's been patiently waiting for me to sort my shit out) whacks those ruminations in the ass and fluffs my pillow and pulls the blanket up to my chin and pats me on the head and says, "good boy," and I fall back asleep like it never happened.

The result of all this growth is that I am no longer comfortable with obesity. Not because its ugly or other people may be offended by it or because I can't find clothes that fit without looking like I'm wearing the couch cushions. Not because of any of that. It's because I finally know who I really am. I know how to do my work. I know that I'm good at what I do. I know that I'm not a fraud (hello, imposter syndrome, have you fucked yourself yet? No? Well, could you go fuck yourself please?) Most of all, I have come to a quiet, uncinematic, gentle, almost miraculous knowledge that I am a good person. This has led to a secondary miracle: I'm not performing anymore. I'm not on stage all the time. For fifty-four years, I've been trying to impress someone who doesn't even exist. Who never existed. Now I've stepped down off that stage and the relief is hard to process. The locus of my self-worth has shifted from external (applause) to internal (the heart of the performer).

If you are an obese person, I feel you. I too have struggled to go out my front door. To sit in a booth at a coffee shop like a normal person. I've described other people as normal (see the previous sentence) without even realizing how abusive that is to my own self-worth. The physical pain of obesity is terrible. My knees are shot. My feet hurt. My back hurts from carrying around an entire other person in the most awkward way possible. A slight incline will leave me winded and gasping. I am always looking for a place to sit down. I get tired just from standing up to cook. Getting out of a chair is an act of sheer willpower and sometimes it takes a couple of tries. Putting on my socks is an insane painful contortion.

But all that stuff I said I learned or revealed in therapy changes things. The fact is, for a long time, I'd kind of given up. I'd kind of accepted that I was going to die trapped inside this cocoon of fat. Soon. I'd accepted that it was inevitable. Imminent.

But it's not. If my boy fell into a pool and couldn't swim, I'd dive the fuck in to save him because I love him. I owe myself that same kindness.

The thing is, if you really want to change, you have to fall in love with yourself. If you truly love yourself, not as a narcissistic dickhead, but just quietly. Just normally. Just maybe even, not actively hating yourself. If you do that, some aspects of your life will change as a matter of course. That sad morbid inevitability will vanish.

Here's the epilogue: this isn't an epilogue. It's a preface.

I lost ten pounds in the first month of 2023. Imagine two bags of sugar sitting on the counter. Pick them up. That's a lot. I didn't do a lot of exercising and it's winter in Chicago (and even in Alabama) so I'm not walking outside unless the house is on fire. I didn't go on a diet. Diets are stupid. In fact, I just had fried catfish for lunch with a side of pasta and slaw washed down with Milo's Sweet Iced tea. I'm not exactly counting calories. I just kind of watch what I eat and the new me, the new self (hi, it's me) sometimes puts his hand on my shoulder and says quietly, Hey, I think that's enough. Most importantly, I own a new dignity, a new and rare charity toward myself that comes from a simple truth: I love who I am, and I want to live.

I have to. I have more books in me. I have camels to fight.

### APOLOGIES

I cannot prove the soup at Bar Andalou contained a rodent of any kind, especially not a rat. My apprehension at the appearance of the bifurcated ping-pong ball sized skull and inwardly curved cheddar cheese-colored teeth caused me to leap to a conclusion which has no basis in fact. It was more likely a squirrel, which is just a rat with a blowout.

Mormons do not automatically have more than one wife. Also, asking them if it works in reverse is rude.

Mormons do not autmatically wear magical underwear.

Adelaide Hunter is not my second wife, nor is our relationship anything exceeding that of my wife's cool friend who reads books and listens to classical music. She is friends with famous classical musicians and artists and we get along.

No animals were harmed in the making of this book.

T. Bernardi is not an instructor of Misinterpretative Dance. He's a competitive doily designer.

The Mormon Tabernacle Choir is a historic musical organization comprised of talented singers and a fine religious organization, not, as one may infer, a cabal of white privileged cackling Karens though I don't know why one may infer that as they are not mentioned in this book, per [My Attorney].

I am truly sorry for cursing out the shirt salesman at the bazaar next to the guard shack full of machine guns at the Temple of Esna.

Barcelona is pronounced BAR SEH LON UH, not BARTH EL OWN AH, unless you actually live in Catalonia, or are an argumentative, pedantic, boorish, dickwad.

I would like to apologize to the staff of Don Fernando's for my behavior and for what I am certain was an inadequate tip.

I may have exaggerated the extent to which I tormented my dear friend, Bob, by asking him to 'give us a twirl'.

I am deeply, ardently sorry to The Judge and his lovely wife for ruining their silver nniversary napkins in such spectacular fashion.

I cannot prove God and Satan are besties—yet.

Not all of my family is biscuit forward, but tracking down the healthy eaters on even the lowest branches of my family tree would take a million years.

Thre is no such thing as a 700 dollar bill in Belize.

Todd is not necessarily a terrible name and if you are named Todd, I cannot prove your parents hated you at birth.

## Apologies

I cannot prove the soup at Bar Andalou contained a rodent of any kind, especially not a rat. My apprehension at the appearance of the bifurcated ping-pong ball sized skull and inwardly curved cheddar cheese-colored teeth caused me to leap to a conclusion which has no basis in fact. It was more likely a squirrel, which is just a rat with a blowout.

Mormons do not automatically have more than one wife. Also, asking them if it works in reverse is rude.

Mormons do not autmatically wear magical underwear.

Adelaide Hunter is not my second wife, nor is our relationship anything exceeding that of my wife's cool friend who reads books and listens to classical music. She is friends with famous classical musicians and artists and we get along.

No animals were harmed in the making of this book.

T. Bernardi is not an instructor of Misinterpretative Dance. He's a competitive doily designer.

The Mormon Tabernacle Choir is a historic musical organization comprised of talented singers and a fine religious organization, not, as one may infer, a cabal of white privileged cackling Karens though I don't know why one may infer that as they are not mentioned in this book, per [My Attorney].

I am truly sorry for cursing out the shirt salesman at the bazaar next to the guard shack full of machine guns at the Temple of Esna.

Barcelona is pronounced BAR SEH LON UH, not BARTH EL OWN AH, unless you actually live in Catalonia, or are an argumentative, pedantic, boorish, dickwad.

I would like to apologize to the staff of Don Fernando's for my behavior and for what I am certain was an inadequate tip.

I may have exaggerated the extent to which I tormented my dear friend, Bob, by asking him to 'give us a twirl'.

I am deeply, ardently sorry to The Judge and his lovely wife for ruining their silver nniversary napkins in such spectacular fashion.

I cannot prove God and Satan are besties—yet.

Not all of my family is biscuit forward, but tracking down the healthy eaters on even the lowest branches of my family tree would take a million years.

Thre is no such thing as a 700 dollar bill in Belize.

Todd is not necessarily a terrible name and if you are named Todd, I cannot prove your parents hated you at birth.

### ACKNOWLEDGEMENTS

This book required a surprising amount of research, given that I'm basically talking about what actually happened to me. That research meant talking to people and asking dumb questions. Without the patience and deep knowledge of Egyptologist Achmed Rizaldi, I'd never have understood the culture of every day Egyptians. Abner Serd was a first reader with the valuable ability to recognize when I was cheating and being lazy and encouraged me to rewrite certain passages to make them hit better. His frustration and amusement at my inability to remain in tense was understandable. Courtney Collins was a first reader who pointed out when I was being a ludicrously convoluted moron or underwriting. She also paid attention to when I was repeating jokes, which meant I had to cut thirty-four thousand words. I must acknowledge my second-wife, Adelaide Hunter, for the way she re-organized our trip and for having powdered electrolytes on hand when I was dying from heatstroke. I must thank my children for being so damn awesome that I wanted to impress them. My sister and my Alabamily keep me and support me and feed me Conecka Sausage by the pound and I love them. Minders, I'm sorry about the poop. My mother helped to embue me with a sense of humor and Mom, I'm really sorry for all the cussing. My best friend, Lt. David "Biscuit" Haynes deserves a shout out for basically launching my career by being a cop and making me host a radio show with him. Finally, I have to thank my first wife, [My Attorney], who puts up with me and was there by my side through every trip telling me to hurry up.

## ABOUT THE AUTHOR

Born in Birmingham, Alabama in 1964, Christopher "Bull" Garlington is a beloved storyteller whose books have brought readers the joy of highly literate fart jokes, Zombie-based telephone sales, and transglobal non-corporeal skills-based guild-societies. He is best known for his travel memoir, *The Full English,* his work as a columnist for various online and print magazines, and for his writing at All American Whiskey.

Garlington lives in Chicago with [his attorney] on the far north side where he divides his time between writing and staring at things. These two efforts are often indistinguishable. He is an amateur chef, an ambitious if not exactly gifted gardener, an amiable neighbor, and a bad, though willing, dancer. You can learn more about Garlington by visiting his website: www.bullgarlington.com

### DID YOU LIKE THIS BOOK?

Well, *thank you*. I was hoping you'd get a kick out of it. If you did, if you laughed out loud or snickered, even *once*, I'd say that's a win for both of us. Finding just a *sliver* of joy in the endless soul crushing madness is a bonus these days. I am overjoyed if I made you laugh.

Maybe I could convince you to pass it on? I mean, look: most people live in an endless rushing river of cold anxiety, bone cracking worry, and endless dread. Making them laugh does more than just bring joy into their life. If a person laughs, even once, it changes their whole demeanor–sometimes for a minute, sometimes for a whole day. They walk around the office with a bounce in their stride. They wave at strangers. They smile for no damn reason. There's great value in this. It is, I am convinced, the surest and most effective way to connect people. When people feel connected, they make better decisions, they consider the bigger picture. They grumble less, and they help more, and even just the teensiest little bit of such behavior, even a sliver of kindness, is powerful. It ripples outward from the smile, from the wave, from the returned grocery cart, out into the nearby world, igniting sparks of kindness in others. Smiles are contagious. Laughter is contagious.

What I'm asking you to do, in no small way, is to save the world. I know it sounds ridiculous at first, but hear me out. *Give this book away.* You're done with it, right? Hand it to your funniest friend. Give it to a co-worker. Throw it at your most ardent enemy. Hell, hand it to a perfect stranger and say: I loved this book. I laughed my ass off. Take it. Enjoy it. Pass it on.

I mean, you can also keep the book and just use the QR code on the facing page to send anyone to download their own free excerpt. You could even tear it out and use it as a bookmark. Tape it to the fridge. Get it tattooed on your arm. You do you. But pass it on. Spread joy.

Save the world.